The Nation-State
the formation of modern politics

The Nation-State

the formation of modern politics

edited by
Leonard Tivey

St. Martin's • New York

© Leonard Tivey 1981

St. Martin's Press, Inc., 175 Fifth Avenue, New York, NY 10010
Printed in Great Britain
First published in the United States of America in 1981

ISBN 0-312-55941-0

Library of Congress Cataloging in Publication Data
Main entry under title:

The Nation-state.

1. National state — Addresses, essays, lectures.
2. Nationalism — Addresses, essays, lectures.
I. Tivey, Leonard James.
JC311.N289   1980   321′.05   80-26635
ISBN 0-312-55941-0

Contents

Preface

The idea for this book arose from conversations among members of the Department of Political Science at the University of Birmingham in 1978. The interests of the people concerned varied widely, as would be expected, since we teach different parts of the discipline. However, we had all found ourselves dealing with some problem or development concerning the nature of the state or of nationalism, and so the enterprise seemed feasible. We hope that the result will serve as an introduction for students and as a contribution to discussion for the general reader.

The essays were written in 1979 and early 1980, and were discussed in a contributors' seminar as drafts were produced. We did not expect to achieve any uniformity, or indeed harmony, of outlook. The discussions served rather to bring about a measure of common awareness — of the history, world-wide nature and deep problems of our subject. It is hardly necessary to say that the views in the essays are those of their respective authors, and not of any collectivity, in the Department at Birmingham or anywhere else. Faults of general conception, planning and presentation are the responsibility of the editor.

The seven authors at the University of Birmingham would like to record their gratitude to Hugh Tinker, who agreed to join us when the work was well under way, and to Gordon Smith who stepped in at a very late stage to provide some considerations about the future. Without their help there would have been severe deficiencies, and we are much in debt to them both for the substance of their contributions and for the cooperative spirit in which they joined us.

The volume could not have been produced without the consistent high quality of the secretarial work of Marjorie Davies and of Frances Landreth, in the office of the Department of Political Science. My particular thanks as editor go to Douglas Rimmer, of the Centre of West African Studies, University of Birmingham for his patient and

viii

thorough advice, which has removed a few absurdities and clarified many obscurities; and to Marjorie Tivey for help with particular points.

Most of all, however, my gratitude goes to the other eight contributors, who not only agreed that the project was practicable, but wrote and rewrote, reflected and discussed, in order to bring it to fruition.

University of Birmingham   LEONARD TIVEY
September 1980

Contributors

CORNELIA NAVARI is a lecturer in the Department of Political Science in the University of Birmingham, with special interests in international theory and in European integration. She has published articles on knowledge and the state and on the contemporary state system; and edited (with J. Mayall) *The End of the Post-War Era: Documents on Great Power Relations 1968–1975* (Cambridge University Press, 1980).

ANDREW ORRIDGE is a lecturer in the Department of Political Science in the University of Birmingham, with special interests in contemporary political theory and in sub-state nationalisms. He has published articles on aspects of Irish politics and on theories of nationalism.

LEONARD TIVEY is a senior lecturer in the Department of Political Science in the University of Birmingham, with special interests in British politics and in political aspects of industrial affairs. He has published *Nationalisation in British Industry* (Cape, 1966 and 1973) and *The Politics of the Firm* (Martin Robertson, 1978).

MARTIN KOLINSKY is a senior lecturer in the Department of Political Science in the University of Birmingham, with a special interest in West European politics. He has published *Continuity and Change in European Society* (Croom Helm, 1974), is co-author of *Social and Political Movements in Western Europe* (Croom Helm, 1976) and *Social Change in France* (Martin Robertson, 1980) and has edited *Divided Loyalties* (Manchester University Press, 1978).

HUGH TINKER is Professor of Politics in the University of Lancaster, with special interests in Asia and the politics of race. He has been an honorary fellow of the Institute of Local Government Studies, University of Birmingham. He has published many books, some of which deal with problems of nationalism, including *The Union of*

Burma (Oxford University Press, 1957), *India and Pakistan, a political analysis* (Praeger, 1962 and 1967), *Ballot Box and Bayonet — people and government in emergent Asian countries* (Oxford University Press, 1964 and 1969), and *Race, Conflict and the International Order* (Macmillan, 1977).

ARNOLD HUGHES is a lecturer in the Centre of West African Studies and an attached member of the Department of Political Science in the University of Birmingham. He has a special interest in political change in Black Africa, and has published articles on Gambian and Nigerian politics and on aspects of pan-Africanism.

ANTHONY WRIGHT is a lecturer in the Department of Extramural Studies and an associate member of the Department of Political Science in the University of Birmingham. He has special interests in socialist theory and in labour history, and he has published *G.D.H. Cole and Socialist Democracy* (The Clarendon Press, 1979).

GEOFFREY OSTERGAARD is a senior lecturer in the Department of Political Science in the University of Birmingham, with special interests in political theory and in libertarian socialism. He has published *Power in Co-operatives* (with A.H. Halsey; Blackwell, 1965) and *The Gentle Anarchists* (with M. Currell; The Clarendon Press, 1971).

GORDON SMITH is Reader in Government at the London School of Economics and Political Science, with a special interest in the politics of Western Europe. He has published *Politics in Western Europe: A Comparative Analysis* (Heinemann, 1972 and 1980) and *Democracy in Western Germany* (Heinemann, 1979); and is co-editor of the journal *West European Politics.*

Introduction

Leonard Tivey

Swooping in from Mars, invaders of this planet would no doubt have many preconceptions. Whether they would guess that the earth's inhabitants were divided into a large number of separate groupings, very different in size, each claiming exclusive control of a patch of the earth's surface, is surely problematic. That this segmentation should seem to the inhabitants entirely normal and an inherent part of the order of things would be an even less likely expectation.

However, such is the condition of mankind. The subject of these essays is the nation-state: that is, not so much the division itself as the form it has assumed. Though people have always associated in some sort of localized units, their congregation into nation-states is a modern development; indeed, in its fully fledged style it is essentially contemporary.

Writings on nationalism and on the state have not linked the two as often as might have been expected. Though most of the essays in this book emphasize one or the other, taken together they bring the relationship into focus. The essays share this common subject but they do not share a common viewpoint, either in promoting or denigrating the idea of the nation-state, or in any other matter.

Since the essays are concerned with a duality, a beginning may be made with some preliminary observations about the two phenomena.

STATES

The state is a specific type of political formation — that is, it is not *any* sort of polity or political system. For instance, there were in earlier times sets of social arrangements that relied so much on customary rules and on enforcement by social pressure that no real

1

central authority existed within the community. Such rudimentary systems scarcely amounted to states. Again, in contemporary times the relations *among* states make up a political order but there is no supreme state. Whatever it is, the United Nations is not a state. Thirdly, there are within many institutions methods of rule, forms of government, types of political activity that clearly do not add up to a state. Some of these other institutional structures, such as churches, sporting organizations and multinational businesses transcend the frontiers of states. So politics is more than the state.

Though some of the earliest societies might not contain states, there certainly developed means of governing tribes or other human groups that might, in retrospect and with some generosity, be called states. This does not mean that such authorities were thought of in ways at all similar to the way in which modern people think of their states. Characteristically, the system of rule would be centred on a personal ruler, chief, king or emperor, and though there are many examples of other arrangements, they too were based on custom, religion, legend or magic. Only the Greeks managed to think about politics in its own terms. Detailed, rigid and autocratic administrative systems were built up by some rulers, such as the Pharoahs and the Incas, focussing of course on the supreme or god-king. But for most of the world and for most of the time, social and economic organization was a localized affair, with coercion applied mainly from outside and perhaps accepted as a necessary protection.

Three structures deserve special mention. The term *city-state* is applied to the cities of ancient Greece and Renaissance Italy, and to other similar political units. The title is deserved (retrospectively of course) since independent constitutional government was their essential attribute. Secondly, the largest political formation has been the great empire — overriding local rule by military force and leading to structures sometimes vast in extent, which in the greatest and more enduring examples, such as Rome, bring about the dissemination over wide areas of customs, law, culture and civilization. They may be called *empire-states* for convenience. The third structure, that of Western Europe in its middle ages, contained the Holy Roman Empire, founded by Charlemagne around 800, and numerous kingdoms, dukedoms, and lesser authorities, and the Roman Catholic Church claiming both independent control of religious matters and the right to judge the propriety of secular rule. The kingdoms of medieval Europe contained an apparatus of government that often aspired to statehood, but that was enmeshed in a system that did not allow it sovereign powers. What all three structures certainly lacked was the idea of the nation; whether or not they were states, they were not nation-states.

The word state came into its modern usage in Europe at the time of the Renaissance. From its Latin root it became *estat* in old French, and eventually *Staat* in German, *état* in French and *state* in English. The English word 'estate' has a similar derivation. The factor of land or territory is common to both terms, and both descend from a feudal system in which forms of landholding were fundamental to the political structure. However, Quentin Skinner notes in early usages the absence of 'the distinctively modern idea of the State as a form of public power separate from both the ruler and the ruled, and constituting the supreme political authority within a certain defined territory'.

The crucial element is that of an 'independent political apparatus' distinct from the ruler, and which indeed the ruler has a duty to maintain.[1] This is the central conception of the modern state. There is ultimately an abstraction, capable of existing in perpetuity, but in practice it needs to be operated by an authoritative government, which can change.

This apparatus of continuing government embodies a system of law (at first derived from customary practices) backed by force. In Europe in the middle ages laws might be defined, and enforced, by civil authorities of various types (the emperor, kings or princes, feudal lords) or by the Church. The emergence of the modern state brought with it the idea of sovereignty — a single authority both for making laws and with force to sustain them — within a sharply defined and consolidated territory. The first part of the story of the rise of the nation-state is therefore the story of the rise of sovereignty. In Europe this meant the removal of entrenched rights and powers of lesser authorities — nobles, barons, local or regional autonomies, customary privileges — and the removal of the political jurisdiction of the Roman Catholic Church. The achievement of sovereignty involved long and confused struggles, and was nowhere a simple process. The sovereignty of the unified state was commonly brought about by the sovereignty of a particular state institution — in Europe's 'age of absolutism' that of monarchy (and hence that of the great dynasties, Romanoff, Hohenzollern, Bourbon and Habsburg) though eventually in Britain the legal sovereignty of Parliament was decisive.

But such solutions were overtaken by a more fundamental political development — the basing of political legitimacy not on divine right nor on existing law, tradition or customs, but on contemporary choice: on the will of the people.

NATIONS

It is not appropriate to detail here the spread of democratic ideals or to examine the means for their fulfilment. The creation of the United States of America and the revolution in France were heralds of the new doctrine. The democratic revolutions, however, brought with them another new doctrine — nationalism. The famous opening words of the United States constitution of 1787 'We, the people of the United States . . .' (that is, not the states themselves, and not *any* people) are significant, and so is the retrospective interpretation by Abraham Lincoln: 'Fourscore and seven years ago, our fathers brought forth on this continent a new *nation* . . .' The revolution of 1789 proclaimed the Rights of Man, but it led to assertions of the sovereignty of the French people. In the aftermath, the people who should rule (or at least in whose name rule should be exercised) were conceptualized, delimited and moralized as 'the nation'.

The emergence of nationalism was of course another long process. Elie Kedourie confidently asserts that 'Nationalism is a doctrine invented in Europe at the beginning of the nineteenth century'.[2] By that time, however, there were in existence countries that had long-established political and cultural unity, notably France and England. They may be taken as the prototypes. What was invented in the early nineteenth century was the ideology — the belief that nations were the natural and only true political units, the foundations on which states, governments and their policies should depend. Thus arrives the concept of the nation-state as an ideal. Its realization over the world did not take place until the twentieth century, when the great empires of Holland, Turkey, France and Britain collapsed. By that time the ideology had bitten very deeply indeed into people's political assumptions. By that time, too, serious problems were apparent. But these matters are the subjects of our essays.

What is 'a nation', that it should have attracted such honour and respect? By derivation the word comes from the Latin root *nasci,* to be born, and so began with the idea of a people of common breed or place of origin. But an appeal to ethnicity begs many questions in view of invasions, migrations and racial mixtures in the same community. Nor does the social bond of common language provide an answer, for obviously some languages (English, Spanish, German) are used by many nations, and other nations even in Europe (the Swiss, the Belgians) have more than one language, while in Africa and Asia linguistic profusion continues. Perhaps the point to emphasize is that the state itself does not merely reflect the qualities of nations: it fashions them. By a state-enforced educational system, linguistic uniformity can be promoted. Moreover, by nationality laws the state registers an official membership of the nation, equating it with its own citizenship. Legal requirements for nationality look to parentage (as in Roman law) or to place of birth, or both. Acceptance of newcomers is described as 'naturalization'. In some countries, notably the United States, the quantity and variety of immigration made common citizenship a vital instrument of national conscious-ness and loyalty — notwithstanding the retention of other loyalties by sub-groups such as Irish Americans and African Americans. If American nationhood is one of the more remarkable achievements of the idea of nationality, the idea of a British nation was one of the boldest. For the creation of the state of Great Britain after 1707 (the United Kingdom of Great Britain and Ireland was established in 1805) led to a state-defined British nationality existing alongside Scottish, Welsh and even English nationality, still officially recognized in religion and some sports for example. The protean nature of nationality is not confined to its later-twentieth-century developments.

In order to avoid a description of the multiform complexities of actual nationalisms at this stage, and to avoid anticipating the essays themselves, a first understanding of 'the nation' may be achieved by noting the claims of its supporters, the nationalists.

(i)   It is assumed, and if necessary vigorously asserted, that the nation is a natural unit of society: it is inherent and not imposed or artificial. Nor is it really something chosen or voluntary, for though it may admit some new recruits, they are assimilated to an existing body.

(ii) Members of a nation have a great deal in common: there is a form of homogeneity that (unlike citizenship) is not merely formal or legal. The foundations of this unity lie both in shared interests and in shared experiences, recounted in history and embodied in such things as literature, music, sport, cooking, customs and morality. Even religion may take on distinctive national forms.

(iii) Each nation needs its own polity, for otherwise it will not be able to realize the fruits of its character and culture — it will be oppressed. In practice the required polity is usually an independent sovereign state, though there are occasional examples where autonomy or home rule has sufficed.

(iv) All states, of course, control defined territories, but it is really the nation that has an inalienable right to its proper territory or homeland wherein to dwell.

(v) A nation should feel self-confident: it needs prestige and success, and to be respected by others. It needs to stand well in the world.

These claims of the nationalists represent an ideal. They are nowhere met in full. In some cases there is an approximation to the ideal, but in others there is bitter grievance over the absence of one requirement or another. Sometimes nationalists urge their countrymen to stir themselves to greater efforts to achieve unity or prosperity or success or glory. They may sometimes urge emulation of other nations. They will certainly urge resistance, if necessary to the point of violence, against oppression or exploitation from another nation.

An important attribute of a nation, of course, is its own self-awareness. Many difficulties — such as lack of a common language, or a short history — may be overcome if people in a particular place become convinced of their own nationhood. The struggle to assert such nationhood may in fact generate the achievements (military or cultural) and fuse the unity that are necessary to establish the truth of the original assertion.

The general acceptance of nationalist beliefs is, paradoxically, shown by the terms used to describe counter-national arrangements. The most notable term is 'international', which refers to relations or cooperation among nation-states. International bodies and inter-nationalist beliefs do not reject nations or nationalism (though they may restrain excesses). They accept and endorse nations as the entities between which relations take place, and recognize states as their agents. The United Nations is in fact an organization of states, but its name asserts that it is bringing together existing nations, not miscellaneous peoples and groups. So too with terms like supranational, and multinational: they implicitly accept that what is being integrated or linked are states or associations or enterprises that belong to nations. There is a prior assumption of the reality of nations before the attempts to transcend them can be understood.

To get away from these assumptions is difficult. It is not easy even to find a vocabulary. 'Anarchy' implies a rejection of government by force, and is opposed to states in general rather than to particular forms. 'Individualism' is often used in senses that do not oppose nationalism — thus in contemporary politics many advocates of economic individualism and free markets are also strong believers in national prowess. 'Transnational' is sometimes used to imply that nations can be transcended, but it still hints that nations are real. The best available term seems to be 'cosmopolitan', since it at least indicates that nationality as a political criterion might be rejected or ignored or relegated to a place of secondary concern. Cosmopolitanism as a distinctive political cause is very rarely made explicit. It can sometimes be discerned as an underlying attitude — in admirers of dynastic rule or of old conglomerate empires, in the managerial technocrats of some multinational businesses, in some high intellectual élites, in some schools of Marxists, and in some other revolutionaries. The cosmopolitan element is characteristically contingent on the rest of the outlook. Since most ideologies are capable of advantageous alliance with nationalism, there are few circumstances in which cosmopolitanism seems essential, and apart from the examples mentioned it attracts little support.

Thus it is now widely held not only that the nation-state is a universal phenomenon, but that nationalism is the common ideology of the world and is likely to remain so. Many writers of these essays (but not all) accept this judgement of the prospects. Yet there is point for the student of politics in understanding that nationalism *is* an ideology, that its origins and its forms can be explained, and that since there was a past without it, a future beyond it is not inconceivable. To acknowledge its present force or even to recommend its acceptance in preference to alternatives is not to suggest submergence in its values. In 1862 Lord Acton recognized the services of the idea of nationality:

> Although, therefore, the theory of nationality is more absurd and more criminal than the theory of socialism, it has an important mission in the world, and marks the final conflict, and therefore the end, of two forces which are the worst enemies of civil freedom — the absolute monarchy and the revolution.[3]

Acton was a liberal and an optimist. Since he wrote, absolutisms, revolutions and nationalisms have abounded and the cosmopolitan individualism that he respected is not yet with us. Yet his message is significant. It is possible to recognize the role of nationalism, as Acton did, without being a nationalist. Certainly there are grounds on which its premises can be rejected and its morals questioned. It is not quite universal. Ernest Gellner in 1964 accepted that, in contemporary circumstances, nationality is a necessary condition and attribute of man, and a touchstone of the boundaries of political units. Thus nationhood, with statehood as its concomitant, is at present needed to satisfy certain ends. But Gellner also asks '. . . why should men have become particularly concerned about the ethnic rubric under which they survived? (Czechs who settled in Vienna, or Chicago, and in due course became Austrians or Americans, did not find this fate unbearable.)'[4] The pragmatic case for the nation-state is not the same as the nationalist case for the nation-state.

ALTERNATIVES?

Is it possible to foresee a period after that of the nation-state? Can an alternative political formation be imagined? In previous eras, fragmentation was overborne by the raising of great empires. Is there a new way? Already there have been leagues, unions, communities, associations and organizations that try to establish something 'above' or 'among' states and that are intended to have a more or less enduring character. These arrangements begin by accepting existing states, and so have the virtue of practicality. The reasoning behind them has parallels with that behind those states that were created by process of 'unification' — that is, it is argued that the evils of hostility, rivalry and lack of coordination can be overcome by some sort of established rule or authority (albeit one dependent on wide consent) that will modify the absolute independence of states. Radical thinking on these lines looks towards actual federation as an even more effective step towards unity, perhaps ultimately hoping for a 'federation of the world' or some sort of 'world government' as the logical culmination — sometime in the future — of a widening span of effective political authority.

For others, these prospects seem daunting. A world-state is not only a distant possibility but if achieved would be for most people a very remote affair indeed. If it claimed sovereignty on the nation-state model, over the whole globe, it could develop into a system of universal oppression. Moreover, if its rule were to become acceptable it would need the underpinning of a common ideology. Could some version of 'humanism' serve the world as nationalism serves the state? Or, if a more precise set of common beliefs were necessary, would not such a universal dogma become in itself a form of intellectual and moral oppression?

So some look in other directions. In the early part of this century, a school of political writers attacked the sovereign pretentions of the state in favour of a version of pluralism, in which other associations (religious or economic) might attract similar loyalties.[5] In the theory of international politics, David Mitrany argued that the functional requirements of modern society would result in the establishment of numerous overlapping organizations that would eventually limit the effectiveness of independent state action.[6] In neither case was there an adequate explanation of what was to become of the basic role of the state in providing law backed by force, or of nationalist feelings. Nevertheless the growth of organizations that spread beyond the frontiers of states and the development of rapid communications are obvious contemporary phenomena. Theories of the breakdown of the effectiveness of sovereign independence therefore seem to have the merits of feasibility and of realism. They reflect things that are happening. The difficulty is that, for those who seek a way to human salvation, they are inadequate. The bonds on which they rely are not strong enough to restrain the legal authority and military coherence of states.

To move beyond, to question the state itself, is to venture towards anarchy. As previously noted, it is not only the nation-state that anarchists oppose: other forms of state or coercive rule are also rejected. But it is a vulgar error to equate the term 'anarchy' with confusion and chaos, for the anarchists' ideal is a society ordered and organized by free people of their own volition, not through coercion. If nations are natural, as nationalists claim, they would survive in such a world; but if they are not, as most anarchists suspect, then there would be no states to shape them.

The object of reviewing alternatives here is not to suggest they are around the next corner, still less to suggest a preference for one set or another. Indeed, their remoteness may merely reinforce the belief that nation-states are here to stay. Nevertheless, alternatives can be imagined: they have their advocates and their analysts, that is the point. By considering other forms, the nation-state itself can be better understood.

THE ESSAYS

The essays in this volume move from general surveys to particular areas, and then to special problems.

Three essays deal with wide developments. Cornelia Navari examines the emergence of the nation-state, in Europe, and considers how its rise may be explained. Three ways of accounting for transformation are relevant: changes in ideas, in particular the rationalist attack on revelation and on tradition, which subverted the intellectual foundations of the old order; the rise of capitalism, with its emphasis on the individual not tied to particular locations or to particular masters, but able to make free contracts; and the state itself as builder of its own sovereignty and as moulder of the nationality of its inhabitants. So by the beginning of the nineteenth century both states that already existed and states that began to be created turned to nationality as the justification for their existence. The need for nationhood was urgent; fortunately its sources were numerous. Andrew Orridge, in the second essay, continues the story, and in doing so describes and classifies the varieties of nationalism, partly in historical sequence and partly according to the circumstances of origin. All of which emphasizes the protean character of this ideology and its promiscuous habit of linking itself with other ideologies — almost *any* other ideology will do. In the third general essay, Leonard Tivey discusses the implications for the economic order of the political segmentation of the world into states and into nations. The system in which the state is the most conspicuous and powerful human institution not only creates separate 'economies' but encourages nationalist demands for the success of these enclosures, channels ideas about the well-being of society into national and statist forms, and allows the concept of sovereignty to override that of property.

The following essays deal with the condition of the nation-state in three parts of the world. Europe saw the origin of the species, and Martin Kolinsky's essay therefore discusses an advanced stage in its evolution. The question arises whether the institutional developments above and below the level of the state will loosen its dominance, or on the contrary strengthen its role as the essential component of a complex system. Hugh Tinker reviews the rise of nation-states in Asia — the transformation of ancient empires and divided communities into what has become the modern norm. The period of colonialism paradoxically provided the necessary creed — anti-imperialism — on which unity could be built, and bequeathed structures that were capable of recognition as members of the international system. The new nation-states of Africa are discussed by Arnold Hughes. Original assumptions about nation-building have been brought into question for, though nationalism emerged as a powerful doctrine in the colonial period, the independent states have to cope with immense problems of ethnic diversity and severe territorial and resource limitations.

Two essays take up special issues. Socialist beliefs, launched in the nineteenth century, have spread in some form throughout the world; yet their relationship with nationalism remains ambiguous. Anthony Wright argues that nationalism has fared the better — indeed socialism has had to 'nationalize' itself in order to gain political influence. Geoffrey Ostergaard emphasizes that there has always been one tradition of political ideas that flatly rejected the state and its claims: anarchism, or libertarian socialism. It is now allied with another old tradition, pacifism, which rejected the right of states to compel the bearing of arms. These currents of thought at times attract little attention, but emerge periodically in the face of world events.

The book concludes with an essay by Gordon Smith that considers the prospects for the future. The nation-state is beset by very severe problems: externally, in that states are all vulnerable both militarily and economically to outside forces, and internally, in that governments find themselves unable to meet the substantial demands of sectional groups. No type of regime avoids the problems; and yet so far the crisis is not overwhelming, not enough to predict an inevitable decline of the nation-state.

This volume of essays is intended to be introductory. It is important that students should reflect on the place of the nation-state in contemporary affairs, and not take it for granted. It is an essential starting-point. Whether they give most attention to political theory, to institutional studies or to policy-making processes, political scientists need an understanding of this most general political formation. Only then can they grasp the context into which modern political, administrative and economic problems have fallen.

The essays also contribute to discussion. They are obviously not the whole of the story — there are parts of the world not examined and there are critical problems not raised. This book offers beginnings that we hope will encourage further enquiry and reflection.

However, the discussion to which we are contributing is not for specialists only. The nation-state has become the first symbol of political identity. The most common use of the first person plural ('we' or 'our') in political discourse at virtually any level refers to nationality: that is how we have come to think of ourselves. Even if no other way is likely to come into favour for some time, it is surely possible for us to be aware of what we are doing. It helps to measure our predicament.

NOTES AND REFERENCES

1. Quentin Skinner *The Foundations of Modern Political Thought* (Cambridge: Cambridge University Press, 1979) vol. 2, p. 353.
2. Elie Kedourie *Nationalism* (London: Hutchinson, 1960, 1966) p. 9.
3. Lord Acton, essay on 'Nationality' (1862) in *History of Freedom and other essays* (London: Macmillan, 1907) p. 300.
4. Ernest Gellner, essay on 'Nationalism' in *Thought and Change* (London: Weidenfeld and Nicolson, 1964).
5. David Nicholls *Three Varieties of Pluralism* (London: Macmillan, 1974) and *The Pluralist State* (London: Macmillan, 1975); H. J. Laski *A Grammar of Politics* (London: Allen and Unwin, 1925)
6. David Mitrany *The Functional Theory of Politics* (London: Martin Robertson, 1975)

1

The Origins of the Nation-State

Cornelia Navari

A nation-state is commonly defined as a polity of homogeneous people who share the same culture and the same language, and who are governed by some of their own number, who serve their interests. If we ask when such a state of affairs came into being, we should say, at no time. There is no people in the world that shares such homogeneity, where there are no regional or cultural differences, where all speak the same language or share the same linguistic usages and where the rulers do not differ in rank or wealth or education from the ruled. Actual nation-states rather approximate to an ideal type than mirror it, and do so in very different degrees.

If we ask when such approximations began to appear, we should probably say toward the end of the eighteenth century. At that time, France was marked out by de Tocqueville as 'the country where men most resemble one another'. In Britain, the English had already begun to resemble one another by the seventeenth century, but such a state of affairs could not have been present in the country at large before the early nineteenth century. And these were 'advanced'; in Germany it was probably not before the twentieth century that the German people became true co-culturalists, while in large parts of Asia and Africa people living within single polities are only beginning to resemble one another and there remain cultural differences among them so great that, given the common definition, these polities would not qualify as nation-states at all.

If we were to switch our definitional ground slightly and ask at what period in time did the notion appear that governments *ought* to serve more or less fictional entities called 'nations' and when did politicians begin to base their claims to rule on the existence of such entities, we would be on firmer ground. The notion that the state *ought* to serve the nation developed through the nineteenth century. It was at the Congress of Vienna in 1815 that some bourgeois Middle Europeans first put forward the (then) novel claim that ethnicity ought to determine the shape of states. Greece in 1821 was the first to win such a gift. The revolutions of 1830 and 1848 were the first to be undertaken entirely in the name of ethnic groupings; and it was only in 1918 that any government made being a nation-state the basic criterion of political legitimacy and the basic condition of its treating with other governments.[1]

THE OLD ORDER

The pre-nineteenth-century state did not serve nations; it did not even serve 'communities'. It served God, the Heavenly Mandate, the Law of Allah; it served hereditary rulers — the dynasts and the dynasties who were portrayed as God's vicars and whose appointed task was to carry out that mandate. It served a battery of customary laws and institutions, centuries old, which were considered to represent the heavenly order on earth. The fact of what language any dynast's subjects spoke was irrelevant to that task, and the particular cultures of his people only mattered to the degree in which they impeded that mandate. It was civilizations that such mandates were intended to preserve, not the lowly matter of cultures.

The only exception to this general rule among the large civilized political orders of Europe and Asia had been the Medieval Empire in the West, and it was only a partial exception. There, God's mandate had been divided between the papacy and a number of regional monarchs and princes; the one had authority over religious observance, the others over secular affairs. There were no dynasts, as later conceived, but feudatory monarchs who served as 'lieutenants'. Politics had been intensely populist, and the people recognized no clear line between culture, affairs of state and religious life. Medieval politics had been invaded by culture: poetry, sagas, and practices rooted in particular life-style all came to be considered legitimate sources of both political and religious practice. Then, culture had mattered and had provided a source of claims against the political and religious authorities.

But it was a brief-lived exception. The notion of sovereignty and the theory of the divine right of kings had combined to bring it to an end. Sovereignty — that is, the idea that in any community there ought to be only one source of authority — cut across all the shared authorities of the Medieval Empire, leaving the monarch alone as the sole source of rights and claims, while the theory of divine right represented the monarch as the direct, sanctified appointee of God, responsible to Him alone and the only authority entitled to interpret His word. In other words, his new authority was deemed to descend to the sovereign direct from God with no 'cultural' or popular interventions. This theory of rule scarcely served to bring kings and people closer together; it placed them much further apart — hence the heightened sanctity of sixteenth- and seventeenth-century monarchs over their twelfth- and thirteenth-century counterparts. It is no accident that chinoiserie should have appealed to eighteenth-century court society. At no other time did the separate Western monarchies so closely resemble that great empire of the East with its dynastic ruler as the single mediator of the Heavenly Mandate, interpreting God's law and serving itself in the process.

Far from widening the basis of the polity, as has sometimes been suggested, the legal fiction of sovereignty, supported by the seventeenth- and eighteenth-century notion of divine right, rather narrowed it and gave a limited focus to statecraft in Europe. The king personified the state; its administration was his court. It was his interests that this administration served. Its legal disputes were his legal disputes and its territorial claims were his territorial claims, claims derived from inheritance charters and roundabout family trees. Taxation had only two purposes: to undertake war in pursuit of these claims and to support the household of the king. Nineteenth-century revolutionaries claimed with some reason that absolutism had been a step backward from the more genuine populism of the middle ages.

There were pressures in the seventeenth and eighteenth centuries for this base to be widened. Some of the European kings' bureaucrats urged tasks of improvement for 'the good of the community'. In Germany, in the seventeenth century, these groups were called cameralists; in the eighteenth century they were the physiocrats and mercantilists. Under their advice and in varying degrees various European dynasts undertook programmes of improvement, especially in France. They built roads, supported canals, imposed controls in external trade in the name of the community or various of its merchant interests. Mercantilism came to be the name given to this type of support and protection by the court/state bureaucracy and the monarchs who undertook them were called 'enlightened despots'.

But such protection as emanated from the court, such schemes of improvement, were generally limited. They extended to issuing some royal charters, to two instances of state banks and to some public works. The Spanish and many German houses ignored such advice completely, and nowhere was it considered a *necessary* concomitant to rule. Louis XIV was quite liable to sacrifice the reform schemes of his advisers to musty dynastic legal claims, while at least two generations of Hanoverians regarded the interests of Hanover to which they had hereditary entitlements as more important than those of Britain to which they had been merely invited.

If dynasts did not serve their 'nations', we should not, on that account, suppose them to have been remiss. Had they attempted to do so, they would have encountered problems. Their societies were divided into distinct corporate bodies — of peasants, squires, burgesses and aristocrats. These bodies were distinguished by their economic pursuits, by their life-styles, by dress, manners and morals, by different forms of religious observance. Peasants and lords were gathered into congeries of provinces; burgesses into island-like towns scattered among them. Each had its own interests, its communities, its customs, its traditions, its 'liberties', even its names. De Tocqueville, one of its most acute observers, speaks of that time 'when the provinces and towns formed so many different nations in the midst of their common country'.[2]

Language usage differed from region to region, from village to village, and it differed markedly between orders. In France (the most highly centralized country) variants of *langue d'oc* were the languages used beyond the Loire; Breton the language of the west and north; German was spoken in the east; Old French was the popular usage in the Ile de France, which differed from the court French ('modern French') of the aristocracy. English was a polyglot of developed regional dialects; and everywhere the French—English usage of the drawing room was paralleled by a more rude Anglo-Saxon English of the kitchen. Over half the population of the Russian Empire did not speak Russian; and its nobility, itself of diverse Polish, Russian, German and Caucasion origin, spoke French and later German. In the Austrian lands, German was the daily language of the dynasty, the higher bureaucracy and the officer corps, irrespective of their ethnic origins, and Latin the language of edicts into the nineteenth century.

These diversities were not accidental attributes of the *ancien régime;* they were produced by its governing habits and its institutions. The maintenance of law and order, the dispensing of justice, the provision of welfare and economic sustenance — all that we expect the state to provide today — were carried out in the old kingdoms by local corporate bodies. Towns were the units of material production and trade; they had their corporations and their *parlements,* which made law and adjudicated town affairs. Each town had its guilds, which established the terms of production, and 'import' and 'export' duties for the services it provided to the surrounding countryside. Provinces had their great lords, their sheriffs and governors, and variegated manorial or seigneurial systems to keep peace in the country and to manage agricultural production. The seigneuries linked lord and peasant by different complexes of duties and rights; to the lord, duties of peace-keeping and rights to produce; to the peasant, duties of obedience and services and rights to land and water usage. But what linked them also divided them; it was this clear distinction of function that created such great distinctions of manners, of morals, even of language. All these bodies gave obeisance in theory; their 'liberties' made them autonomous and self-regulating in practice. Each developed in consequence its own laws, its own customs and its own interests.

The dynast's role was to defend these institutions and the customary laws that regulated them, and to mediate conflicting claims. He might move against them, but seldom with standardization in view. Attempts to do so tended to spark off revolts and civil wars. The most successful method of eroding old privileges was to create new ones; and the diversities it erased in one direction, it tended to create in another.[3]

These patterns of particularism, diversity and self-rule were mirrored in the emerging American polity across the Atlantic where religious dissenters had carried them. Little aristocratic privilege was to be found there, and minimal feudal practice; the social origins of the dissenters made such practices irrelevant. But New England was a patchwork of distinct townships, each with its own brand of worship, its political vision, its operating charter and governing bodies. Land was not given to individuals but to towns, which established sub-towns of the original settlement. In the South, the governing unit was the county, with its county town, county hall and county court. These new institutions of the new world, so often marked as the source of its modernity, were derived from the oldest institutions of the old world; in the provinces from which the settlers had come there had been little centralization and no royal bureaucracy. They made America a congeries of distinctive and autonomous local communities long before it became a nation-state.

In such societies, where sustenance and security were provided by local bodies and their raison d'etre by religious affiliation, political loyalty was as diverse as language. It went to town, to province, to guild, to overlord, to religious body, and to those who extended protection to these interests. Armenians were the most loyal of the Tsar's subjects because he offered the best prospect of freeing their co-religionists in the Ottoman Empire. De Tocqueville spoke of the American Union in 1830 as 'a vast body which presents no definite object to patriotic feeling'. Patriotism, which he termed 'frequently a mere extension of individual selfishness', had risen up then only so far as the federal state, and he confidently predicted that in any struggle between the Union and one of the states, 'at the present day', the Union would be defeated.[4]

Because of these erratic and shifting loyalties, kings were led to establish their own 'tribe' of civil servants loyal to them. To ensure loyalty, they were often foreigners or the declassed. French intendants were of humble origin; Italians long served as diplomats to French and English kings. The Ottoman Empire developed a separate class (the Janisaries — Christian children, orphaned and raised without any other connections) whose whole future was tied to bureaucratic service and hence to the well-being of the Empire. These 'mamluks' or bureaucratic gentry, divorced from traditional society, without any other calls on their loyalty, form the closest equivalents in that age to modern-day national patriots.

Because of these diverse particularisms, large antagonistic interests within the state chose at times to mediate those interests through the enthronement of a foreign prince, and actively sought one to rule them. William of Orange, the Hanoverian line and the German prince Otto who became the first king of the Greeks are examples of this preference. This was quite apart from the frequent dynastic accidents that brought a Frenchified Mary to the Scottish court, a Bourbon to the Spanish throne, an Italian to the French throne, a Spaniard to the German throne.

In such societies, nationalism had little place. Indeed, since institutions, customs and dynastic habits all cut across ethnic groupings, its expression would have been rather perverse. Religion and dynastic loyalty were the main generators of greater group loyalty. When certain German towns in the sixteenth century rose up against the prospect of a Spanish emperor, this was not because they wanted a German emperor; it was a protest against a Popish emperor. Otherwise, claims were defended or advanced in the name of customary laws and ancient practices by subjects and in the name of *raison d'état* by the dynast, both of which were legal categories.

Given the nature of the *ancien régime*, with its diversities and particularisms, how, we might ask, did the nation-state come about? How did societies structured by institutions, habits and conceptions that so cut across ethnicity become societies in which ethnicity was, and remains, the chief mark of social differentiation? The answer is that all those institutions and habits that made up the Old Order were destroyed. All those customary laws that buried ethnicity under a welter of distinguishing corporate rights and privileges were wiped away. The path to the nation-state is not a growth story, a tale of the evolution of these old social formations. It is a story of their destruction and their replacement by new matter, ideas and types of social relations.

THE FORCES OF DESTRUCTION

The social forces that worked against the Old Order have long been the subject of argument among historians. Ideas jostle with changing economic forms and expanding political authority to produce a cacophony of disputation. The answer to some of this disputation is simple enough: it varied according to time and place. The answer to much of the rest may be found in the types of explanations themselves, which, in fact, do not vary a great deal. Whatever their starting-points, whether an economic historian treating of Languedoc, a political historian treating of Prussia or a social historian treating of Indian religions, again and again we see the motions of the same forces working in different ways.

We see a particular body of ideas, carried by revolutionaries, or imperialists or missionaries, depending on the case in question, attacking long-cherished conceptions. We see those ideas usually in conjunction with some large-scale, or small but crucial, economic alterations that alter in their turn some basic social institution. Finally, almost invariably we see a new sort of governing agent who rationalizes these changes across the whole of society by new laws and standardized practices that are maintained by force.

The elements comprising this tableau have been given generic names. Many ideas or trends in 'thought' that attacked the Old Order have been gathered under the generic name 'rationalism'. The new productive techniques that attacked its productive base have been given the name 'capitalism'. Those new administrative techniques that attacked it by force and rules have been called by some bureaucracy, but this conceals as much as it reveals. Others prefer to refer to this particular phenomenon as 'the sovereign state'.

Rationalism

Rationalism (broadly defined) was a body of thought that developed throughout the eighteenth century, primarily in Europe, where it formed the basis of a critical movement. Its crucial point for the study of human affairs was that it did not begin with biblical exegesis, as such studies often did in the Old Order. It held that the proper study of mankind was Man. As such, it was a form of renaissance humanism; but it was a humanism that had been revolutionized and dynamized by the great seventeenth-century discoveries of the Laws of Nature, to which its origins in fact more properly belong. To the more optimistic, those scientific discoveries held out the hope that Man, a creature of nature, might be found to be in obedience to hitherto hidden mechanisms of self-regulation and, could they be found, a great science of Man might rise to parallel the science of nature. The more perceptive, like the seventeenth-century thinker Thomas Hobbes, grasped how damaging those very discoveries might prove to the legitimate bases of the *ancien régime,* and how necessary it was to discover new bases upon which to found social institutions.

In itself, rationalism was a disparate body of ideas on governance, economics, laws and religion; but all focussed on one central article of faith: that Man had a nature obedient to laws, self-regulating and generally benign. He was led by those laws to perform functions necessary to him, like eating and sleeping, and he was led by them to avoid activities harmful to him, like warring. Rationalists believed further that his social institutions should take account of those laws, should be built upon them and reinforce them.

To get at Man, to know him and to construct his institutions, rationalists developed a distinctive, indeed revolutionary, methodology. Its overriding precept was that the study of Man should begin *de novo,* in complete disregard of the institutions within which he actually lived. Hence their interest in savages and wolf-children, whom they took to be 'original' Men, unspoiled by socialization. They believed, secondly, that such laws as were derived from that study should be the only ordering criteria of social institutions. Indeed, they went further. They believed that all reform should proceed as from a *tabula rasa.* No institution should enjoy favour because it was old. All should be capable of being wiped away if Reason dictated a more sensible or rational way of proceeding. One of their heroes was Jeremy Bentham who believed that all the customary laws of England ought to be recast at once and constituted into a rational penal system. One of their most formidable enemies was Edmund Burke who argued that ancient constitutions had their own wisdom and could only be evolved slowly.

Many students of rationalism have disliked the epithet 'destructive'; they have argued that rationalism was a great breakthrough in consciousness, that its ideas were creative forces, and that rationalists offered their societies necessary and useful aids to its organizations. But this is an 'objective' view; it fails to place rationalists within the social contexts in which they were in fact operating. Those early explorers, encountering primitive societies upon their travels, also delivered to them certain aids that they believed would help their social organizations but that in fact disrupted them. So too did the rationalists behave within their own societies, treating them like so many primitive tribes, criticizing their customs, their self-conceptions, their taboos and religious beliefs. The ideas they developed were almost always in direct contradiction to its own ways of knowledge, of governance and of social relations.

Amongst these were the ideas rationalists developed concerning divine right monarchy. Following Thomas Hobbes and his compatriate, John Locke, they criticized its pretension to descent from heaven and to know God; they disputed its central conception of man as deeply flawed, and its pageantries and annointments. They were not opposed to either monarchy or authority as such;

rather they wished to rid authority of its unnecessary trappings and to recognize it for what it was — necessary to a well-ordered state. They held that to dress it up with annointments and pageantry and pretend it descended from heaven served to make authority uncontrollable and irrational, whereas it might be useful and beneficial.

How did the rationalists suppose that society ought to be ordered? They were generally contractarians or constitutionalists. They believed the old mystical bonds of heavenly descent on to a prearticulate social order ought to be replaced by a limited and rationalized contract between ruler and ruled, a literal set of rules re-thought *de novo,* in which the ruled would give up such freedoms as all would agree were harmful to a well-ordered society, such as murder or theft or the carrying of arms — and only those freedoms — and consign these 'natural' rights to a sovereign in return for security and order. Such a contract, they believed, would replace the weak, contentious bond of superstition by the stronger bond of Reason.

But the very notion of a rational bond was deeply inimical to divine right monarchy, which was based precisely on annointment, descent and religious sanctions. Moreover, it was inimical to monarchy altogether. For what was the implication of the rule of Reason? If authority was not to descend from heaven, if it did not need to rest upon the accident of heredity, if it should not rest upon dynastic marriage, then any man or body could be sovereign. From there it was but a short step, the step from Locke to Rousseau, to claim that monarchy was not really necessary at all. The rationalists were demanding, in short, that divine right monarchy reconceive itself to the point of no longer existing.

Surrounding divine right monarchy was the privilege system and the ornate ranking of men in society, on which the rationalists were absolutely withering. Where, in nature, thundered Rousseau, did one see such an ornament of rank? Where did there exist in nature the Noblesse de l'Epee, de la Robe, the intricate distinctions of dukes, baronets and knights that made men as distinct from one another as they were from the population at large? For some the attack on privilege was undertaken in the name of reason; for others it was undertaken as part of the attack on divine right monarchy. It was also an attack on patronage and preferment, and was part of schemes for more rational administration. In other words, it was considered by most rationalists to be an addendum to more central ideas, and anyone not acquainted with the Old Order might share this view. Indeed much more time is given to expositions of rationalist thought on monarchy than to its criticisms of privilege.

But if the attack on divine right struck the Old Order at its head, the attack on privilege aimed straight at its heart. For in the Old Order dynastic monarchy was a kind of fiction imposed on top of an intricate privilege system inherited from the past. It was this privilege system that actually administered the country. The entire manorial system and its elaborations depended upon privilege; its basic economic organization was bound up with the distinction between lord and peasant. Its provinces were managed by great lords. To alter the self-conceptions of monarchy might not have affected this system at all, as the institution of enlightened despotism perhaps demonstrates. But the attack on privilege was an attack on much of the social structure of the country at large.[5]

The attack against the Old Order from below was to be supported from an unexpected quarter, the physiocrats and their more distant cousins, the agricultural improvers, scientists among whom the English were particularly adept. As a school, they are often separated from Enlightenment thought, or at least from its political parts, but at the time they were not considered so distinct in their animating elements, merely in their focus. The attention of the physiocrats and agricultural improvers was directed toward the material well-being of society.

According to the physiocrats the real basis of a polity's wealth lay not in its gold mines, not even in trade or commerce, which was rather turn-over wealth. It was agricultural wealth that sustained trade and promoted commerce, since it actually resulted in the production of things that had not existed before. Thus, they pressed for more rational means of agricultural production and urged its furtherance by the court/state bureaucracy.

What this meant was new techniques of cultivation, new tools, crop rotation, large fields, different patterns of fallow, and by implication a more educated peasantry and more involved landlords. Moreover, and perhaps more to the point, the improvers wanted whoever could to have freedom to buy and sell land, and equal taxation by land, not by estate or status, to equalize the tax burden. They demanded nothing more or less than the complete abolition of all forms of serfdom, of the rights of tenure, of all the customs that had grown up over centuries as part of the regulation of relations between the lord and his tenant.

The mild recommendations of the agricultural improvers implied, indeed, even more. For the peasant was but one part of a complex of which the landed aristocracy was the other half. To abolish all feudal customs meant in effect to abolish the aristocracy as a separate caste and to make the aristocrat nothing more than a land owner, if indeed he had land at all.[6] Thus the agricultural revolution came into alliance with and supported from a different angle the attack on privilege, and widened the basis of the attack, while together the two sought to wipe out all the structures within which the vast majority of the people lived.

Down to the latter part of the eighteenth century, the rationalists had confined their attacks to governance and its collateral institutions in the country. The customs of town life were left relatively untouched; guild structures, customs and duties had appeared irrelevant to their task. But, in 1776, there was published the rationalist epic that was to unite town and country into a single uniform structure of thought, obedient to the self-same laws and requiring the self-same structures — Adam Smith's *The Wealth of Nations*.

The particular body of thought operative here came to be called political economy. Its central precepts are well known. According to its chief adherent, the economic life of a country at large, in all its parts, is self-regulatory. It has its laws, the laws of supply and demand, where price is determined by the interaction of the two. These do not require false maintenance or protection. Indeed to interfere with them would stifle the natural workings of the invisible hand. What the political economists wanted was the utmost freedom, of establishment and of price, and the end to protective tariffs, customs and duties that impeded that movement.

What appeared most under attack in these writings were the mercantilist policies adopted by enlightened despots, that is, state interference with the workings of the economy and tariff legislation. Some, indeed, have seen in *The Wealth of Nations* almost a singular reference to despotism — making economic 'liberalism' everywhere the ally of political liberalism.

Yet official mercantilism was not the most restrictive of the restrictive practices of the Old Order and national tariffs were not the only tariffs. What was as much or more under attack were all the minute privileges and regulatory practices of town, regions and guilds with their multifarious licensings, price settings and impediments to the free movement of goods. The political economists were demanding an end to all this; and the demand for 'laissez-faire' as it was called, was one of the most destructive demands made of the Old Order.

These attacks on the court and the multifarious structures of town and country life were accompanied by demands that the customary laws of places be rationalized into common codes: one fair at Nemingen inspired more than a dozen different rationalist schemes for its better management. The whole was crowned by virulent attacks on religion — the linchpin of these old orders — which set the tone for nineteenth-century scepticism and undercut the only bond that held all their structures together.

The general recommendatory tendency of these ideas taken together was toward *dismantling*. Whenever men attacked the Old Order, they thought almost invariably of wiping its institutions away, not reforming them. Few expositions appear in rationalist literature of new institutions or new institutional forms. To the degree in which the rationalists' ideas influenced state legislation or the interpretation of custom, the laws tended to lift previous restrictions rather than establish new ones. This tendency was inherent in rationalist thought; in much of it, indeed, it was explicit. For, starting with a belief in self-sustaining natural laws of man's behaviour, they felt that fewer and simpler structures would be sufficient to inform that behaviour. Man's natural instincts and the benign self-regulatory aspects of his nature would fill the empty space spontaneously.

The thinkers propounding these ideas began to gather in coffee houses in the 1730s. By the 1760s, they formed a distinct school of thought and had begun to circulate in salon society where their ideas gained a certain notoriety. In its language and reformist programmes the French Revolution was an entirely rationalist creation; and, despite the restoration of the divine right Bourbon monarchy, rationalist ideas came increasingly to be accepted as common wisdom. In England, by the time of the repeal of the Navigation Acts in 1849, they had become common sense. They were carried abroad through the rest of the nineteenth century by imperial reformers and even by missionaries. Even the Tsar was forced to adopt some rationalist schemes after the abortive revolution of 1905.

So influential did rationalism become that whenever men of those times asked what forces were causing the Old Order to crack, to pass away and to be replaced by a new one, they almost always answered 'illuminism' or 'free-masonry' (after the secret society that propounded rationalist ideas). They came to see it as the chief, often the only force working against the old social formations. But for rationalists to have appeared at all, some erosion must already have taken place; and for dismantling to have become the order of the day, the old formations that were being dismantled must have already lost some, at least, of their vital functions.

Capitalism

Capitalism involves satisfying wants through the use of money; it also implies a type of society in which money is the chief mode of exchange, the measure of value, the satisfier of wants. In feudal society, the basis of exchange is reciprocity, defined by oath or promise. The two systems are mutually antithetical: where money is in widespread use, where it is easily gained, it will make oath and promise unnecessary; it will enable some men to rethink their promises, to change their habitats, to look elsewhere for protection and justice. It will create masterless men who can float freely in the interstices of such society. Whenever money penetrates a system built on barter and promise, it will serve to disrupt it. It is this fact that has so often made money subject to strict regulation and religious sanction.

Because of its disruptive influence and the strict social controls on its use, money was in Europe and elsewhere often purveyed by those who lived outside society — by Jews, by Armenians, Greeks and foreign Chinese, by 'land agents' or commissioners who were not culturally part of the societies in which they operated. To concentrate the use of money in the hands of those who were culturally different served to limit its harmful effects on society at large. Hence also the persecution periodically suffered by such groups, in the name of the protection of traditional society.

If capitalism disrupts traditional society, it also creates, in those who rely upon it, a peculiar characteristic: it makes them more or less alike. Money has its own rules and makes those who rely upon it similar in their interests, outlooks and ways of thought. They are not distinguished by all those particularisms present in traditional society. They differ only in that some may have more money, others less, not in their attributes, names or customs. It is no accident that it was the Dutch who looked most homogenous, most like a nation in the seventeenth century, for it was the 'nation' that was most dominated by mercantile values.

Before the great gold discoveries of the New World, when the money supply of Europe was limited, it was handled in any quantity only by banking circles and banking families who had a more or less effective monopoly on its control and circulation. The techniques of banking had moved outward from Italy in the thirteenth century to Flanders, but the great Lombardy banks retained their pre-eminence and mastered the field well into the fifteenth century. During this early phase of capitalism, capital existed within the bounds of traditional society without doing more than eroding it at the edges. Indeed, capitalism was incorporated into it and quasi-feudalized. Those who handled it became a special 'caste' of their own, operating within fixed rules, serving the royal houses and securing money for the trade pursuits of small industries and traders who, in their turn, formed particularist quasi-feudal associations.

Even then, however, particularly in the seafaring countries of the Atlantic seaboard and in the northern Italian city-states, it had begun to affect the social structures to a degree, and if the particularly extreme forms of feudal structure like serfdom were practically unknown in those parts after the thirteenth century, this was due largely to their being the points of access for money supply and trade.

After the sixteenth century, the money supply of Europe dramatically increased, and money was handled not just by banks, but also by groups of much larger-scale trading companies that were enabled to grow. Trade became a serious capital pursuit. The circulation of money became much more widespread and it circulated in quantity among the upper orders. It did not disrupt the caste system at this stage; indeed, if anything, it served rather to confirm it. Yet within those castes it effected distinct changes. In England, where mercantilism was relatively advanced, wealth became an important stepping-stone to power and rank, and everywhere in the seventeenth century the new sovereigns, to secure the loyalties of the aristocracy and badly needed incomes for themselves, began to sell offices for money rather than for service, bypassing hereditary entailments and creating new offices for the purpose. In France, there grew up two new castes of nobility who had bought their ranks, castes to which entry was easy and that shared many values and characteristics of the burgher or mercantile class, however much its members sought to escape the taint.

From the 1690s to the 1740s traders, to maximize their profits, began to import raw materials to have them turned into finished goods at home — the cottage or putting-out phase of capitalism. During this period, money began to circulate much more widely over larger parts of the countryside in Europe at large and its effect was proportionately spread to the structures of the countryside. More peasants, put in the way of work, began to acquit their feudal dues by money, not in kind or service. They began further to request complete acquittal of their dues by large payments, which would leave them free of overlordship, in effect 'owners' of their land, while great lords began to pay workers for service on 'their' estates, thus neatly reversing the old feudal relationships.

Where these practices were effected they disrupted the ancient constitution, the whole structure of rights and duties; they began to make the old customs appear irrelevant, antiquated and outdated. In whose jurisdiction did the man of property fall? For the aristocracy, these practices entailed a decline in its real duties and left it only with a show of privilege or rank without any real responsibilities. Hence, in part, the tellingness of the rationalist attack upon it.

By the end of the eighteenth century, the Old Order had begun to change where these processes were effected from below and within, but still it contained those changes by elaborating its own structures not by radically altering them. New groups came into prominence under old heraldries; the outward show was elaborated and its inner essence eroded, but its form was still recognisable and its rhetorics in place. If the Old Order accommodated itself to capital, so too did capital accommodate itself to the Old Order; pre-nineteenth-century capitalisms worked essentially within the interstices of traditional society. The 'great transformation', as Karl Polanyi has called it, was effected by capital-intensive industrial capitalism.

Unlike the previous forms of capitalism, according to Polanyi, industrial capitalism required special conditions for its operations. These conditions derived from the cost of industrial plant; to defray such costs and to make industrial operations pay, the proto-industrialists required a steady and reliable labour supply, a steady and reliable supply of raw materials and a market sufficient to absorb the product in large quantities.[7] Eric Hobsbawm has put the latter first and has marked as an essential precondition of English industrialization the possession by England of an overseas empire.[8]

Industrialization, in short, required just those sorts of movements that the customary laws and guild and town privileges of traditional society impeded.

Where such freedoms existed, they were enlarged upon to draw people off the land and into the factories. Where they did not exist they were created by the lifting of serfdom. These changes destroyed the peasant *qua* peasant. They turned him into a paid worker, a man not tied to land or locality. If mercantilism and the putting-out system had created sporadic groups of masterless men, industrialism created masses of them.

Town artisans at first attempted to compete with mechanised production by ruinous price cuts; thereafter they were either absorbed or, like the English handloom weavers, simply destroyed. They took some guild practices into the factory with them; the early Krupp steel works in 1830 had twenty-seven different artisan groups among scarcely a hundred workers. But the guild as such gradually disappeared as the artisan became a factory worker. It was replaced in England by the Friendly Society, a workers' cooperative that protected the worker by means other than those used by the guild to protect the artisan.

The new system required markets to be freed of their feudal restrictions; towns gave up their duties and customs. It needed transport to move goods to markets; from the 1860s in America there was a movement of large populations from East to the West, effected by offering free transport and cheap land, so that the railroads would later be used for the transport of goods. Together these developments transformed the relations of the townships, stringing them, as one writer observed, like beads on a thread to hang around the neck of some great emerging city, which then performed the services previously offered by each locality.[9] By such means, it either destroyed or altered the notion of locality and the particularisms that had grown with it.

These practices were carried abroad where raw materials lay waiting for exploitation, or where railroads were waiting to be built, and, wherever they were located, we may see the same transformations at work. If Ludlow gave up its privileges, so too did Oudh. If 'ownership' was being expanded at home and common lands broken up, this was the same process being imposed for the same reasons rather further away, to the ancient system of land tenure in India, to the tribal lands beyond the American frontier, to the tribal lands in Africa. If handloom weaving was destroyed in England by a flood of mass-produced goods, a flood of those same goods destroyed Indian weavers. If the traditional society had been broken up at home by the introduction of mining, so mining broke up tribal structures abroad, in Africa, South and Central America.

At home, this process was called industrialization; abroad it was called imperialism. At some levels, what was involved differed little. The abuse of natives abroad and the destruction of traditional communities, structures and life-styles was being paralleled by the self-same abuse of natives at home, by the destruction of their traditional communities and traditional life-styles there. What differed was the form of relief sought; English workers battled for 'representation'; Indians later on were to join battle to rid India of 'foreign rule'.

As the new class formed and expanded its activities, as its numbers became larger and its wealth impressive, so too its organization, its wants and its ideas began to take on concrete political forms. The language of its reforms was almost always rationalist and its conceptions were informed by rationalist conceptions. What Locke, Adam Smith and Arnold Thaer supported by Reason, capital supported by interest, giving rise to a not surprising suspicion that the one was but the epiphenomenon, the cloud of vapour given off by the other.

Under their pressure, the ancient political constitutions began to be reformed. In one after another of the European polities from the late eighteenth century through the nineteenth century, divine right monarchy receded. By revolution or evolution, it was altered to take on new forms, contractarian or constitutional. Privilege and rank receded to give way to different rank based on wealth, ranks occupied by those of different values and interest while, below, the swollen ranks of masterlessmen, deprived of traditional communities, turned their political interests and loyalties in new directions, more fitted to their new circumstances. The Friendly Societies gave way to trade unions, to savings banks and to cooperative stores. American farmers founded the Grange, their southern compatriots founded the Ku Klux Klan, and all began to battle for representation in the state machine, which appeared increasingly as the most effective device for intervention on their behalf.

Of particular interest in this respect is the East India Company, one of the great chartered companies of the mercantile era. In 1833 it was deprived of its monopoly on the Indian trade, and to preserve its position in the altered circumstances it also took to involving itself in government at new levels. It began to take on untoward concern in the moral status of the princes of the Raj, their efficacy as governors, the well-being of their subjects. One by one these princes were required to accept ameliorations of their rule; by mid-century they were being unseated and deposed and the Company took over their administrations. It was a strange parody of what was happening in Britain.

If rationalism and capitalism were powerful allies in the transformation of the Old Order, they did not work alone. Where each worked in its own sphere or together, they generally looked to the state machine to further their interests or conceptions. Where each worked unevenly or sporadically, the sovereign often generalized those uneven tendencies into general norms for the whole of society. But the state was no mere agency for these tendencies, as is sometimes portrayed. De Tocqueville long ago pointed out that even before rationalist tendencies struck France, even before capitalism, which had in his time not yet even a generic name, the sovereign state had already begun to work on the structures of traditional society.[10] Indeed, if rationalism and capitalism struck deepest in the sovereign state, this was in part because the state, itself, had prepared the way.

The sovereign state

The destructive tendency of the sovereign state on the many authorities of traditional society lay in its claim, where that claim existed, to be the *sole* source of authority. The very idea of such a single source was antithetical to them; it challenged the claims of traditional customs and rights merely by existing. In Eastern Europe, where kingship had kept more of its medieval characteristics of lieutenantship and where the idea of sovereignty did not have much influence, and in the empires of the East where the Heavenly Mandate was deemed to be reflected in society as well as in the celestial dynasties, the monarchical principle subsisted together with aristocratic, feudal and religious structures without disrupting them. Indeed, it is precisely the absence of the notion of sovereignty that accounts in part for the persistence of such structures in the East. In the West, especially in France, where the idea of kingship came to be tightly bound up with the notion of sovereignty, it almost immediately demanded subordination, the reduction of rights and privileges and the subjection of the church.

When the *stats princip* first began to work upon traditional society, and sovereigns began to base their claim to rule on the idea that there ought to be only one source of authority, they aimed at taming only those elements that stood most in contradiction to them — aristocratic independence and papal interference. On the former the state acted sometimes by sheer force of arms, more often by the less risky expedient of exchanging privilege of an honorific or financial sort for the privilege of independent rule and administrative duty. Thus, sovereigns bestowed court favour and court privilege in return for a limitation of extensive feudal rights in the country at large. They gave honours to be gained at court to tempt the aristocrats to remain there and extended their own efforts at justice, poor relief and defence to edge the aristocrats out of their positions in the country of their domains. Thus aristocracy began to gain rank and fortune without any of the risks, duties or tasks that everywhere used to be thought their logical concomitant, while the seigneurial courts, desmesnes and county towns, deprived of major local luminaries to animate them, could not fight against being bypassed, adapt to new tasks when required.

Religion was determined at court and religious homogeneity at first was enforced to prevent dissidence. Hence, religion might switch with the monarch. In 1685, Louis XIV revoked the Edict of Nantes, achieving religious uniformity. To ensure the enforcing of royal edicts, the sovereign moved against the towns to limit the rights of self-defence. This was particularly important since towns were often centres of religious dissidence.

In towns where there had existed the elected bodies of the *corps de ville* and the general assemblies, the right of appointment to the latter was claimed as the right of royal appointment and given or sold to local notables as a royal privilege. In 1692 in France the right to hold municipal elections was abolished and the municipal posts were put up for sale. This was not so much to curtail the 'liberties' of the towns, for they could be bought back again; it was part of the policy of financing the court. But it undermined the independence of the towns and eroded their structures, not to mention their prosperity.

In France where the ordinary courts, the *parlements,* were free and independent of royal authority, kings used the expedient of 'exceptional' courts of justice, which were appointed to try cases involving the king's authority and interest. These exceptional cases were enlarged to cover affairs of the public domain and what was theoretically an exception became a fixed rule. As the rights to try of the traditional courts declined, so too customary law declined; positive, standard laws edged them out and replaced them.

Where the king took away duties or engaged in such practices that these duties declined, they either were not performed or they had to be performed by a central agency, a bureaucracy. The growth of bureaucratic power follows *pari passu* the growth of kingly or state power and the extent and depth of one will always match the extent and depth of the other. In France, this system took the form under Richelieu of a Royal Council and some thirty provincial intendants who handled all the ordinary administration of the provinces. John Law, the Scots Controller-General taken on by Louis XIV to set up a French royal bank, declared himself amazed in 1704 to find that the entire kingdom was ruled by thirty men and that 'your Parlements, Estates and Governors simply do not enter into the picture'. Their tasks steadily widened throughout the eighteenth century as town and country bodies became increasingly viscerated.

As more and more of the country came to be governed by royal edict and common codes, rather than by the discrete customary local laws, the customary laws declined. In 1806, the French state wiped out even the last vestiges of the old laws of the post-feudal society through the imposition of a complete new legal code that rationalized all the royal edicts of the past into a fully organized and coherent system — the Code Napoléon. It was Bentham's dream come true.

The more that diverse customs, local particularisms and independent institutions were eroded, taken over or edged out of their prerogatives, the more that those that remained looked anomalous, or dangerous. The more the sovereign ruled, the more exceptions to that rule stood out and presented themselves as unpalatable and as potential or actual centres of resistance. The seventeenth-century English government found mere compromise with the Scots sufficient to maintain its sovereignty. By 1707, it found a separate parliament there unacceptable, and managed to get it removed. By the mid-eighteenth century, the Highlands, rendered by this action more exposed, were being cleared and the highlanders shipped out or massacred. What was palatable in the seventeenth century had become intolerable by the eighteenth century.

The erosion of local dialects and language diversity was everywhere the result of royal edict and bureaucratic action. In 1539, by the Edict of Villiers-Collerets, Francis I made the *langue d'oïl* the state language, and Richelieu founded the Académic Française to mould and control language usage. In 1790, Joseph II attempted to extend German to Hungary. In 1879, the Hungarian Education Act made it compulsory to teach Magyar in all primary schools. In 1887, the Russian bureaucracy imposed Russian as the language of instruction in state schools.

It was the French state dynamized by the Revolution that abolished the feudal regime entirely in its decrees of 4 August 1789. It abolished the system of internal tariffs in 1790. Under the name of anti-combination laws of 1791, it dissolved the guilds and merchants' companies. In 1793, it standardized weights and measures. In 1795, it gave the French a uniform system of taxation. It cancelled all the laws of primogeniture and entail, thus destroying the last vestiges of the feudal system of rank and privilege. The Napoleonic armies carried this style of bureaucratic centralization, levelling and standardization into Central Europe; and the new regimes established by Napoleon in the Rhineland abolished serfdom, customs and guilds on the French model. The whole battery of the old customary laws was wiped away by the imposition of variants on the Code Napoléon. When Hegel insisted that it was the state that created the nation, he was looking backwards to the history of France, not forward to the history of Germany.

When Germany was unified 'from above' in 1870 and the Reich was formed, this way of proceeding did not appear to most Germans to be at variance with the experience of their Western neighbours — a substitution of Union 'by force' for the 'organic growth' of France and England. It appeared to be a repetition of it, differing only in that it was less bloody. Here, as there, the state was moving outwards into diverse feudal remnants of the old order, dissolving them, making all obedient to the same law.

In the 1860s, 70s and 80s, the state machines of Hungary and Russia began to adopt these self-conceptions and forms of operation. They began to move against the traditional communities of their realms. Serfdom was abolished in Russia in 1861. The Hungarian administration, under the name of Magyarization, enforced Hungarian as a common language. In 1889, the Russians took away the school and university privileges of Armenians and Baltic Germans.

Today's new nations of Asia and Africa are often distinguished from the 'old' nations of Europe on the grounds that their nations are artificial creations out of diverse tribal and cultural groupings. Let us remember the Hungarian law of Nationalilties, promulgated in 1868: 'All citizens of Hungary form a single nation — the indivisible unitary Magyar nation — to which all citizens of the country belong irrespective of nationality.'[11]

THE NEW CREATIONS

The progress to the modern nation-state was not simply a tale of the withering away of old institutions. In their wake, the forces destructive of the Old Order left new creations — new institutions and new types of social relations — that knit society together in new ways. They were ostensibly simpler but they were on a much larger scale.

Rationalism created the idea of the 'citizen' — the individual who recognized the state as his legal home. It created the idea of a uniform system of law throughout a country. It created the idea of legal equality, where all citizens have the same status before that system of law. It created the idea of the state that exists to serve those citizens. It created the idea of loyalty to a larger group than clan or caste. Capitalism created the 'mass' — the masterless men who are free to sell their labour — and hence the material conditions for modern citizenship. It created the conditions for mass communication among them. It created classes and class distinctions of its own, to be sure, but it tied those classes together by an intricate division of labour. It cast that division of labour over vast territories, bringing hitherto distant regions into immediate functional relationships; the Western grain producers of America became dependent on Eastern finance, on Eastern markets, on Eastern transport. It created the need for continuous monitoring of all these complex interdependencies.

The state created common languages and common education systems, and enforced common legal systems existing within clearly defined state boundaries. It created state tariffs at those boundaries, state debts and state banks managing state-wide currencies. It created national bureaucracies and national armies that socialized people from different regions and classes.

These features are the characteristic features of the modern state; they are the features that make it modern. They are also the characteristic features of the nation-state; the nation-state was created by them. The modern state and the nation-state are coextensive phenomena. In the process of development, modernization and nation-building imply the same programme.

Not all states that claim to be nation-states display these characteristics: India still has diverse regions of diverse peoples; Malaysians still speak different languages; Africans still give some loyalty to tribe. But their leaders and many of their citizens wish to approximate these features. They wish to develop bureaucracies and capital plant. They wish to develop common education systems and common taxation systems. They wish to develop uniform people speaking uniform languages. The claim to be a nation-state is, in these circumstances, the statement of a goal and the outline of a political programme; and the appeals they make to their still fictitious nations are appeals to implement that programme. To the degree in which it is implemented, they too will become nation-states.

NOTES AND REFERENCES

1. The United States made this condition. It was one of President Woodrow Wilson's Fourteen Points for the peace settlement after 1918. The French Revolution was undertaken in 'the name of the Rights of Man and the Citizen', abstract rights belonging to all men, not merely Frenchmen and not on account of their being French. Nationalism was the legatee of a failed universalism.
2. Alexis de Tocqueville *Democracy in America* (1835) (trans. H. Reeve; London: Longmans 1862) vol. 1, p. 389.
3. The erosion of local privileges was effected in part by fixing and elaborating aristocratic privilege. See Perry Anderson *Lineages of the Absolutist State* (London: New Left Books, 1974) for an exposition of the habits of absolutism.
4. de Tocqueville, *op. cit.* Vol. 1, pp. 461–2.
5. Rousseau's *Discourse on the Origins of Inequality* (1755) ought to be given equal status with his *Social Contract* (1762) as a major transformer. The notion that inequality was in large measure unnatural, a social creation, was much more shocking to eighteenth-century thought than contractarian ideas, with which privilege could cohabit. Of course, Rousseau was not a ratinalist in a narrow sense. He had grave doubts about progress and civilization. But his major political writings attempt to start afresh, ignoring or condemning what actually exists.

6. Many aristocrats earned their income entirely from the performance of services, for example from mill rights or rights of passage. To these groups, rationalist ideas were absolutely antithetical, whereas to those who had large land rights they were often welcome.
7. The argument is laid out in detail in K. Polanyi *The Origins of Our Time: the Great Transformation* (London: Gollancz, 1945).
8. In his *Industry and Empire* (London: Weidenfeld and Nicolson, 1968), which is an attempt to relate the two.
9. Henry V. Billows (a New York minister) 'The townward tendency' in *The City* (1872) p. 38; quoted by Thomas Bender *Community and Social Change in America* (New Brunswick: Rutgers University Press, 1978) p. 110.
10. de Tocqueville *The Ancien Regime and the French Revolution* (first published 1856. London: Fontana, 1966). De Tocqueville's study was among the first to question the notion that rationalism alone had undermined the *ancien régime*.
11. Quoted by F. H. Hinsley in *Nationalism and the International System* (London: Hodder and Stoughton, 1973) p. 55.

FURTHER READING

General expositions of the development of the nation-state are Hans Kohn *Nationalism, its meaning and history* (Princeton, NJ: Van Nostrand, 1955) and, for specific aspects of that development, Charles Tilly (ed.) *The Formation of National States in Western Europe* (London: Princeton University Press, 1975). For a sociological comparison of the different forms the Western state has taken during its evolution, see Gianfranco Poggi *The Development of the Modern State* (London: Hutchison, 1978).

On the growth of the state, the classic is A. de Tocqueville *The Ancien Regime and the French Revolution (1856;* London: Fontana, 1966). A good introduction is J. R. Strayer *On the Medieval Origins of the Modern State* (Princeton, NJ: Princeton University Press, 1970). See also J. H. Shennan *The Origins of the Modern European State 1450–1725* (London: Hutchison, 1974); and Ernest Barker *The Development of Public Services in Western Europe, 1660–1930* (London: Oxford University Press, 1944). H. Seton-Watson *Nations and States* (London: Methuen, 1977) carries the story outside Europe; and, since the United States is often neglected in general reviews, A. Schlesinger *Political and Social Growth of the American People, 1865–1940* (New York: Macmillan, 1941).

On capitalism, see Karl Polanyi *Origins of Our Time: The Great Transformation* (London: Gollancz, 1945), which should be read together with S. Pollard and C. Holmes (eds) *Documents of European Economic History, Vol. 1, The Process of Industrialisation, 1750–1870* (London: Edward Arnold, 1968). More detailed studies are Neil Smelser, of the Lancashire cotton industry, in *Social Change in the Industrial Revolution* (London: Routledge and Kegan Paul, 1962) and Martin Kitchen *The Political*

Economy of Germany, 1815 — 1914 (London: Croom Helm, 1978).

On why nationalism might have followed upon these changes, see Ernest Gellner 'Nationalism' in his *Thought and Change* (London: Weidenfeld and Nicolson, 1964).

On rural change, see Jerome Blum *The End of the Old Order in Rural Europe* (Princeton, NJ: Princeton University Press, 1978) and Eugen Weber *Peasants into Frenchmen* (London: Chatto and Windus, 1977).

On rationalism, W. E. H. Lecky's *History of the Rise and Influence of Rationalism in Europe* (first published in 1865) remains one of the more comprehensive accounts. More modern accounts are Carl Becker *The Heavenly City of 18th Century Philosophers* (New Haven, Conn.: Yale University Press, 1932), for a general review of Enlightenment ideas, and R. Bendix *Kings or People: Power and the Mandate to Rule* (London: University of California Press, 1978) for changing political ideas.

2

Varieties of Nationalism

A. W. Orridge

Let us first of all explore the nature and limits of this subject by examining two propositions: that nationalism is distinctively modern and that it is very widespread.

Feelings of support for political institutions and of attachment to culture and regions are found, of course, wherever the activities of men have been recorded. A sense of patriotic attachment was felt by the citizens of Athens for their city, by Romans for their city and empire, by the Germans and Jews of antiquity for the cultural groups to which they belonged. Whenever empires have been built by conquest, the conquered peoples have resisted and felt hostility towards the invaders. Often they have taken whatever chances they could find to drive out the alien rulers, even after many years of imperial rule. In all periods and places, men have felt an affection for the people, customs and physical surroundings among which they grew up. However, none of these amounts to modern nationalism. An attachment to the habits, neighbours and scenery of childhood may be almost universal, but no one has any genuine feeling of neighbourliness for all the inhabitants of a country the size of England or even of smaller nations such as Denmark, nor do they have an intimate acquaintance with all the customs and scenery of these countries. Wider cultural similarities have sometimes attracted devotion of a patriotic sort before recent times, but this was rarely reflected in political structures. Ancient Greeks and Germans were aware that they were different from other peoples, but their political units were cities and tribes, often in bitter conflict with one another, and only external threat produced even temporary unity. The notion that there is or should be some intimate connection between broad

39

cultural similarities and political organization (a central element of nationalism in all its many forms) would have seemed very strange, and would have been very far from political reality, in most times and places before the last two centuries. A medieval European monarch, for example, would have been mystified by the notion that he should rule only, or even mainly, people of similar cultural origins to himself. (For the moment there will be no further effort to define nationalism. The reason for this will become clear towards the end of the essay.)

The distinctively modern character of nationalism is accepted by most who have investigated the subject, but there are great differences about the period when it arose. Some see the French Revolution and its aftermath as the crucial period, while others are prepared to find nationalism as far back as the thirteenth and fourteenth centuries.[1] To take only one example that is likely to be familiar, many instances of English national feeling can be found in Shakespeare's histories, although this of course reflects sentiment in Elizabethan England, not the earlier period in which the play is set. For instance,

> This happy breed of men, this little world,
> This precious stone set in the silver sea
> Which serves it in the office of a wall,
> Or as a moat defensive to a house,
> Against the envy of less happier lands,
> This blessed plot, this earth, this realm, this England . . .
> [*Richard II,* Act 2, Scene 1]

The sensible approach to this dispute is not to look for any particular age as *the* period in which nationalism appears, fully formed, for the first time, any more than it would be reasonable to expect to find one period when modern socialism, bureaucratic administration or democratic politics appeared. Complex political phenomena such as these emerge slowly over long periods of time and their roots, predecessors and prototypes can be found long before they reach the forms we know today; hence the arguments of those who find nationalism in the fourteenth century. But, on the other hand, they only achieve their characteristic modern forms at a much later date; hence the arguments of those who propose that nationalism is a creation of the early nineteenth century.

It needs little space to establish the widespread nature of nationalism today. Almost all the 150 or so member states of the United Nations claim to be nation-states, with varying degrees of plausibility, as the title of the body indicates. Our very word for inter-state relations is inter*national* relations. Nationalism lies at the roots of some of the most important features of the politics of the period in which we live. The immense increase in the number of independent states since 1945, the result of the dismantling of the empires of European states, has among its major causes one of the varieties of nationalism, anti-imperialist nationalism. Even between communist or socialist states, which sometimes claim to have overcome nationalist tensions, the divisions between China and the USSR, between the USSR and some Eastern European states, and between China and Vietnam, display strong elements of nationalism and are as severe as any disputes between Western industrial nations. However, while there is much nationalism, just as clearly it is not all the same, and indeed one of the most impressive features of modern nationalism is the range of circumstances in which it has gained purchase. Let us now turn to examine this variation.

A SEQUENCE OF NATIONALISMS

There have been many attempts to classify nationalisms.[2] This does not mean that all the existing ones are inadequate and will eventually be replaced by one universally agreed and complete classification. In some fortunate subjects, such as zoology, complicated entities such as creatures fall into distinct groups and within each group individuals are so similar to one another that one classification on the basis of these groups will serve most purposes — the classification into species. In less fortunate subjects, such as political science, complicated entities such as cases of nationalism are always significantly different from each other in some respects, and thus they can be classified into different groups for different purposes. If the analyst is interested in the history of political ideas, he will classify nationalisms according to their relationships to periods of political thought or to other sorts of political philosophies. If his interest is in certain historical periods, he will find most useful a classification that connects nationalism to particular epochs. If his concern is with the social roots of nationalist movements, a classification that relates nationalisms to the classes and groups most likely to support them will be most appropriate. No one of these classifications is necessarily better than any other, none is equally useful for all purposes. Here, nationalisms will be classified partly in a historical sequence, in order to demonstrate the linkages between the different varieties, and partly according to the political circumstances in which they take root, to emphasize the adaptability of the basic notions of nationalism.

Historically, the first and most influential kind of nationalism has been that of the nation-states of Western Europe. Certain countries in this area, especially England and France, but also the Netherlands, Denmark, Sweden and to some extent Spain, were the prototypes of modern nationalism. Over a long period of time these states evolved in the direction of what we now know as the nation-state. Their possessions expanded and contracted, sometimes covering quite large areas of Europe, as with England, France, Spain and Sweden at various periods. But at their core lay a sizeable population with a degree of initial cultural similarity that increased as time went on, such as England within the later United Kingdom or the possessions of the crown of Castile in the Iberian peninsula. With varying degrees of success, the rulers of these states encouraged internal unification. They did not do so with the conscious aim of constructing a nation-state. The effort to standardize national languages was motivated not only by patriotic pride in the national culture but also by desire for state prestige and administrative convenience. The power of independent regional potentates was destroyed to ensure the security of the central state. Internal administration was unified and made more effective to increase control over the population, and to ease the collection of taxes for warfare. Religiously distinct cultural groups such as the Jews and the Moslem Moriscoes in Spain were expelled because of domestic hostility and internal security in an age when religion was of deep political significance. But the result of these variously motivated policies was the creation of states that had at their centres a large population with a common language, a common sense of identification with the state and, by the standards of the time, a strong and coherent administration. Often these states possessed outlying territories that did not share these features, such as Ireland, Catalonia or Brittany. Often they possessed extensive territories outside Europe, as with England, France, the Netherlands and Spain. But, as everyone recognized, these were states that were identified with particular cultures. The name of the state and of the culture were the same: England, France, Spain. Elsewhere in Europe states took the name of more limited regions within larger cultures, such as Bavaria and Prussia within Germany, or they were known by the name of the ruling dynasty, as with the Habsburg Empire. These first nation-states were also necessarily the first examples of modern nationalism. Their core populations felt an attachment to the state and the nationality that was their primary political loyalty. At times of war or international tension, this sense of common destiny was reflected in both popular mood and official propaganda.

These nation-states were among the most successful countries of the eighteenth and nineteenth centuries for a host of reasons. Their internal unity (administrative and otherwise), compared with other states, made it easier to raise revenue for warfare. Their core possessions were less open to rebellion and disaffection to foreign rivals than the possessions of more dynastic states. There is an economic argument of long pedigree that economic growth is best promoted where there are few internal barriers to trade in the shape of regional differences in tolls and taxes, weights and measures, and commercial law. The Western nation-states varied in the extent to which they fitted this description but some of them were certainly among the most economically successful countries of this period. In wartime, national enthusiasm aided the formation and fighting capacity of armed forces (although most states had many non-nationals in their armies and navies before the nineteenth century). During the period after the French Revolution, when ideas of liberty and self-government spread throughout Europe, states whose ruling groups shared the same cultural identity as the mass of the population at least could not be accused of oppression through alien rule, whatever other infringements of liberty they committed. When pressures for representative government and an extended franchise developed in the nineteenth century, these states did not face the problem of threats to the unity of the state from culturally distinct and potentially disloyal groups to the same extent as purely dynastic states. The general argument of nationalism is, in effect, that all states should take the form that these prototype nation-states had taken as a result of a complex and largely unintended pattern of development. Nineteenth-century nationalism in all its forms was a response to the prestige and success of these states and used them as an example, but the aspects of the original nation-states that were used as models varied greatly with the situation of the national group.

Some of the larger European cultures responded to the political and economic success of the larger nation-states, their great-power status and prosperity, and attempted to equal them. The large but politically fragmented cultures of Germany and Italy produced movements for political unification so that these too could become nation-states occupying their 'rightful place' alongside the English and the French. For each the Napoleonic Wars were crucial. The many states of Germany and Italy were swept aside by the French citizen armies inspired by national sentiment, even the most powerful of them such as Prussia. Invasion and political domination followed defeat and were often accompanied by wholesale remoulding of political boundaries and internal administration and, in some cases, absorption into the French Empire. The only states capable of resisting the French were Britain and Russia and these also had at their centre a substantial and patriotically motivated national group. The lesson was not lost and the movement for unification took root in both Germany and Italy with the retreat and defeat of French power, although it was not achieved for half a century. When it came, it was the result of the astute manoeuvring in war and diplomacy of the most powerful independent state in each culture, Prussia and Piedmont, in the period 1850—1870, each led by a masterly political strategist, Bismarck and Cavour, and supported by widespread popular feeling. Each also met opposition within the national group. Prussia faced competition for primacy within Germany from the Habsburg Empire, but the latter was less economically dynamic, less politically and militarily potent, and weighed down with extensive non-German possessions. Even after a unification that excluded Austria, many parts of the German Empire insisted on the retention of privileges — Bavaria, for example, possessed its own king and diplomatic service. In Italy, the papacy refused to recognize the sovereignty of the Italian state for decades after the annexation of the Papal States of central Italy in 1870. Catholics were forbidden to vote or stand in elections until the first years of the twentieth century and the status of the papacy was not settled until the Lateran Treaty of 1929, which established the tiny Vatican City as an independent territory. Once some degree of unity had been achieved, both powers set about attaining what they believed to be their rightful place on the European and world stage, competing with other great powers for extra-European empires and attempting to 'complete' unification by claiming areas of German or Italian culture not yet within the national state. This self-assertion promoted in its turn a more conscious and bombastic nationalism on the part of the older nation states as a response.

Other culturally distinctive groups in Europe responded to rather different features of the prototype nation-states: the common cultural identity of rulers and ruled, national rather than dynastic or alien government, and the liberal and democratic values that were most closely associated with these states, especially the concept of the sovereignty of the people. From the beginning of the nineteenth century, culturally distinctive groups within larger states responded to these aspects of the early nation-states, attacked the states to which they belonged because their rulers were alien, and demanded some degree of self-government. In the simplest cases a distinct region inhabited mainly by one cultural group was governed by a larger state whose ruling groups were of a different cultural composition. Straightforward secession of the region could provide an answer to this kind of nationality problem, as happened with Norway, united with Sweden before 1905, and with some of the Balkan possessions of the Turkish Ottoman Empire during the nineteenth century, such as Greece. Often, however, the problem was much more complicated than this.

If the nationalist image of the world were reflected in political reality, the map would consist of states based on culturally distinctive groups occupying homogeneous, compact and mutually exclusive national territories. But in parts of Europe, especially central and eastern, this was and still is far from reality. The result of many centuries of conquest and population movement was that many cultural groups were geographically intermingled in a complex pattern. While some of the larger groups, such as Czechs or Hungarians, might have some core territory in which they were the overwhelming majority, such as Bohemia or the Pannonian Plain, there would also be many parts of the 'national territory' of which they demanded independent control that contained other nationalities in large numbers, and these were not usually willing to accept permanent subordination. Hence there developed a multitude of intricate and baffling nationalist claims and counter-claims. Hungarians claimed, and obtained, substantial autonomy for 'Hungary' within the Habsburg Empire, but historic 'Hungary' included not only Hungarians or Magyars but also Croats, Czechs, Germans, Rumanians, Serbs, Slovaks and Slovenes. Czechs demanded autonomy for the traditional possessions of the Bohemian crown, but north-western Bohemia, later to be known as the

Sudetenland, was densely settled by German speakers, economically powerful and traditionally dominant, who wanted continued Austrian control, or even unity with a Greater Germany. For almost every nationality claiming independence and self-determination, there were smaller groups within the same area wanting continued association with the larger state to preserve their privileged position or at least restrain the excesses of the larger nationality, or demanding to rejoin their fellow nationals outside the territory. Eastern Europe was not the only area of the continent to face these problems. In the United Kingdom, the claim of the nationalist Irish for an independent and united Ireland met and still meets the bitter hostility of the Ulster Unionists. In Finland, the Finnish-speaking majority battled with the traditionally dominant Swedish speakers and both fought for autonomy from Russia, whose Tsar had been Grand Duke of Finland since the end of the Napoleonic Wars.

By the beginning of the Second World War many of these groups had gained independence by their own efforts: Bulgaria, Greece, Ireland (excluding Northern Ireland), Norway and Rumania, for example. Others, perhaps the largest number, had gained some degree of independence as a result of the defeat or collapse of some of the great Eastern European powers in the First World War. Austria-Hungary was dismantled. Ottoman Turkey lost almost all its remaining possessions in Europe and had to experience its own nationalist resurgence to maintain an independent existence. Russia temporarily lost territory in Eastern Europe. Czechoslovakia, Estonia, Finland, Hungary, Latvia, Lithuania, Poland and Yugoslavia all gained, regained or extended their independence in this way. However other groups, equally as active as the successful groups, never gained independence, and yet others soon lost it. The Catalonians and Basques in Spain forfeited what limited autonomy they had achieved with the victory of Franco in the Spanish Civil War. Some of the nationalities of Tsarist Russia that had produced nationalist movements in the period of turmoil between 1916 and 1922 were suppressed with the victory of the Bolsheviks and had to be content with the autonomy allowed by the complex Soviet nationalities policy. Other former possessions of the Russian Empire, such as Estonia, Latvia and Lithuania, enjoyed two precarious decades of independence before returning to Russian possession after the Second World War. The success of such nationalities has therefore depended at least as much on the fortunes of the larger power they confront as on their own efforts, and the application of a sufficient degree of force can halt their progress for decades. Also independence rarely solved all national conflicts. A supposed nation-state such as Czechoslovakia began its independent life with more non-Czechs than Czechs within its border. The two other major groups were the Germans (24 per cent of the population), the traditional opponents of the Czechs, and the Slovaks (16 per cent of the population), a slavic group speaking a language closely related to Czech but at a generally lower level of economic development and previously subject to the Hungarian crown.[3] Problems with Germans in particular dogged the new state, especially after the rise of the Nazis in Germany itself, until the difficulties served as the pretext for the annexation of the Sudetenland by Germany in 1938. This was rapidly followed by the secession of Slovakia and eventually the absorption of what remained of the Czech state into German hands as a 'protectorate'. Almost all the states of Eastern Europe faced minority problems of this sort in the inter-war period, usually intensified by the cultural connections of the minorities with one or another neighbouring state. These conflicts have been eased to some extent since the Second World War by the mass expulsion of Germans from many East European states, including Czechoslovakia. But the character of the regimes that have governed these countries since the 1940s also has something to do with the relative quiescence of national minorities. The most liberal of these states, Yugoslavia, faces very substantial nationality problems today. Western Europe has also experienced a resurgence of this kind of nationalism as formerly authoritarian regimes have decayed allowing old nationalist tensions to resurface, as in Spain, and as previously quiescent nationalities, such as the Scots and the Welsh, have begun to show interest in political autonomy. The ideology of nationalism opened a Pandora's Box of potential European nationalities that is not yet empty.

The appeal of the nationalist picture of the world has proved to be as great outside Europe, especially in this century, as within Europe. Once again the adaptability of nationalism has been strongly evident. The list of models to copy and modify was now extended and included not only the original nation-states but also states that had used nationalism as an ideology of development towards great power status and as an ideology of freedom from foreign oppression. These were to find application in yet more varied circumstances.

The presently most prominent extra-European form of nationalism is the anti-imperialist nationalism of the former colonial possessions of European powers. The African, Asian and American dependencies of these powers adapted the nationalism of liberation for their own purposes. In defining themselves as oppressed nationalities they attacked European imperialism in terms of its own rhetoric, and furthermore a rhetoric whose most prominent supporters within Europe were the greatest imperial powers, Britain and France. Anti-imperialism began to take on a nationalist guise in some colonies in the late nineteenth century and these movements grew in numbers and in strength throughout the twentieth century, gaining potency from factors such as the development of educated indigenous classes, the supposed settlement of European nationality problems on the principle of national self-determination after the First World War, and the growth of socialism in Europe. However, as with the dependent nationalities of Europe, the strength of the metropolitan power was at least as important as the support of the nationalist movement or movements in determining the fate of a colony. Before the Second World War, colonial revolts and disturbances were often put down ruthlessly, and powerful mass movements such as the Indian Congress had to struggle hard for even limited concessions of local self-government. After the Second World War, however, it was clear that the European imperial powers were very far from invincible, that they had been greatly weakened by the war, and that the dominant power in the West was now the United States, a country that saw itself as an opponent of traditional political imperialism and was not willing to prop up the ailing empires of its allies. By the middle of the 1950s, the great European empires were being more or less voluntarily dissolved and by the 1960s many instances of decolonization owed as much to the desire to be rid of empire as they did to local nationalism.

However, despite the parallels that these nationalist movements drew between themselves and such European peoples as the Czech and the Irish, what had happened was not so much the reawakening of nationalities as the adaptation of the ideas of nationalism to new purposes. Beneath the nationalism of politically dependent groups in Europe there usually lay some authentic sense of cultural unity. The potential Czech or Irish or Hungarian national territory may have contained groups opposed to the national movement, but the population that supported the movement did possess some common and often ancient culture in the shape of language, religion, customs and sometimes institutions. Whatever problems the new state might face, there was no doubt that some substantial element of its population did feel a positive sense of being Czech, Irish or Hungarian. In many of the African and Asian cases, however, matters were rather different. What united the nationalists was frequently not so much a sense of common belonging as a feeling of common distance from the white rulers. In Africa especially, the colonial boundaries within which the nationalist movements developed did not contain people of common culture but peoples of a number of different cultures placed in a similar political situation because of the pattern of Europe conquest and administrative division. Often these peoples had a pre-colonial tradition of conflict with one another. Frequently the colonial boundaries cut across cultural lines, placing some peoples partly in the territories of one imperial power, partly in the territories of another. The nationalism of such culturally diverse colonies was in reality more of a feeling of hostility towards the alien ruler than a sense of internal unity. Indeed it is only a little too strong to suggest that anti-imperialist nationalism is the accepted modern form of the age-old protest against the recent and still alien conqueror. This has become even clearer in the post-independence period. Many ex-colonies have faced severe problems of internal unity, with actual wars of secession in the worst cases, such as Pakistan, the Congo (Zaire) and Nigeria. For these states yet another facet of the nationalist model has become attractive, the nation-building and developmental nationalism of some European states, as they attempt to imbue their diverse populations with a sense of unity and loyalty to the state.

Not all colonial nationalisms took precisely this shape. In some cases ancient and coherent cultures were conquered and formed the basis of distinct colonies or semi-colonial territories. Cases of this sort, such as Egypt or Vietnam, could adopt the nationalism of liberation almost without alteration. The ancient cultures could be interpreted as nationalities with little difficulty and the newly independent states, whatever other problems they faced, did at least possess substantial core populations whose national identity was not in doubt.

Other non-European areas also possessed ancient and extensive cultures but were never actually annexed by a European empire, countries such as Japan, Turkey and China, and these also responded to European power and prestige by borrowing and modifying the ideology of nationalism. For some of them the nationalism of renewal and assertion represented by Germany and Italy was attractive. They also were old cultures with a history of political and military strength that felt humiliation and weakness in the face of the Western great powers. In the Japanese case the response was the transformation of the ancient identity into an aggressive and expansionist nationalism that sought to equal and displace the European great powers. Other ancient cultures had been much more deeply penetrated by European states, although not actually conquered. Here both the great power and liberation varieties of nationalism could find their adherents. Left-wing movements could phrase their nationalism in terms of anti-imperialism and fellowship with other victims of Western economic and political dominance, as with the Chinese communists, from their inception after the First World War until the present day. Right-wing movements in the same countries could express their nationalism as a desire for regeneration and equality with the older nation states, as with the Kuomintang (Chinese nationalists) when they were the internationally recognized government of China from the mid-1920s to the late 1940s.

Extra-European nationalism did not involve those of non-European origins alone. The imperial powers not only conquered vast areas of the globe that were already densely inhabited, they also planted larger numbers of Europeans wherever space and climate permitted. Here once again nationalism displayed its adaptability. Some areas of settlement fought wars of independence from the metropolitan powers — the United States against Britain and many of the states of Latin America against Spain. The nationalism of liberation was appropriate in these circumstances, stressing the differences between the colony of settlement and the country of origin and the right of the former to its national independence. However these wars were fought at an early stage in the development of modern nationalism — in the late eighteenth century in North America and in the Napoleonic Wars and their immediate aftermath in South America — and the use of straightforward liberal arguments about freedom and representative government were just as important as nationalism. Indeed in both cases there was considerable doubt about nationality. Many people doubted the possibility of uniting the diverse and then isolated ex-British colonies into a lasting state. In the Latin American wars against Spain, there was little agreement about the entities that should achieve independence. The most prominent revolutionary leaders, Bolivar and San Martin, hoped for vast states covering the territories of several contemporary Latin American states, but opposition and pure distance and terrain caused these to fall apart into something like the present-day map of Latin America in a short period of time. Later, both these countries and the United States faced the problems of integrating populations of diverse European and non-European origins into a single society, a task still not completely achieved in the case of black and native Indian populations.

Other European colonies of settlement attained their independence by concession from Great Britain rather than by war: Australia, Canada, New Zealand and South Africa. The growing sense of distinctiveness of the settlers again expressed itself as a sense of nationality, but in a less intense manner than in the case of anti-colonial nationalisms and in a way that maintains in a steadily weakening form many of the old connections. In two of these cases, Canada and South Africa, the situation is complicated by the presence of whites whose culture of origin was another European power — France and the Netherlands respectively. Both these groups have found the nationalism of liberation appropriate models for their own political aims at certain times — the Boers when they resisted the establishment of British rule in their territories at the end of the nineteenth century and the French Canadians over the last fifteen years or so. The South African situation is of course yet further complicated by the anti-colonial nationalism of its large black population.

The process of copying and adaptation is by no means at an end. As the nationalism of liberation of the dependent European nationalities once served as a model for the colonized areas of Africa and Asia, so the anti-colonial nationalism of these continents now serves as a model, with suitable amendments, within the Western world. In Europe, the heartland of nationalism, the example of decolonization in the Third World has fertilized the rhetoric and self-image of the more radical elements in the nationalisms that have emerged on a substantial scale in recent years in culturally distinctive areas of larger states, such as Scotland and Wales. These elements sometimes refer to their cultures as 'internal colonies', drawing a parallel between themselves and Afro-Asian peoples. Some groups in the Americas — native Indians and blacks — have also drawn the same parallel and some of their leaders have portrayed them as imperialistically oppressed nations, although this idea has faced the difficulty of specifying where the national territories might be. In Latin America, the long-lived hostility to the political and economic dominance of the United States is now often expressed by radicals in the language of colonialism and neo-colonialism, and their nationalism sees the nationalism of African and Asian ex-colonies as its natural comrade.

This thumb-nail sketch of the variety of nationalisms does not do full justice to the range of forms that exist. The various types that have been discussed are not completely distinct. A given country can display several types in sequence. Serbian nationalism was originally a separatist movement against the Ottoman Empire. Once independent it indulged in irredentist and expansionist claims against surrounding states and eventually became the basis of the nationalism of unification of the South Slavs whose contemporary political form is Yugoslavia. Different kinds of nationalism can be found side by side in the same place. In South Africa the Boers resisted British imperialism as a nationalism of liberation, and continued to resist British influence in South Africa, but the blacks in the same territory today oppose both Afrikaner and English-speaking whites as a potential anti-colonial nationalism. Enormously different kinds of cultural groups can see themselves as nations: dispersed minorities living in many countries, such as the Jews before the establishment of the state of Israel; numerically tiny groups with a distinctive territory, such as the Icelanders; and entire civilizations consisting of a substantial proportion of the human race, such as the Chinese. There is not space to give more than a mention to the pan-nationalisms that attempt to gather together a number of culturally similar nations, such as Pan-Slavism, Pan-Arabism or Pan-Africanism. No classification could do complete justice to such diversity.

THE DEVELOPMENT OF NATIONALISM: A PROCESS OF COPYING AND ADAPTATION

This diversity is also the reason why so far a task that some might feel to be a basic condition of a chapter such as this has not been attempted: the definition of nationalism. Nationalism is not a set and defined ideology or kind of political movement that can be exactly described and that is transferred whole from place to place. Rather it is a few simple ideas about the relationship between states and cultures that first emerged as a response to the prestige of countries such as France and Britain. It is adopted and adapted by political leaders in a wide range of situations who emphasize very different elements of the original models. In this way the different kinds of nationalism multiply and each in turn can become the model for other kinds of nationalism, which in their turn also borrow and modify the idea. In these circumstances it is pointless to expect more than a limited relationship between all the various kinds of nationalism or to hope that some clear-cut classification will encompass all the diverse situations in which the concept of nationality and the relationship between nationality and state have been important.[4]

This process of borrowing has been made easier by the range of other philosophies and ideologies with which nationalism can be combined. It is the task of other chapters in this book to explore these relationships in more detail but this malleability of nationalism should be briefly mentioned here. The idea that separate cultures deserve some political recognition can be used in the defence of an immense range of interests. Aristocracies in distinctive regions of nineteenth-century European states could defend their provincial privileges against a centralizing administration in these terms on the grounds that the privileges were part of the national distinctiveness, as happened in the early stages of some of the smaller European national movements. Liberals can demand an end to alien government in the name of the democratic self-determination of nationalities. Powerful states and their dominant groups can defend their expansion and aggression in terms of the strength and destiny of their particular nation in a highly competitive world. Radical socialists can combine nationalism with the struggle against economic domination and underdevelopment. In certain extreme forms nationalism can shade off into racism, the notion that nations are not just culturally different from one another but also biologically different, an idea that usually carries the implication that some races are superior to others. The relationship between racism and nationalism was closer in the nineteenth and early twentieth centuries than it is today, partly because of the horrendous consequences of racist nationalism in the Second World War, partly because it is no longer plausible to argue that the differences between very many nations correspond with differences of a biological kind. Nonetheless, wherever undoubted racial differences exist, extreme varieties of nationalism tend in the direction of racism, as with the National Front in contemporary Britain.

SOCIOLOGICAL EXPLANATIONS

We have seen, then, that nationalism is widespread, that it is very malleable, and that the various forms are connected more by a sequence of borrowing than by close similarities of form. Some central questions remain: Why should there have been so much borrowing of this particular set of ideas? Why is it that some version of nationalism has proved attractive in so many circumstances? Are there some general factors that explain its massive appeal? There are some available answers to these questions but in examining them we move to another level of analysis, that of sociological theory. This is a complex area and the arguments cannot be fully examined in an introductory discussion. At most the theories can be roughly outlined and some suggestions offered about the problems that they face. It should be emphasized that sociological theories rarely have a one-to-one correspondence with individual cases. The application of the theory to a given instance requires a detailed knowledge of the context and many supplementary factors.

There are two major kinds of sociological answer to the problem of the widespread appeal of nationalism and both of them make the assumption that nationalism must be closely connected with other features of modern society. Nationalism emerges in modern Europe and spreads throughout the rest of the world along with other such characteristic features of modern life as industrialization, science and technology, rapid communications, the involvement of the mass of the population in political life, and large-scale bureaucratic administration. This connection, the argument runs, is surely not a coincidence. There is some intimate linkage between nationalism and these other developments, which are often linked together under the single label of modernization.

The first kind of theory, that of *uneven development,* suggests that the link has to do with the irregular nature of the process of modernization. As all these changes have swept over the world, some places have done better than others. At any point in the last 150 years, some areas have been more industrialized, more prosperous and more powerful than other places. Nationalism, it is argued, is the response of the less favoured areas as they assert their independence or, if already independent, their equality with the favoured areas and their right to share in the benefits of modernity. Thus the Germans and the Italians responded with nationalism to their weakness in the face of their more modernized Western neighbours in the nineteenth century. In a rather different way, the smaller European nationalities that lacked independence opposed the more powerful states that controlled them. In the twentieth century, this reaction spreads to the possessions of European powers in Asia and Africa, and so on. As a matter of fact, it is not at all clear that the divisions between nations correspond at all well with the undoubted unevenness of modernization, but even if they did, another crucial question would remain unanswered. The uneven development creates the units that become nations — more and less developed areas — and provides the motivation for the inhabitants of the less developed areas to object to their status, at least in theory. But why should their reaction be nationalism, which in all its many forms is at least an attempt to create a state in which culture defines membership of the state and in which 'the people' are in some way the basis of legitimacy? Why should the response not be instead a reassertion of traditional aristocratic leadership or a desire for socialist world unity? The uneven development theory explains the hostility to a position of weakness, but not the precise form of response to this position.[5]

For an answer to this question we must turn to the other argument linking nationalism and modernization, that of *social cohesion*. This approaches the issue in a rather different way. The states that preceded those we know today were held together in a certain way. Their constituent units were not citizens — individuals with separate and equal membership in the state — rather, as was shown in the first chapter, they were composed of institutions. In the case of medieval Europe, these institutions were manors, monasteries, guilds, towns, religious orders, nobilities and the like. Men were born into these institutions, or at any rate took their place in them at an early age, and lived out their entire lives within them. These institutions also defined the position and indeed personal identity of the individual for almost all purposes. Political units, such as kingdoms, were made up of relations between institutions of this sort bound together by traditional obligations and oaths of allegiance. There was no need for any widespread sense of common identity among the whole population. It was enough that they were within these institutions and that the institutions were bound to a certain lord. In fact towns and manors could be transferred from lord to lord with little damage to the activities of those involved.

In contrast, the societies that we know today are much more fluid. Geographical and social mobility occur on such a scale that few people live out their lives in one locality or one social body. We move house, we move from family to school, from school to workplace, from workplace to workplace. It is no longer enough for political units to be made up of relations between rulers and institutions on the one hand and between institutions and individuals on the other. The institutions are no longer sufficiently rigid and all-encompassing. Furthermore, industrialization and urbanization bring in their train demands for political equality and political participation, making the mass of the population much more politically relevant than ever before. It is therefore of great utility if the state can appeal to a sense of common identity among those it rules. It then ties them to each other and to itself and is much more assured of their political loyalty. For the individuals, otherwise rootless and confused in a constantly changing social world, it provides a sense of political identity. In the absence of this widespread sense of attachment, the state's capacity to withstand the stresses of war or economic difficulty will be reduced by the danger of indifference or even outright disaffection. Nation-states are thus less liable to failure in the face of difficulty than multi-cultural states and their domestic politics are freer of certain kinds of tension. This makes them attractive as models and provides greater survival capacity, hence the widespread appeal of nationalism and the number of states claiming to be nation-states.

This theory will not tell us why, say, Basques choose to adopt the Basque identity rather than the Spanish, or why the Scots, after centuries of apparent satisfaction with a British political identity, should turn in large numbers to the idea of a political reflection of Scottishness. But the adherents of this argument would probably claim that it is not intended to explain any particular case in detail. Rather it offers general reasons for the superior long-term survival capacity of states that roughly correspond with nations. It suggests that the cogency of nationalism is to be found in the way that it ties the population to the state, and hence can be called the social cohesion explanation of nationalism.[6]

The reader must be left to make his own decisions about these theories in the light of the other chapters of this book and the suggested reading. Neither of them is in any simple sense completely wrong, although they may be defective or lacking in many ways. They do, however, share one central insight, which provides an appropriate point on which to conclude this survey. A phenomenon as widespread as nationalism, which seems to coincide with so many other aspects of the modern world whenever they occur wherever they are found, is no mere accident or set of unconnected instances. The nation-state and nationalism are inherent features of our age and, whatever changes they may undergo or new forms they may assume, their demise is not an immediate prospect.

NOTES AND REFERENCES

1. The opposite sides of this debate may be sampled in E. Kedourie *Nationalism* (London: Hutchinson, 1961) and some of the contributions to C. Leon Tipton (ed.) *Nationalism in the Middle Ages* (New York: Holt Rinehart Winston, 1972).
2. A range of classifications of nationalism is discussed in A. D. Smith *Theories of Nationalism* (London: Duckworth, 1971) Ch. 8.
3. The figures are for 1931 and are taken from *Chambers Encyclopaedia* Vol. IV (London: Pergamon, 1967) p. 333. Minority statistics for all European states in the 1930s can be found in R. W. Seton-Watson *Britain and the Dictators* (Cambridge: Cambridge University Press, 1939) pp. 322–3.
4. This account of the variety of nationalisms as linked by a process of borrowing and adaptation, rather than by replication, owes much to the similar account of the process of modernization offered in Reinhardt Bendix 'Tradition and modernity reconsidered' *Comparative Studies in Society and History, 9* (1966–7) pp. 292–346.
5. The leading recent proponent of this theory is Tom Nairn in *The Break-Up of Britain: Crisis and Neo-Nationalism* (London: New Left Books, 1977) Ch. 9. Its roots however can be traced back through twentieth-century Marxism.
6. An account of nationalism that contains many of these themes is E. Gellner *Thought and Change* (London: Weidenfeld and Nicolson, 1964) Ch. 7.

FURTHER READING

The following suggestions are confined to widely available introductory works likely to be found in most sizeable libraries.

Comprehensive and balanced accounts of the ideological and historical background of modern nationalism are Hans Kohn *The Idea of Nationalism* (New York: Collier Macmillan, 1944) and Boyd C. Schafer *Faces of Nationalism, New Realities and Old Myths* (New York: Harcourt Brace Javanovich, 1972). Rather briefer than these is K. R. Minogue *Nationalism* (London: Methuen, 1967).

It would be impossibly lengthy to list works on all, or even the most important, examples of nationalism, but representative cases of the various types can be studied in the following: G. Procacci *A History of the Italian People* (Harmondsworth, Middx: Penguin, 1973) Chs 11 – 13; Hajo Holborn *A History of Modern Germany, Vol. 3, 1840 – 1945* (London: Eyre and Spottiswoode, 1969) Part 1; William V. Wallace *Czechoslovakia* (London: Ernest Benn, 1977); R. Emerson *From Empire to Nation: The Rise to Self-Assertion of African and Asian Peoples* (Cambridge, Mass.: Harvard University Press, 1960); G. Pendle *A History of Latin America* (Harmondsworth, Middx: Penguin, 1963) Chs 7 – 9; R. Pipes *The Formation of the Soviet Union. Communism and Nationalism, 1917 – 1923* (Cambridge, Mass.: Harvard University Press, 1964); S. Payne *Basque Nationalism* (Reno: University of Nevada Press, 1975); K. Webb *Scottish Nationalism* (Harmondsworth, Middx: Penguin, 1977).

For sociological theories of nationalism, see Tom Nairn *The Break-Up of Britain: Crisis and Neo-Nationalism* (London: New Left Books, 1977) Ch. 9, which represents the uneven development viewpoint, and Ernest Gellner *Thought and Change* (London: Weidenfeld and Nicolson, 1964) Ch. 7, which combines elements of this and of the social cohesion theory.

Two overall surveys with a wealth of examples are H. Seton-Watson, *Nations and States* (London: Methuen, 1977) and B. Akzin *State and Nation* (London, Hutchinson, 1964). Finally, two widely available works should be mentioned. E. Kedourie *Nationalism* (London: Hutchinson, 1961) is stimulating but argues a thesis that not all students of the subject would accept, and A. D. Smith *Theories of Nationalism* (London: Duckworth, 1971) is comprehensive but likely to prove rather too advanced for the beginner.

3

States, Nations and Economies

Leonard Tivey

The other contributions to this volume discuss *state* and *nation*; the object of this essay is to examine a third concept, that of 'an economy' and to show its connections with the other two. To begin, the early development of relevant matters will be sketched. Then the history of the state's concern will be discussed, in the form of a critique of the conventional account. The implications of the nation-state for property rights and for social reform are then outlined; and finally the culmination of things is presented.

There must always have been some economic aspect to human existence, in the sense that wants (material or otherwise) must have been provided in some way or other. The way wants are provided is now described as an 'economic system', but for most of history the practices seen from the twentieth century as economic in purpose were closely entangled with other activities — religious, customary, political — of the time. For the most part, too, the scale of organization for the identifiable economic activities was not great, the household that provided its own food being very common at all periods. There are numerous cases, some very famous, where *trade* was extensive and important, but even so agriculture remained the predominant activity of society.

In primitive societies, for example, material wants of food and shelter — subsistence — were provided by activities such as hunting, foraging, stock-raising and crop-growing organized as customary practices of tribal or village communities. The unit of rule (which was possibly rudimentary) had no difficulty in encompassing the economy as a whole: indeed it was usually embedded in the same set of customs and beliefs. Trade between these units existed and may have involved money, but it was concerned with a very limited range of goods.

In ancient times the range of government varied from small city-states to great empires. The overwhelming form of economy was agricultural, with households, including servants and slaves, providing for their own wants. Specialist trades, dependent on exchange for their subsistence, were important in urban life. Both before and within the great Mediterranean empires, trading in specialized goods became extensive, and at times wine and grain were traded over long distances. Trade was essentially between individuals, perhaps through intermediary merchants, but bound by customary practice and often by political regulation. The regulation was motivated by ethical beliefs and political pressures rather than any sophisticated attempt at economic management. Significantly, the vast irrigation projects of some ancient civilizations required despotic political systems to manage them.

In the feudal system of medieval Europe there were no simple sovereign authorities; nevertheless the territorial span of the higher political levels of the system — that of the Emperor, or the kings of France or England — was very much wider than that of basic economic units. Compared with that of the ancient world, the life of the middle ages was even more dependent on agriculture, in which families and manorial villages were largely self-sufficient. Trade grew in importance in wool, cloth, metals, furs, wine and so on, but even at its maximum there were few circumstances in which it rivalled localized agriculture as a means of subsistence. Indeed, much trade depended on fairs, which were only held at particular times of the year. There was no abstention by rulers from concern with economic affairs, but the rulers consisted of a complex hierarchy, linked by complex allegiances. Their bureaucratic efficacy was low in economic as in other matters, and their financial resources were difficult to mobilize. The normative rules embodied in natural law, reinforced by divine authority and conveyed by the Church, were in effect the most important political control in economic life. They might be enforced with more or less rigour, indeed, by princes or by ecclesiastics; but at most they were clumsy instruments of policy. The system of property, feudalism itself, united politics and economic life in a relatively rigid way. Rulers of all sorts might wish to promote prosperity, perhaps by establishing peace and stability, for the revenues of their own households would benefit from it. Nevertheless even the most powerful of them had limited administrative and financial resources.

In spite of their many differences and even bearing in mind the sophistication of some economic arrangements, all these pre-modern economic systems were 'containable' within the political units of the times. We may marvel at the extent of long-distance trading involved; but trading it was, not complex productive organization. Politics and economics were both institutionally and conceptually intertwined, and so the economy could be conceived as 'within' the polity. Ancient Rome was dependent on tribute for its daily bread, and some places such as Venice or the Hanseatic cities might depend on trade for their prosperity. But such a degree of dependence was not normal, and the difficulties that political authorities might have had in coping with its problems lay more with the underdevelopment of economic understanding or with lack of administrative capabilities, not in the territorial range of authority. In any case, less was expected of them.

The change that is most important for political systems in the modern world lies in the growing complication and interdependence of economic life. In some places the economy can still be contained within a political unit — a superstate — but mostly it cannot. This transformed relationship is crucial, and is now well noticed, but its consequences have not yet been fully appreciated.

Other essays are concerned with the arrival of the post-medieval sovereign state. The concern of this essay lies more with the emergence of the 'liberal' state — that is, with the sort of state where liberalism implied limitation of state functions. This is by no means the only feature of liberal politics, and most twentieth-century liberals would dispute its primacy, probably putting freedom of expression to the fore. But the limitation of the state's role meant not only its separation from religious concerns (at least to the extent of religious toleration) but also from intervention — 'interference' — in economic matters. The promulgation of such a doctrine required as a first step the disentangling, at the level of operative concepts, of activities that had hitherto been parts of a whole. Economic affairs had to be separated from other matters; trading and production had to be distinguished, and work separated from leisure.

However, the doctrine of economic liberalism did not mark the first post-medieval stage. Naturally enough, perhaps, the emergence of the distinctive sovereign state in Europe brought with it ideas about trading designed to support it. These ideas may be called mercantilist. But mercantilism was not a single economic doctrine.[1] It was rather the belief that trade and perhaps production should be used as an instrument to sustain a polity. It reflected a growing awareness of state requirements, a search for means of making a success of sovereign states. One early doctrine was that of bullionism, so called from its stress on the importance of precious metals. Often, export of gold and silver was restricted, and traders (primarily foreigners) were encouraged to bring these metals into the realm, with the ultimate destination of the king's exchequer. By Tudor times in England, the idea had become one of an advantageous balance of trade — more exports than imports — in order to enrich 'the country' itself. The policy measures advocated, and those put into effect however, were variously conceived and did not amount to a general European practice.

Mercantilism, whatever it was, was sharply attacked by Adam Smith in 1776. His views on what was necessary to promote the *Wealth of Nations* mark the beginning of a new era in economic thought. The industrial and commercial revolutions were visible to all, and many accounts of modern economic history find it convenient to begin about this point.

THE CONVENTIONAL HISTORY AND ITS SHORTCOMINGS

The vital importance of Adam Smith's work in the history of ideas — 'it was the end of everything that came before and the beginning of everything that came after'[2] — has led to the establishment of a widely received account of the development of political economy beyond this point. It may be briefly stated. It tells of a period in which the ascendancy of the economic doctrine of laissez-faire led to the political doctrine of the minimal state, and how this was gradually eroded by varius forces — by the intellectual attacks of 'new' liberals, socialists of various types, New Dealers, and Keynesians, and by the arrival of democratic mass politics. This period was therefore succeeded, for better or worse, by state intervention, public ownership, demand management and high public expenditure, and these implied in turn a political system based on bureaucracy and corporatist pressure groups. In short the last 200 years embodied the rise and fall of the liberal state.

This conventional description is not untrue, but it is inadequate and hence misleading. It lays far too much stress on economic doctrines about the role of the state, and it neglects two major factors:

(i)   It does not begin, historically speaking, soon enough. Of course, all historical 'starts' are arbitrary. Yet the natural inclination of economists to begin with Adam Smith and the industrial revolution ignores the nature of 'the state' itself. The story must start at least with modernity and sovereignty.

(ii) Even more crucially, it neglects the nineteenth-century emergence of nationalism, and its rapid acceptance. It underrates both its emotional significance in providing human satisfactions (i.e. 'public goods'), and the force of its moral imperative, patriotism, as supposedly overriding individual or group purposes.

These two matters need elaboration.

(i) The modern state is an abstract, specifically political, entity. Its abstract nature is vital, since it is thereby enabled to 'exist' independently of mundane circumstances, in the guise of L'Etat, the Republic or (in Britain) the Crown, and to loosen and perhaps dissolve its connection with any particular dynasty or set or rulers. In the view of Quentin Skinner,[3] its emergence is linked with the rediscovery in the Renaissance of politics and government as distinctive human activities worth attention as such, and not entirely derivable from other human activities and moralities, or indeed from religion. The distinctiveness of politics and the state predates the similar emergence of economic or business life as something that might be not only practised, but understood independently as a system on its own.

The key doctrine of the new politics was the sovereignty of this impersonal 'state' (not necessarily of particular rulers, who might be transient) in all civil matters, and its eventual divorce from religion. Of course, abstractions do not govern. Sovereignty was achieved by monarchs who asserted the supremacy of their rule by force —by dissolving monasteries, by consolidating territory, by enforcing taxes, by defeating separatists and baronial challengers. But absolutist monarchs prepared the way for other forms of unified rule, constitutionalized or even democratized, but still, in the modern era, claiming to be operating a state.

The first importance of this doctrine for economic life was that it made economics secondary and subordinate; man's primary status was that of citizen. It also began the creation of a secular way of life, and this eventually opened the way to a similar attitude to economic matters. As the state became the only authoritative body for dealing with civil relationships, then it stood ready to serve economic ends whenever these were perceived to be matters of common concern. The main arena of linkage for economic life was bound to be the state, not only in the territorial sense, but also conceptually, because the state could shape the forms it took — by what it allowed as well as what it forbade, by the institutions such as companies or trade unions available to the citizenry.

In Britain and in some other countries the reforms that were sought were the removal of existing mercantilist restrictions, but the state was also the agent for the removal of customary feudal relationships and local controls. It was the effectiveness of state justice that made the elimination of other jurisdictions possible. Markets of some sort must exist in any exchange economy, but even when laissez-faire beliefs most prevailed, it was the duty of the state to provide the right conditions — to establish a *free* market, which means one ruled by certain regulations (about contract for instance) but not others. Later in the nineteenth century it was necessary for the state to make special arrangements (easy incorporation and limited liability) whereby the main organizations of economic life, business firms, could be created.[4] The onus for economic development lies with the state at all stages: it may make things worse rather than better, but economic life does not proceed regardless of whatever the state may do.

The trouble with starting the story at Adam Smith or thereabouts is that it takes too much for granted. Indeed taking into account prior doctrines of physiocracy or of mercantilist writers does not provide a remedy, for their assumptions are also statist. It is not merely that liberal economists assume the continuance of some limited state functions: they appeal to the authority of the state for reform, and they take its claims to territorial sovereignty as normal. Here begins the idea of 'an economy' — that is, an economic system within boundaries. The boundaries are political frontiers, but they are increasingly assumed to be in the nature of things, and thus the economic world like the political world takes on the character of a set of separate units — indeed, the same units. A very great deal goes on economically across the boundaries, but so it does politically and culturally. The commercial expansion of the early modern period — by the Dutch, for example — did not take much notice of boundaries. Nevertheless, this period marks the beginning of the territorial consolidation characteristic of modern states.

Certainly the idea of the state territories providing at any time a set of closed systems is absurd. There was always extensive trade between people in different political units, and the rise of sovereign states was accompanied by great expansion of world trade. It was the age of capitalism, a new commercial civilization. But the outcome of all the changes was clear: a division of the world into a collection of sovereignties, and trade classified as international or internal. Though international trade was encouraged during the free trade era, the distinction between foreign and domestic trade never lost its clarity. The political concepts of imports and exports applied to capital funds as well as to other goods. Similarly, rulers had endorsed currencies in all historic times, and the gold standard ensured their compatibility until the twentieth century. Nevertheless, sovereign states equipped themselves with central banks, and eventually found themselves in charge not merely of currency in a narrow sense, but of monetary affairs in general. In the twentieth century this responsibility has become a matter of its relationship with banks and other major credit-issuing bodies. States endorse particular currencies — pounds, dollars, yen, pesetas — and these only are legal tender (i.e. must be accepted) within their territories. The exchange rates between such state-endorsed currencies are of consequence to the welfare of residents in the various countries, and so states must either accept some automatic regulator such as the gold standard or attempt some form of management. The extent of governmental involvement has increased, to the distress of bankers and some economists; but the truth is that it was the assertion of sovereignty that created the possibility of such developments. The seeds were sown long ago.

A similar sort of delayed action, of even greater importance, arises in the role of states for the movement of people. From all sorts of motives people desire to move around: as travellers and as temporary or permanent migrants. By the nineteenth century most feudal ties were being abandoned and there was massive migration, often for demonstrable economic reasons. The labour market, that is to say, began to assume a worldwide character. But the liberal state was a territorial state, and asserted its sovereign right to determine not only its rightful citizens but eventually its residents and even its visitors. For the personal linkages of feudalism there was substituted a set of areas between which the movement of free men was regulated and often restricted. There can be little doubt that on balance the development of the state system vastly increased the mobility of labour compared with anything that prevailed before; but there can similarly be little doubt that it now provides a means, of remarkable if not yet decisive severity, of controlling the patterns of human settlement, and hence of economic development. Certainly it is the large movements of people occasioned by economic forces that are most likely to be curtailed.

Since the state by definition embodied a system of law and government, it became a centre of bureaucratic skills and a focus for information and calculation. Its territory and its citizenry determined the extent to which many forms of social information were gathered — its authority enabled compulsory censuses to be taken, for example. Much fact-gathering, of course, was for the administrative purposes of the state itself. Thus much knowledge about human affairs is segmented state by state at the earliest data-collecting stage; indeed, the perception of reality and the awareness of problems has become impregnated with statist assumptions. These prior conceptions have become vital to the nature of economic thinking, at both the professional and popular levels.

From these necessary features of the state and its institutions, there arises its most important political characteristic — its salience. It is by far the most prominent feature of the social landscape. Human beings grow up into a world in which sovereign states are universal. After the spread of the European style of polity over the world there seemed no other possible structure of things. And since the state does claim supreme earthly power, it can scarcely be surprising that it has been increasingly called upon to provide what people want. Sovereignty was the vital quality; the claim to supremacy overrode any doubts about efficacy. What at any time states might be unable to do could conceivably be remedied by better techniques of government, greater understanding, and so on. There was no recourse to which people might turn if at any point the state failed — no rival, no alternative, no superior.

The decline, in the West, of universal religious faith and hence in the authority of the Church was, of course, decisive in isolating the state in its lonely eminence. Many citizens adopt entirely secularist outlooks and need satisfaction in this life: they expect no other. Those who do not nevertheless find it necessary on grounds of toleration to deal politically with others in secular terms.

The creation of sovereignty occurred in a period of intense religious concern. Its arrival was necessitated by conflicts opened by religious controversy. At first, then, its salience — indeed, its dominance — was intended to serve the cause of social order and stability. The death of God was not proclaimed until the nineteenth century (and it might be a false report). But when it came it left the state alone with its claim of omnicompetence. Self-reliance and self-realization might well be urged, but men in their troubled search for betterment could still see one great power — the state, remote and awesome. Could it be made accessible?

(ii) It was the idea of the nation that provided access. In his work on the *National System of Political Economy,* first published in 1841, Friedrich List[5] attacked Adam Smith for allegedly favouring a 'cosmopolitan economy'. The attack was misplaced, for Smith clearly assumed the state system as he found it — in his remarks about the need for good government and for adequate provision for defence, for example. List accused Smith and other free traders of assuming what had not yet been achieved, a 'universal union and a state of perpetual peace'. They ignored, in his view, the division of the human race into separate national societies.

List's prescription, of course, was a form of external protection, potentially temporary. The objective was the prosperity, independence and power of the nation as such. Only through the advancement of nations (large nations, for small ones could not hope to achieve much) could individuals or humanity at large themselves advance in culture, prosperity and civilization.

The economic devices favoured by List achieved some acceptance in practice, though his arguments were disputed by liberal economists. The custom of seeing economic matters through the medium of the nation, however, became all-pervasive. It may be doubted whether the classical liberal economists thought very differently, in spite of their individualist principles. The case of Wilhelm von Humboldt is no doubt special, but illustrative nevertheless. His book *The Limits of State Action* of 1852 advocates a very low level of state activity.[6] Nevertheless he spent much of his life as a Prussian civil servant, building up the state educational system. His motives appear to have been patriotic: he did not abandon his desire for diversity and self-reliance, but his reverence for the nation grew. Free trade and free enterprise began as features of an *individualist* economic philosophy, but they are now more commonly recommended as policies to be adopted by states on behalf of nations; indeed some advocates of such things put them forward in a fiercely patriotic guise.[7] Since protectionists and economic planners also justify their schemes by appeals to national well-being, differences in economic philosophy are reduced to disputes about tactics.

For the nationalist, economic development is a matter of pride and of patriotic duty. Prosperity and, even more, the signs of prosperity are marks of collective achievement. League tables are produced, ranking countries in order on various economic criteria; and it is implied that relative position is the matter in question rather than, say, the actual contentment of people. Moreover, economic development is regarded as a means not only to standing well in the world, but as a basis of military power. Economic success is a precondition of advanced technology, and this is needed to ensure security — national security, that is.

Since war is one of the oldest human activities, it may seem unfair to associate it with nationalism, a relatively recent phenomenon. Nevertheless most wars are between states that claim to embody nations. In the twentieth century it has become hard to find warfare sustained for any period without involving nationalist conflict. The economic effects are enormous. Apart from its direct consequences on manpower and technology, modern war has legitimized breakthroughs in the level of taxation and new techniques in state control of the economy. It is not a question of a simple causal chain from nationalist spirit to wartime experiments. There is also the need for warring states seeking to achieve new levels of mobilization to encourage nationalist emotion. But there is a connection, and it is very important in accounting for the level and acceptability of state activity.

What is more clear is the association between nationalism and culture. In some anthropological sense, culture (language, common history) may be taken as the foundation of nationalism. The economic importance of this association is often neglected. At one level it provides the style, the design, the aesthetic content of many products; and it provides the occasion and the need for much creative activity. It provides stimulus, that is to say, to the worlds of art, entertainment, sport and even fashion. There are already, and could be, plenty of other localisms or traditions that also fuel the imagination in these activities. Nevertheless, at present national feelings of some sort are most prominent, and so help to supply the wants of people.

There is a more significant level: the level of personal identity. Nationalistic products not merely supply wants; nationalism characterizes a want in itself. It forms, names, embodies an emotion that is widely and very deeply felt: a feeling that a person belongs to something, is not alone, is part of a great community. Sometimes this feeling is regarded as non-material and therefore non-economic. The inference could not be more foolish.

Economics is about the means to human satisfaction. The means are scarce, and should be husbanded. Among the means are the conceptual resources of the age — the stock of ideas that can be used to make up the understanding people have of their fellows, their environment, the world. In a primitive society, resources of this type are short and the social constructs of myth and magic are confined to tribe and locality. In modern times, the development of arts, sciences and learning has provided greater intellectual resources. Nevertheless they still need to be used; the available concepts have to be fitted to people's perceptions and desires. It is an adjustment process, a sort of market.

So nationhood is an idea that itself provides for a want. It is a 'public good'. It does not stand alone, but it is in regular demand and fairly good supply. It is substitutable at the margin for other 'goods' that meet this human craving. A family tradition might serve; or a religion; or a deeply felt vocation. Nationalism is not eternally indispensable, but at present most people use some of it. It will stir people into activity, into achievement. It will induce them to cooperate with some of their fellows and to rival and emulate others. These are not trivial economic factors. Moreover its symbolism, and its emotionality, shape the way people think and feel, and so not only mould economic demand into particular forms, but also determine what responses can be made to it. In other words, the more obviously commercial demands of people are deeply affected by priorities and attitudes derived from ideological beliefs, of which nationalism is at present the dominant feature. The way supply is organized is also fashioned to conform to such beliefs.

The state, although ultimately of an abstract nature, is nowadays normally described in mechanical terms. It has 'machinery' of government and it is subjected to 'pressure'. In part such language is required in order to make its affairs intelligible to people in an era when they think in such terms about most things. But it also means that the state takes on an almost physical character. It can do things, if it is so impelled. It is strong and powerful, but it needs to be operated. Alone it would be robot-like; it needs the company of a thinking and feeling being. The symbiosis of nation and state is a mind/body relationship — a ghost in a machine.

Thus the main impact of nationality on the economy lies in its role as the 'inner' directing force of the sovereign state. The sovereignty enables the state to rule over economic activity; but the state is supposed to respond, not to a set of miscellaneous individuals, but to a nation with specific character and wants. It is this quality that makes the state seem more homely and approachable — no longer divine, no longer aristocratic, but a thing of the people — and a thing like themselves, speaking the same language and acknowledging the same customs.

In contemporary Western politics the effectiveness of the nation is secured by the mechanics of democracy, by voting. In many countries such systems do not prevail. Nevertheless, they do not abandon the nationalist ideology: far from it. The connection in these cases between nation and state apparatus is often somewhat mystical, but for that reason it is likely to be insisted on even more fervently.

At all events state and nation are now linked as servants of Man's highest ambitions. As mentioned, there is a sense in which the state has become a god-substitute; if so, nationalism is the religion-substitute. But they are substitutes, and for the most part they pursue mundane secular lives, only rising to the level of fanaticism or worship in crisis or among extremists. It is precisely this quality that makes them so important in economic matters, for these too are mundane and secular. Even in the modern era, states and their rulers were once distant and dignified; but now, in the twentieth century, nations expect them to deliver the groceries.

PROPERTY AND STATE: POSSESSIVE NATIONALISM

The long erosion of the feudal economic and political system in Europe saw the rise of not only a free market and a set of sovereign states, but also a property system to match. Instead of the complex mesh of personal ties and customary rights over land, there was created an arrangement whereby ownership rights were concentrated in a single freeholder.

In practice, as any glance at property laws will reveal, things never became all that simple. In principle, however, the political system of unique authority within territorial limits was reflected by a property system in which authority again was unique. The changes were not swiftly brought about. But after the enclosure movement in eighteenth-century England, the post-Revolutionary reforms in France, and those of Stein and Hardenberg in Germany,[8] the single owner became normal. The freeholder determined the use, acquired the fruits, controlled access, and could transfer any or all of these rights, in relation to the property. To begin with it was territory (land) that was most in question, though the rules have also been applied to other goods, material and immaterial.

The connection between political sovereignty and property rights is crucial. Under feudalism, the rights of political rulers were similar to and dependent on the rights of others with respect to land. The establishment of states with sovereignty and law-making institutions enabled the other property rights to be transformed. Given the existence of powerful legislatures, the property laws could be redeveloped, no doubt in the interests of the rising bourgeoisie. The state-power remained, however, and what was changed once could be changed again, perhaps in other interests. Property rights thus became secondary rights. Sovereignty and (in large measure) property are both exercised in recent times by abstract entities — by states and by corporations. Under the philosophy of the liberal state, the two concepts have been kept apart. The dichotomy between things that are 'public' and those that are 'private', which was one of the conceptual foundations of such societies, was used to distinguish state property from other property; but sovereignty was generally believed to be something else entirely. It involved a different type of law, and was about ruling people not about owning things.

It has become apparent in recent times that the two are not so disparate. They both sustain titles to possession, very clearly in the cases of land or minerals. Though it may be faced with problems, both domestically and from so-called multinational firms, the modern state is usually in a position to assert the primacy of its own proprietary rights. It is not surprising therefore that those who have other property rights should try to influence state policy. If they fail there is little more that can avail, for sovereign independence means that not merely legal transfer of ownership but revolutionary expropriation is legitimate. In practice, it is often not so much transfer of freehold that is in question, as its limitation by planning laws or taxation.

The pressures that impel states to take this view of their sovereign rights are similar to those affecting other social and economic activities, and need not be elaborated. It hardly need be said that nationalist beliefs are also involved. Nationalists see the nation as a moral being that has not only an incorporeal existence and rights but an indissoluble connection with 'the country' and everything in it. Such an attitude does not lead directly to state ownership or control, but it does create a certain vulnerability in that direction. If some asset, some piece of property is not serving the nation and enhancing the standing of the nation in the world, then existing arrangements might well be overridden, to promote national success. Moreover, foreign ownership is regarded with suspicion or hostility; it is a phenomenon that strikes hard against the nationalist image of what the world should be like. Independence is believed to be at stake, and this is still a major ambition of nearly all nationalisms. In December 1974 the United Nations (which is, of course, an organization of nation-states) adopted a 'Charter of Economic Rights and Duties of States', which included 'full permanent sovereignty' over national resources in its territory and its right to nationalize foreign-owned property.[9]

So property arrangements that might seem to be advantageous on 'pure' economic grounds are hard to achieve. In fact, property rules serve a good deal more than narrow economic purposes. They are symbolic; they create status; they are part of a political network of rules. Perhaps the whole concept of property is too limited. Possession is only one way — a rather extreme one — of determining who can do what with what. Within states, laws about obstruction, planning, nuisance and employee rights, for example, are also relevant. So are, increasingly, the practices and conventions of administration, along with what are usually called restrictive practices in industry. A member of an organization may own or possess nothing with it but control many things by virtue of status.

Similarly, developments in the world of sovereignties are leading to a set of relativities rather than a collection of absolutes. Militarily it is probably true that few 'independent' states can now defend themselves. It is certainly the case economically that very few can develop themselves, or even sustain themselves. Economic sovereignty — the possession of the physical and human resources of a territory — is now limited by many 'external' factors; moreover these are not merely market forces, but include specific rules from international organizations — for example, the General Agreement on Tariffs and Trade. In other words, the analogy of property and sovereignty continues, for both are being refined, restricted and divided.

However, this is to anticipate a little.

SOCIAL REFORM AND THE NATION: A QUESTION OF FEASIBILITY

The increase in state functions and consequently in the size of the state bureaucracy is one of the most obvious features of twentieth-century political developments. It is well accounted for in the conventional history,[10] and it is unnecessary for this essay to go into any detail. Before turning to the culmination of it all, however, a few remarks about the state and society are needed.

The idea of a set of human relationships prior to, and independent of, any form of rule, government or state emerges (or re-emerges) in the seventeenth and eighteenth centuries in Europe — in terms of political theory, conspicuously in John Locke's notion of the state of nature as a tolerable state of affairs. This conception may reflect the earlier era in which custom was the effective determinant of what people did. It echoed the belief that for the English — and perhaps other peoples — there was a traditional order of things that existed naturally and had not been created deliberately either by contract or conquest. Whatever its ancestry, the belief in 'society' as a fundamental concept, of which politics and economics were facets, led to the further restructuring of knowledge — to a science to understand this order (sociology) and to an ideology claiming to operate at this broad level (socialism).

These developments might be expected to be hostile to the nation-state, and in some philosophical sense perhaps they are. It is true, moreover, that change — reform or revolution — is commonly urged on *social* grounds, to create a new society, to bring social justice, to ensure social progress or at least to minimize social evils. These causes take on a moral urgency: they tend to regard the political or the economic as mechanical or amoral systems, not catering for the whole person. The criteria and the concepts tend therefore to be wide, even universalistic.

But in practice the outcome has been different. The nation-state has been strengthened, not weakened. The importance of state-collected information for economic understanding has been mentioned. A. D. Smith puts it more strongly: 'The study of society today is, almost without question, equated with the analysis of nation-states; the principle of methodological nationalism operates at every level in the sociology, politics, economics and history of mankind in the modern era.'[11] Thus when the social ideas move to the stage of application, the reality to which they are applied is that of the nation-state.

Some concepts may serve to illustrate what happens. 'Equality', of course, is served directly by the modern state in that it provides some equalities — of legal status, of voting — to its citizens. These equalities of citizenship are used in turn by people to try to bring about other equalities (of opportunity, for example), but of course these must be found within the ambit of citizenship. The reduction of remote inequalities does not have the same urgent appeal as that of those seen near and clear. Similarly, if a notion of 'community' is to find embodiment, then existing customs and current experience are usually most useful. It certainly requires a high level of inter-communication, and so common language and culture are highly relevant. Perhaps all true communities must be small — certainly many communitarians rally to the cause of sub-state nationalisms. Nevertheless, there is usually a close fit between nationality and many community values.

It seems to be a matter of feasibility. In the first place, the state can provide a readily available administrative system that can be extended from providing, say, police services to providing public parks and medical services; and the tax system can be used for distributive purposes. But secondly, the nation can provide a vehicle for morality and emotion that is nevertheless usually large enough to be thought of as 'a society'. With such instruments and within such a span, beliefs about better societies can find expression. By concentrating in this way, moreover, they can find acceptance, and alliance, more easily.

The economic consequences are formidable. Administrative and financial provision to meet social responsibilities and adjustments to reduce inequalities (between families or between regions) are all focussed on the state, partly because it has legal efficacy and partly because it is the appropriate nationwide instrument. 'Social services' are by no means the only causes of the high level of state activity, and the state was a dominant institution long before they grew; but there is no doubt of the part they played in the build-up. Contrary to what might have been expected at one stage in the history of ideas, 'society' did not turn out to be an enemy of the state.

THE CULMINATION

The idea of 'an economy' can be discerned, retrospectively, at least as far back as that of a sovereign state. It is with the second half of the twentieth century, however, with the science of macroeconomics and the craft of economic management that it comes into its inheritance. An economy is not of course completely self-contained, but it is in some sense a bounded system with a life of its own, which can be comprehended as such. Clearly the mere existence of a state with its frontiers and citizenry and of a nation with its culture and its people gives rise to the idea of a half-enclosed system, with its own set of interdependencies, quite apart from the capacity of a government to step in and manage it.

Along with the prescriptions of the free economy and minimum government there was created the science of economics — that is, the conception of the economy as a distinct operation, with a claim to understand the rationale of that operation. Such a science, whatever its first indications, was always likely to lead to a sort of technology — at first no doubt tinkering with the system as it was, and later bolder attempts to redesign it. Laissez-faire — though certainly believed in by some people — was not consistently practised for long anywhere. Most of the classical economists admitted the possibility of exceptions, and these exceptions tended to accumulate. Moreover, the conventional history is essentially a history of Britain and the United States, and while these were pioneer industrial countries, they were not the only ones, and the role of the state was always more emphatic in other places, including France and Germany.

In spite of the assumptions about self-interest common in economic theory, and supported by much observation of economic behaviour, the political instrument of the state has maintained its ascendancy. Perhaps this can be explained by some version of the logic of self-interest but, however that may be, the moral claims and the institutional structure of the state have proved dominant forces for economic life. Intellectual and social change may take place of their own accord, but it is to the state that conservatives, moderates and revolutionaries alike all turn as the mediator of economic forms.

In consequence there emerged the familiar features of twentieth-century economies. The key factor was the pressure for a very high level of economic mobilization, pressure brought about by the modern preoccupation with earthly well-being. In one version the marks of effectiveness are to be sought in full employment and welfare; in another, rapid innovation and commercial success are the things to look for. But nearly always economic slack and slow progress (for example, in contemporary Britain) are regarded as bad. The number of services or industries actually run by state agencies varies a good deal, but the norm is high. Many of these (such as education) constitute back-up services for the directly productive organizations of society — firms. On the whole, industrial firms do not undertake much of this sort of support service directly in Western societies, except where it can be done by financial means (such as pensions). There are notable exceptions, but the company town is not very common. The multiform outcome has obvious liberal advantages. But the high degree of state involvement in the provision of support services has made the state a productive agent of greater or lesser efficiency. As sophistication has grown and the pressure for economic advance has continued, the arrangements have become more and more interdependent and the need to ensure their economic effectiveness and purposefulness grew. The state became a sort of macro-enterprise.[12]

As mentioned, even the early modern state tended to become the best provider of data and information about economic matters. It became customary to think about economic policy matters in nation-state terms, perhaps as a matter of habit, since other things were also discussed in that way. The twentieth-century range of data — national income, employment, capital formation and so on — was perforce in nation-state form. Just as the idea of 'an economy' became, via macroeconomics, a statist conception, so 'our economy' became a nationalist one. The education, health, welfare and orderliness of society, which had become essential investments to improve output, could also be transmogrified into social and national achievements, that is forms of economic output themselves. Paradoxically, the success of nationalism in making itself seem 'natural' made it less noticeable and so, by a sort of default, it opened the way to the popularity of other forms of analysis (of class, for example), since they became the more overt (or even 'artificial') divisions of mankind.

CONSEQUENCES

The image of an economy coextensive with a nation-state is a very persuasive one. It must have reality, for the nation-state is likely to be a currency area, and both state and nation have imposed common characteristics on business life within their span. The belief that 'an economy' exists is a powerful force for making it so.

But it also contains much illusion. The conditions of pre-industrial periods, when the various forms of polity could readily encompass the bulk of economic life, have departed. The spread of trade and colonization over the world from the sixteenth century began the process. The dependence of the industrialized countries on food imports from the new countries and tropical zones in the nineteenth century was a decisive step. In the twentieth century, however, the highly mobilized economies have needed to look to increasing international specialization to sustain the pressure for continual economic improvement. To keep getting better, at the high level of activity now customary, means extending the division of labour even more radically and rapidly taking up new developments from elsewhere. Constant innovation is necessary to sustain the expected rate of progress, yet it cannot be adequately generated within any nation-state except the United States. Energy resources, especially fossil fuels, and mineral reserves are unevenly spread and need to be internationally traded to fit the pattern of usage.

There are attempts to restrict these developments, and they are not entirely without effect. If a nation's appetite for increasing prosperity can be moderated, perhaps by a widespread preference for stability, then some measure of the customary independence may be retained. The grounds may be conservationist; or a feeling that too rapid social change leads to personal insecurity and social intolerance; or a preference for continuing the same employment patterns. The instruments are usually some form of economic protection, against imports and immigrants, and the choice is not necessarily irrational. However, though there are some attractions, this route can scarcely satisfy the nationalist desire for high standing in the world, for having at least as good a life as that of other nations. So the nation-states' economies are faced with a dilemma: to succeed they need to become less national.

One of the major successes of the nineteenth-century state was the invention of the business firm, in place of individual or partnership traders. Created by company or corporation laws and by employment contracts, it enabled large organizations specifically devoted to economic (that is, production and trading) activities to be built up, with some autonomy in the social system. Legally they remain creatures of the state and politically there is often pressure on them to serve the purposes and ambitions of the nation.

It is the rise of the multinational firms that raises problems for the nation-state. In fact, businesses that operate in several countries are not new, and many flourished in the nineteenth century. What is new, perhaps, is the scale of some of them in absolute terms, and the effectiveness of internal communication systems that enable them to be managed from a central headquarters. At all events, these businesses create, not mere dependence on international trading, but a sort of organizational overlap with the nation-state pattern of the world. Even worse from the nationalist point of view, there is another focus of economic calculation. Is what is best for Unilever the same as what is best for the Netherlands? Is the optimum policy for Rio Tinto Zinc the same as that for Papua New Guinea? Many bland assurances claim that they are. But if they are not, the political theory of sovereignty and the moral theory of nationhood both assert that the business enterprise should come second. It would merely be scandalous to suggest that if the interest of all individuals likely to be affected were calculable, the precedence might not always be sustained.

In fact, the exercise of legal sovereignty can remove these enterprises from all but the weakest states. It is the consideration of economic advantage that deters such action. Their importance in the context of this essay lies in what they show about the developing nature of economic life, the way it begins to lie athwart the structure of traditional political units, that is of nation-states. There is in addition an international political structure in economic affairs —

the International Monetary Fund, the World Bank, the General Agreement on Tariffs and Trade, the United Nations' economic commissions, and the European Economic Community. They are all built on existing nation-states, but given appropriate political conditions they can develop, with finesse, a degree of authority of their own. Formally (legally, that is to say), these international bodies are indeed put together by nation-states and can be taken apart — or rendered ineffective — by the same nation-states. The question is whether by their usefulness, their endurance, their esprit-de-corps, they can build some autonomy for themselves in the scheme of things.

So in spite of its culminating integration with the machinery of the nation-state in an internal sense, the idea of 'an economy' finds itself in some difficulties. It is not of course the case that states are no longer capable of exercising any control over their economies or of the forms taken by economic life within their boundaries. Things have not yet reached that point, though if some trends continue it may well come to that. So far it merely means that they can no longer be sure of having everything their own way.

NOTES AND REFERENCES

1. D. C. Coleman (ed.) *Revisions in Mercantilism* (London: Methuen, 1969).
2. William Letwin *The Origins of Scientific Economics* (London: Methuen, 1963) p. 228.
3. Quentin Skinner *The Foundations of Modern Political Thought* (Cambridge: Cambridge University Press, 1979) vol. 2, pp. 349—58.
4. L. Tivey *The Politics of the Firm* (London: Martin Robertson, 1978) Chs 1 and 2.
5. Friederich List *The National System of Political Economy* (1841) (trans. Lloyd, 1885; Longmans, 1904).
6. Wilhelm von Humboldt *The Limits of State Action* (1854) (edited Burrow; Cambridge: Cambridge University Press, 1969).
7. For example, in Britain, the Institute of Economic Affairs, devoted to the promotion of free-market economics, sponsored essays entitled *Rebirth of Britain* (London: Pan Books, 1964).
8. F. L. Nussbaum *History of the Economic Institutions of Modern Europe* (New York: Kelly, 1968)
9. The General Assembly adopted the text of the Charter as resolution 3281 (XXIX) on 12 December 1974. See the *Yearbook of the United Nations* (1974) vol. 28, pp. 381—407.

10. See, for instance, G. K. Fry *The Growth of Government* (London: Cass, 1979); and S. Fine *Laissez-faire and the General-Welfare State* (London: Oxford University Press, 1956).
11. A. D. Smith *Nationalism in the Twentieth Century* (Oxford: Martin Robertson, 1979) p. 191.
12. An enterprise, that is to say, in an even narrower and cruder *economic* sense than the concept of the state as a purposive enterprise deplored by Michael Oakeshott in *On Human Conduct* (London: Oxford University Press, 1975) part III.

An advertisement by Mobil Ltd., a multinational oil enterprise, in *The Guardian* on 25 April 1979, and in other papers about the same time, vividly illustrates the concept of a state as a macro-enterprise:

Tired of hearing hard-luck stories about companies which need assistance from the taxpayer? Here's a good-luck story for a change — worth £40 million a year to Britain. When major industrial investment projects are in the offing, national governments like to deal themselves in on the game. Because Europe is a unified market, there's often a choice of countries in which new plant could be built; and the winning country collects a new European export business. High stakes. ,

A few years ago, Mobil in Britain came up with a plan to invest in a new refinery plant which would enable us to export petrol to Europe in the 1980s. The trouble was, we weren't alone: other Mobil companies in Europe had a good case for building the same plant in their own countries. But the European market wasn't big enough to support more than one new Mobil plant.

And that's where the governments showed their hands. Every European government offers incentives to attract industrial investment: tax reliefs, grants, low-interest loans. All high cards.

But Britain held some nice cards too. Like a 100 per cent tax write-off of the investment cost over one year. And Britain placed the ace — a £10 million grant towards the interest on money borrowed for the project, provided it was built here to an accelerated timetable. That was the decisive card. And now the new plant is under construction at our refinery in Essex. In the 1980s it should be boosting the balance of payments by £40 million a year — a handsome return on the taxpayer's outlay.

We ought to put *our* cards on the table: as a competitive private enterprise company, we're far from enthusiastic about some forms of government intervention in industry.

But when international investment is at stake, governments are in competition with one another. Just as companies have to keep their products competitive, a national government has to ensure that its *country* stays competitive.

And every ace counts.

FURTHER READING

There are obvious classic works that are fundamental to this topic, such as John Locke *Second Treatise of Civil Government* (1689) and Adam Smith *Wealth of Nations* (1776). It is important to include Friederich List *The National System of Political Economy* (1841; Longmans, 1904) for a forthright statement of the nationalist view of economic priorities. General works on the state, sovereignty and nationalism recommended for the two previous essays are again relevant.

The rise in state activity is explained, with particular reference to the United States, in Sidney Fine *Laissez-faire and the General-Welfare State* (London: Oxford University Press, 1956). Geoffrey Fry gives an account of *The Growth of Government* (London: Cass, 1979) in Britain that clearly presents the received history of ideas. J. M. Keynes' essay 'The end of laissez-faire' in *Essays in Persuasion* (London: Macmillan, 1931) was a contribution to that history.

Property can be better understood through R. Schlatter *Private Property — the history of an idea* (London: Allen and Unwin, 1951; New York: Russel and Russel, 1973), and the collection of essays edited by C. B. Macpherson, *Property* (Oxford: Blackwell, and University of Toronto, 1978).

Multinational business concerns have generated a large literature. The best introductions are C. Tugenhadt *The Multinationals* (London: Eyre and Spottiswoode, 1971; Harmondsworth, Middx: Pelican, 1973) and R. Vernon *Storm over the Multinationals* (London: Macmillan, 1977). A general discussion relevant to some of the trends mentioned is in Daniel Bell *The Coming of Post-Industrial Society* (New York: Basic Books, 1973; London: Heinemann, 1974; Harmondsworth, Middx: Peregrine Books, 1979).

4

The Nation-State in Western Europe: Erosion from 'Above' and 'Below'?

Martin Kolinsky

The centralized nation-state was the outcome of political evolution, of which some aspects have been discussed in previous chapters. Whatever the merits of the nation-state, it became apparent in the twentieth century that it did not prevent the mounting horrors of war, and that alone it could not ensure economic prosperity. As a result, efforts were made to develop new political devices. The preferred solution among those of liberal outlook was the 'international institution'. The aftermath of the First World War saw an attempt at institutional order through the League of Nations; the close of the Second World War brought the United Nations and a range of other more specialized bodies, some almost worldwide, others of lesser scope.

In Europe, the cradle of the nation-state, the most advanced attempts to develop a new institutional order are to be found. Some close attention to its experiences is vital. The idea of the nation-state as an ultimate, compelling reality was brought into question in Western Europe by the Second World War more widely and profoundly than had been the case after the First World War. The governments that had fused extreme nationalism and dictatorship, Nazi Germany and fascist Italy, were buried in the war of aggressive brutality they had unleashed. International relations were restructured by alignments of states dominated by the new military superpowers. The battered nations of Europe were corralled into one or other of the two great blocs as world politics became dominated by the Cold War. In the West, the nation-states retained their sovereignty (or gradually attained it in the case of the Federal Republic of Germany), but had to recognize the limitations on its exercise given their military, economic and financial dependence on the United States of America. Moreover, the perception of the threat of totalitarian communism, soon after the harrowing struggle against Nazism, made closer coordination of policies desirable and necessary to protect the shared values of democracy and liberty. Although the notion of a politically united Europe proved to be a fragile flower, important international structures were established such as the Organisation for European Economic Cooperation (OEEC) in 1948, which was transformed in 1960 into the Organisation for Economic Co-operation and Development (OECD), the Western European Union (WEU) in 1954, the North Atlantic Treaty Organisation (NATO) in 1949, the European Coal and Steel Community (ECSC) in 1952, Euratom in 1958, and the European Economic Community (EEC) in 1958.

The various organizations differed in type, as will be discussed later in the chapter, but represented permanent alliances for specific purposes of policy alignment and coordination. The real issue was not surrendering political sovereignty but ascertaining common goals and finding methods of working together. The outcome was that the operation of government in Western Europe was not merely determined negatively by dependence on the United States. It was also influenced in a positive manner by participation in the increasingly dense network of international organization. For the newly created state of Western Germany, participation in European integration was a means of acquiring respectability and legitimacy, both requisites for the removal of the Occupation Statute and for winning independent, sovereign status. For Italy and the smaller countries, participation in the European organizations also represented a gain in status and a strengthening of their political integrity. Participation meant a defined place in the international order, formal recognition of its voice and interests, security and material benefits and, most important of all, a basis for positive action and influence. Dependence on a large neighbouring state, as was later to be repeated in the case of Ireland vis-à-vis Great Britain, was reduced and replaced by an acknowledged, formal (proportionate) equality.

However, the situation appeared to be more complex to British and French governments. Under both Labour and Conservative administration, Britain was not interested in anything beyond multilateral, loosely structured cooperation and consequently remained aloof from the initial phases of European integration. However, the economic success of these institutions, and the search for a new political role in Europe, led to a reversal of policy by the leaders of both major parties in the 1960s. The situation in France was almost the opposite, with governments seeking military independence while accepting some degree of economic integration with neighbouring countries. Nevertheless in both cases the network of international organization created a new environment for governments and significantly modified the traditional notion of national sovereignty.

THE CHANGING NOTION OF SOVEREIGNTY

Sovereignty means that the state is the ultimate source of authority, law and legitimate force within its boundaries. However the boundaries are not impermeable, and no state can be taken in isolation: its industry, energy, raw materials, finance and trade are dependent on world circumstances; its society is penetrated by international trends and influences. The exercise of sovereignty is further conditioned and modified by membership of international organizations, the obligations incurred there and the concern for maintaining positive relations with a great variety of other states. In reality, therefore, sovereignty is a more diffuse and indeterminate notion than was understood when the British Empire flourished and European states could act as world powers. There are some who are concerned that the development of supranational integration in the European Community (EC) will lead to a complete transfer of powers, so that countries such as Britain will become reduced to the status of provinces. Such a surrender seems most unlikely, as is discussed later, because of the reassertion of the authority of the nation-states within the Community. The somewhat paradoxical consequence of 'integration' in the EC is that national governments dominate the decision-making and policy-making processes.[1] The Commission, representing the supranational element in the Community, is relatively weak compared with the representatives of national governments (the Council of Ministers) and of national civil services (Committee of Permanent Representatives, COREPER). Moreover, national parliaments have for the most part not established effective methods of controlling ministers in their dealings at Brussels, so that the authority of national governments is enhanced by the executive-to-executive relationships created in the Community. The diffusion of sovereignty is accompanied by a strengthening of central governmental powers.

The traditional meaning of sovereignty in unitary states has also come into question from 'below' by moves towards regionalism, autonomy and federalism in various countries. Although it did not arise from sub-state nationalism, the most significant change occurred in Germany with the establishment of the Federal Republic after the fusion of the western zones of occupation. West German federalism, which arose from special circumstances, is discussed in the next section. While such a solution is advocated by only minorities elsewhere (in Britain the most prominent are the Liberal Party and the Edinburgh daily newspaper *The Scotsman*), pressures for regional reforms have been widespread, even in the staunchest of unitary states. The situations in Britain, France, Italy, Belgium and Spain are reviewed briefly below.

The causes of sub-state nationalism and regionalism are various,[2] and each case has its unique aspects. Suffice it to state here, without attempting to elucidate causal explanations, that the pressures for decentralization, and in some cases for autonomy, arose from the overwhelming concentration of powers in central government at a time when the growing interdependence of states seemed to bring the capabilities and functions of the traditional structure into question. It is somewhat paradoxical that while interdependence reinforces the concentration of powers (because the action is at a government-to-government level), it represents at the same time limitations on traditional capabilities (in economic, military and diplomatic spheres), which in turn reinforces the questioning of the validity of such concentration of powers. In Britain, for example, the sense of political and economic decline, while leading to membership of the EC, also contributed to the erosion of some of the links between Scotland and England. It was in this context of change that the rise of Scottish nationalism stimulated in the 1970s intense discussion of the political alternatives of devolution, independence, and even federalism.

The changes occurring 'above' the level of the state, are not without consequence for the patterns of authority and political integration within national structures. There is posed the question of the redistribution of functions for the sake of greater administrative efficiency and democracy:[3]

How to relieve the congestion of affairs at the centre?

How to promote regional development and planning to reduce socio-economic imbalances?

How to encourage democratic participation at sub-state levels?

Although internal decentralization provides greater scope for cultural and regional diversity, recent experience in Britain and France suggests strongly that unitary state governments are determined to maintain full control over whatever measures of change are introduced. The political circumstances affecting the trends of change in various countries are examined in the next section, which is followed by further consideration of the problem of interdependence and the various national interpretations and reactions to it.

Pressures for decentralization: sub-state nationalism and regionalism

Most of the constitutions of the Western European countries provide for a concentration of powers in central government. In contrast to the unitary states, there are only three examples of federalism: Switzerland, Austria and West Germany. The Federal Republic of Germany, established in 1949, consists of eleven *Länder* (including West Berlin). Legislative powers were distributed between the federal and the *Länder* governments. The former has exclusive power in foreign affairs, citizenship, currency and communications, while sharing powers (concurrent legislation) with the *Länder* in less vital matters. The powers of the *Länder* are considerable, including control of education, cultural affairs (radio and television) and police. Moreover, the implementation of federal legislation is largely accomplished through the *Länder*. Hence the importance of the *Bundesrat*, the second parliamentary chamber in which each *Land* is represented according to its size. The *Bundesrat*, which has a suspensory veto on bills passed in the *Bundestag*, serves as a meeting-place for officials of the central government and of the *Länder*. With the exception of Bavaria, regionalist feeling is not pronounced, and there are constitutional provisions to even out regional discrepancies. In conformity with the aim of 'unity of living standards' in all *Länder,* the federal government redistributes certain taxes in favour of the poorer states. In Bavaria, with its special historical and political traditions, there is a strong sense of particularism. Although the Christian Social Union (CSU) is a permanent coalition partner of the Christian Democratic Party (CDU), it is by no means passively acquiescent, and there have been threats to form a separate national party of the ultra-conservative right. The political ethos of the CSU is notably on the right-wing of Christian democracy and its powerful leader Franz-Josef Strauss has led the opposition on such important issues as the *Ostpolitik.* Although his ambitions to become the Chancellor-candidate were long frustrated, he was sufficiently influential to undermine two CDU leaders (Barzel and Kohl) and in June 1979 finally reached the top position in the Christian Democratic coalition. It is his extremely powerful base in Bavaria, the second largest state of some eleven millions, that has enabled Strauss to stay for so long in the forefront of national politics.

Although the decentralization of power involves elected parliamentary forums (the *Landtage*), there has been a constant decline in their legislative power and a growth in the bureaucratic coordination of federal/*Länder* relations. Kurt Sontheimer has summarized the process in the following words:

> The practice of co-ordination and co-operation in German federalism which is supported by innumerable treaties and administrative agreements between the Laender and between the Federation and the Laender is carried out mainly without the Laender parliaments. Federalism as it is practised is to a great extent a matter for bureaucrats, not for politicians, and it has withdrawn in part from parliamentary control.[4]

The tendency, therefore, is towards a certain degree of *recentralization* of power with a strong element of administrative devolution. The main actors on the *Land* level are the minister—presidents and officials of the *Länder* ministries. The tendency towards recentralization has been reinforced by several other trends. The problem of terrorism, for example, has necessitated much closer coordination among the *Länder* police authorities and federal security bodies. The issues of university and educational reforms have also prompted efforts at greater coordination, as have economic questions. In all these areas, the federal government has taken initiatives both for closer cooperation with the *Länder* authorities and to establish greater control for itself. Indeed, with the internationalization of European economies becoming ever more pronounced — within the European Community and in terms of dependence on world trade — the need for consistent *national* economic policy is keenly felt in Germany. Moreover the huge success of the German economy, and the financial transfers reducing regional discrepancies, have largely overshadowed such problems as the growing obsolescence of much industry in the Ruhr area. Such decline is offset by the extremely rapid development of *Länder* like Baden-Wurttemberg, which used to send its surplus labour across the border to work in Alsace, but by the mid-1960s reversed the direction of migration as its industries grew to contribute nearly one-sixth of the Federal Republic's gross national product.

The trends toward recentralization have weakened the parliamentary structures of the *Länder,* but have not undermined the federal system as such. The federal institutions (*Bundesrat, Länder* executives, Constitutional Court, and the constitution itself) remain viable, and political party organization is well adapted to the federal organization of the state. Unlike the situation of the Weimar Republic the legitimacy of the political system is not in question. Nevertheless it is clear that federalism as practised in West Germany is not static, and there is a movement towards a degree of recentralization. This contrasts with the situation in Canada, where there is a pronounced shift to the provinces (Quebec nationalism, Alberta economic strength). It contrasts also with the situations in which many European unitary states have found themselves, where the pressures for decentralization have been often strong enough to pose the question of altering the established constitutional order. These pressures are strongest when reinforced by nationalist claims (Scotland, Corsica, the Basque country, and in Belgium) though regional feeling based on aspirations for economic development are also prevalent in such diverse areas as the west of France, the south of Italy and the north of England.

The rise of nationalism in Scotland and Wales resulted first in the *Royal Commission on the Constitution 1969—73* (Kilbrandon Report) and then in legislative proposals for devolution. The intense and prolonged debates on these proposals were marked by backbench revolts that seriously embarrassed the Labour government and contributed to its final downfall in March 1979. Considerable government activity during the 1970s was focussed on the implications of the Kilbrandon Report. In addition to working out the extremely complex devolution proposals, the cabinet and cabinet office committees were concerned with mounting regional economic pressures. Development agencies were established in Scotland, Wales and Northern Ireland, and regional policy generally became much more active. Grants for industrial location and other aids under the Wilson/Callaghan administration of 1974—79 rose to over £400 million a year.

Inevitably the effect of government attention to the Celtic peripheries, especially to Scotland, created concern in the less affluent English regions. It was most pronounced in the north of England, which felt that it was in as much need of assistance as Scotland but had less political influence on the government. Not surprisingly, then, Labour MPs from the North East joined the backbench rebels in voting against key aspects of the government's devolution programme, and lobbied for the establishment of a Northeast development agency.[5] The repercussions were felt further afield. Although the West Midlands was not as directly worried by the devolution proposals, the sharp decline in the prosperity of the region led to growing resentment at not being included in the government's category of assisted areas. The Birmingham Chamber of Commerce, for example, has consistently argued that the city has lost its growth industries by years of government direction of investment away from the industrial heartland. Moreover, it cannot even tap the European Regional Development Fund, because Westminster did not include it among the assisted areas. The resentment is underlined by a feeling of political weakness: unlike traditionally poor areas the organization of a regional interest grouping through one of the major parties had not been necessary in the past. However, in its situation of declining prosperity the lack of a special channel to government bounty was keenly felt in the West Midlands. These were the reactions of people concerned with industrial and planning problems, but they were not more widely articulated into mass-based political demands. Since political expressions of regional identity did not emerge in other parts of England either, there were no parallels with the Scottish and Welsh nationalist movements. For the latter, devolution was seen only as a step along the way to independence, despite the fact that in the government's view devolution was set out as a means of responding to aspirations for democratic participation at an intermediate (regional) level of government. In fact this, rather than national independence, was consistently the most popular option in Scottish opinion polls. Despite the scrapping of the Labour devolution bill, the question of change in the political and administrative relationships of the constituent parts of the United Kingdom remains open. Whatever the future outcome, however, it seems unlikely that decentralization measures will reduce the essential controlling and mediating capacities of central government in Westminster. This expectation is supported by the French experience, where the 1972 regional reforms were by no means as far-reaching in their implications as the changes envisaged in the Scotland Bill.

Unlike Britain, French government concern was impelled less by nationalist movements than by a need for a new administrative framework for promoting regional economic development. The administrative reform was limited because the intention was not to replace the existing pattern of *départements,* established by Napoleon, but to bring them into association for planning purposes. The potential political significance of the regions was curtailed by rejecting direct elections. Instead the regional councils represent for the most part the established political interests of the parties and the local notables.[6] Nevertheless the *départements* are too small on their own, given the urban—industrial development of France and the economic pressures exerted on it by Common Market competition. The relatively simple solution sought in the 1972 reforms — the coexistence of regions and *départements* — could lead to greater tensions if nationalist or regionalist feeling should develop more strongly, perhaps in response to prolonged recession, in sensitive areas such as Brittany, the midi, or Corsica. Even if that does not happen, it has become increasingly clear that strong-minded regional élites, such as those in the Pays de la Loire and in the Lyon area, want more scope for themselves and less constraint from Paris.[7]

In Italy, the situation is dominated by the division between the industrial North and the underdeveloped South (the *Mezzogiorno*), a problem recognized in the Treaty of Rome, which established the European Economic Community, as calling for special measures of assistance. These have come from both the European Investment Bank and the European Regional Development Fund. Despite these actions, which have conjoined with three decades of Italian government development projects, the Mezzogiorno remains a special problem, whether measured in terms of its low contribution to gross national product, its poor living standards or its high rate of unemployment. The regional disparities in Italy have remained the most pronounced in the European Community, and continue to impede Italy's progress toward greater economic stability. As the Community has recognized from the beginning, it is not merely an Italian problem but is a serious threat to the aim of creating integration, which requires greater similarity in economic performance, standards of living and social opportunities.

Constitutionally Italy is a unitary state with regional administrations. As a reaction against fascism, the 1947 constitution provided for regions as an integral part of the organization of the state. But the establishment of the regions was held back until 1970 because of the fear on the part of Christian Democratic governments of Communist domination in the central regions of Emilia, Tuscany and Umbria. However, the shift to centre—left coalitions in the 1960s finally resulted in the introduction of the regions because of the insistence of the Socialists when invited to join the governing coalition. There are twenty regions, each with a council elected by proportional representation as in national elections. The council elects its executive and presiding officer. The legislative powers include agriculture, health services, planning and cultural affairs — a range considerably less than those of the German *Länder*, or even what was contemplated in the Scotland Bill, though Italian regions do have limited powers for raising revenue. Five of the regions, including the islands, are defined as special and have somewhat wider legislative powers. An area of particular concern for all regions is industrial policy, which is determined by central government, although the regions are responsible for small business. The division is a cause of friction because the regions argue that it is impossible to establish development plans without being able to influence industrial policy. Nevertheless, dynamic regions such as Piedmont have approved regional plans.

The transfer of powers to the regional administrations has proved to be a slow and uneven process. As may be expected, those institutions, such as the employment office, that are important sources of political patronage have proved much harder to decentralize than less vital administrations. Another problem is financial. Regional budgets are mainly financed from a common fund (i.e nationally raised revenue) distributed by central government.

A frequently voiced complaint is that Rome controls the purse-strings too tightly. But there is some evidence that certain regions, particularly in the Mezzogiorno, are seriously underspending their allocations, either because of inefficiency or because of lack of programmes. However, these problems have to be seen in perspective: the slow pace of devolving powers has meant that operative regional government is a very recent phenomenon in Italy. It is far too early to attempt to judge its effectiveness in the urgent tasks of development, planning and administrative reform. It is not made easier by the frequency and apparent intractability of national government crises.

Belgium is another example of a unitary state with pronounced regional differences. The most prominent aspect is a linguistic/cultural conflict between Flanders and French-speaking Wallonia, which has persisted over decades, and which has more recently developed further into a dispute about the status of Brussels. Over the past twenty years, with the decline of traditional steel and mining industries, economic dominance has shifted from Wallonia to the north, which has prospered on American and German investment (the port of Antwerp in particular; Flanders generally because of its less strike-prone and less organized labour force).[8] Whereas the Walloons have reacted by demanding priority action to revitalize their obsolescent industries, the Dutch-speaking Flemings who form a majority of the population (5.3 out of 8.8 million) resent the cultural and political domination of the French-speaking élites and are determined to preserve their newly acquired economic advantages. The long simmering conflict increasingly focussed on the question of Brussels, a predominantly French-speaking city in the southern part of Flanders. The steady shift of population from the city centre to the suburbs has created politically significant pockets of French speakers. The reaction of the Flemish communes has been strong. The government of Leo Tindemans (1977–78) attempted to resolve the tensions with a programme of regional reform that proposed the replacement of the nine provincial administrations by the three regions of Flanders, Wallonia and Brussels, with a number of central government powers to be transferred to elected regional and sub-regional councils. Although it had been agreed that Brussels boundaries would remain within the limits of its existing nineteen communes, the prolonged negotiations over the regionalization legislation were seriously interrupted in 1978 by objections from the Flemish wing of Tindemans' own party (the Social Christians, CVP). Tindemans resigned, but the subsequent elections proved inconclusive, and the stalemate over constitutional reforms continued to the end of the decade.

The irony of the situation is that until his resignation Tindemans was seen in the larger EC context as one of the chief movers of European integration. His sober and cautious report to the European Council, 'European Union' (January 1976), was widely discussed and, though criticized in detail, regarded as heralding a more realistic and useful approach to the problem of European unity. A more fundamental irony is that Brussels, the seat of the Community, has become the centre of conflict over national unity.

The enlargement of the Community to include Spain is likely further to intensify regional problems. First, there is the pressure of Spanish agriculture on the poorer farming regions of France and Italy, in mutual competition over Mediterranean products of cheap wines, and fruit and vegetables. This created strong feeling in southern France and Italy once the prospect of Spain's entry became a reality. Secondly, the poor regions of Spain, such as Andalucia and Extramadura, like the Mezzogiorno, greatly intensify regional disparities within the Community and will strain the limited resources of the Regional and Social funds. Thirdly, within Spain itself, the long-standing violence of the Basque situation threatens national unity and the fragile democratic order. Basque and Catalan autonomy were ruthlessly suppressed during the Franco dictatorship, but in the new constitution of 1978 the right to autonomy of the 'regions and nationalities' of Spain is recognized and guaranteed (article 2). However, somewhat as in Italy, fulfilment has taken longer than expected, and the question of defining the extent of devolution is subject to important political reservations.

Central government control

The trends in the various countries should be seen in the fluid international context. The growth of the world economy, the energy crisis, and the claims of the Third World during the 1970s — notably in the United Nations Committee on Trade and Development (UNCTAD), General Agreement on Tariffs and Trade (GATT) and Lomé Convention negotiations — have contributed towards what has been described as 'the new nationalism' among Western countries.[9] The effect of the 'new nationalism' is to enhance the importance of central government control, which, as is discussed below, is being reinforced by the process of European integration. However, integration carries with it a certain counter-pressure in regions on the periphery or in economic decline to acquire more say in the management of their problems. This may be fuelled by invidious comparisons: the feeling in North East England of coming off second-best to Scotland in benefits and influence; the resentment in the West Midlands at being excluded from regional aids; the feeling in the West of France that not enough is being done to speed decentralization of Paris industries and administrations; the sense of neglect in Alsace, which tends to measure itself against the standards achieved across the border in Baden-Wuerttemberg and Switzerland. It is true that these responses can be managed by central government through generous policies of regional aid and through political pay-offs where appropriate channels have been established. But there remains the question of democratic participation in decisions affecting the regions. For example, the seventy-one Scottish MPs in London are not well-placed to exercise control over the Scottish civil service in St Andrews House, Edinburgh. Nor has regional reform in France represented much improvement because the councils are not directly elected, and the government has strongly resisted pressures to make them more viable political institutions. However, as the case of West Germany illustrates, elected assemblies in themselves are not the full answer to the problem of democratic participation. The decline in the legislative powers of the *Landtage* and the tendency to bureaucratize regional affairs indicate the general difficulty that parliaments have become relatively marginal to decision-making processes in many spheres. The multiplication of regional assemblies in itself will not reduce the possibility that such institutions may be emptied of much of their content and lose their potential influence. The problem is also posed decisively at the level of the European Parliament, as will be considered later.

Pressures for decentralization affect the exercise of state power in that political stability requires attention to the demands of sensitive regions. But the central administration alone has the capacity and information to manage the competition for limited resources and to exercise overall responsibility. Therefore, although its authority may be questioned internally, and its means in the world reduced, the political grip of the unitary state has not faltered, nor is it likely to do so.

INTERNATIONAL ORGANIZATION

The nation-states of Western Europe participate in numerous international organizations, but the European Community is the only structure that embodies the principle of supranational integration. The interpretation of the supranational aim varies from federalism — that is, the creation of a United States of Europe on the model of the USA, with transfer of sovereignty in the fullest sense to a European government — to a permanent association of independent states, retaining their capacity to decide their domestic and foreign policies for themselves, but seeking common ground with their partners by means of consultation and coordination. Whereas very few partisans of federalism remain after the hard realities of de Gaulle's nationalism in the 1960s and the energy crises of the 1970s, the EC has survived as an association of nation-states. Its importance in world trade and economic affairs is not in doubt; it has elaborated a unique legal framework through its treaties and the Court of Justice; and it has strengthened the potential of the European Parliament as a parliament-in-making through the introduction of direct elections. While these supranational elements serve to buttress the Community framework, the limitations have to be stressed as well. The European Parliament is a consultative body and its restricted powers cannot be extended without the agreement of all the governments and parliaments throughout the Community. The Court of Justice has only theoretical superiority over national institutions and does not have means of enforcing its decisions. Of greater importance is the fact that the Commission, which embodies the supranational animus of the Community, lost much of its momentum after its collision with de Gaulle in the mid-1960s.[10] The influence of the national governments, which is exercised through the powerful Council of Ministers and the Committee of Permanent Representatives, has been enhanced by regular summit meetings of prime ministers and presidents. At the same time, the power of central governments has increased domestically because the intergovernmental bargaining, and the legislation arising from it, is very difficult for parliaments to monitor and control.

Despite these limitations, which arise from a tangle of cross-purposes and competitive bargaining about the terms of cooperation, the Community has proved its capacity to survive the shattering of illusions about the progress and prospects of supranational integration. What has endured is the underlying interdependence of the member states and the importance of their multilateral contacts, even in a less than ideal organization. This was symbolized in the first campaign of direct elections to the European Parliament by Mme Simone Veil, who headed the list of the Giscardian candidates. She subsequently resigned from the French cabinet to become the Liberal candidate for the presidency of the European Parliament. In her campaign, which was widely reported throughout the Community, she stressed that as a survivor of Nazi concentration camps, in which her family perished, she saw the European Community as the safeguard of democracy against the threat of a recurrence of totalitarianism. Whether rhetoric or not, it was received as a forceful and emotive restatement of a major theme used to justify the Community (in its most doggerel form it portrays the Second World War as the 'European civil war'!)

The truth, of course, is that the EC by itself has nowhere near the cohesion to affect the basic political structures and trends within the member states. The reasons Germany does not recreate its Nazi past have to do with the establishment of democratic institutions in the western zones of occupation before the new state attained its sovereignty, and with its international situation as part of the Western Alliance. Nevertheless, the Community represents an important aspiration that has imparted a wider sense of identity and belonging, especially to the post-war generations. The European dimension has served as a soft-lining for the new German consciousness, enabling them to look forward without paying more than lipservice to the atrocity of the past. The *crise de conscience* has penetrated little deeper than to instill a certain self-effacement in those political leaders having contact with the external world. But this does not minimize the importance of the Community as an aspiration and as a source of pressure on applicant countries for upholding democratic norms. The further enlargement of the Community to include Greece, Spain and Portugal is a significant test. With luck, the Community may accomplish what the military alliance was unable to do, namely to underpin and strengthen the new, fragile democratic structures of those countries by facilitating their economic development.

The existence of the Community, with its processes of political and economic concertation, contributes in some degree to the cohesion of the wider NATO alliance of fifteen countries. But it is indirect, a spin-off from the multiplicity of contact, rather than an indication of the complementarity of the two organizations. NATO, which is an intergovernmental structure, represents a pooling of common defence and strategic interests under American leadership. In this perspective the EC bloc dissolves into an amorphous assembly of states grouped around a superpower. Even France, which has withdrawn militarily, has consistently recognized its ultimate reliance on American nuclear protection by remaining within the NATO political alliance. Indeed it could be argued that France's maverick diplomacy since the mid-1960s was possible only because it could take that protection for granted.

The achievements of NATO as a military alliance during the Cold War and subsequently have undoubtedly depended on US capabilities in both nuclear and non-nuclear fields. But the political community underpinning NATO exists only in the vague sense of commitment to Western values supplemented with limited co-ordination in foreign policy. To some extent it is in the nature of things, since NATO is defined as being 'composed of sovereign nations which have relinquished none of their independence in the field of foreign policy. Decisions in the Council are not taken by majority vote, but by common consent.'[11] Nevertheless consultation and coordination are imperative for the alliance, and a premium is placed on the exchange of views among governments before decisions are taken so that consultation may influence policy-making.

But alliance politics have shown over the years that in many important respects the principle is as much honoured in the breach as in the observance. As the threat of confrontation receded after the Cuba missile crisis in October 1962 to more abstract concern about the arms balance and arms limitations, the political tensions of the alliance became increasingly pronounced. De Gaulle's desire to develop a French nuclear force and to break through bloc alignments with bilateral understandings and relations was the most unequivocal expression of conflict. Other European countries certainly did not wish to follow suit, and solemnly reaffirmed the military and political value of the NATO community. But they, and particularly the Germans, were no longer happy about dependence on American assurances. The distrust between Adenauer and Kennedy blossomed into full anxiety even before America became completely embroiled in the Vietnam war. The depth of American involvement in Vietnam forcibly reminded the Europeans that American interests lay as much in Asia as in the West, and could be switched away from the latter no matter what their partners thought. This was worse, in fact, than the scare story that America would be inhibited to retaliate (because of its own vulnerability to nuclear attack) if the USSR made a limited thrust into Western Europe. The anxiety about being abandoned, or being unable to influence American policy sufficiently (which could be detrimental to their interests), underlined the weaker partners' concerns about nuclear planning. American control of nuclear weapons and of nuclear policy made it virtually impossible for the Europeans to feel more than third-rate. De Gaulle's path of independent development of nuclear weapons was politically impossible for the Germans to consider, and not practicable for the others, except Britain. The American problem was to keep German (and other) fingers well away from the nuclear trigger, while giving them some feeling of participation. This has been achieved to a limited degree by the establishment of the Nuclear Planning Group sub-committee in NATO, but it remains extremely difficult to balance the elephant — budgerigar duet on the nuclear/political see-saw.

NATIONAL INTERPRETATIONS OF INTERDEPENDENCE

It is evident that notwithstanding the viability of the military alliance, the political community underlying it has not progressed beyond embryonic stages and remains in a state of flux. Economic discussions in various international forums and political consultation in the EEC (a grouping narrower than NATO) partially supplements it, but not sufficiently to create an integral system of military — economic — political — diplomatic coordination. The instability or low-level crisis arises from the unbalanced nature of the Atlantic alliance, as well as from the varying bilateral and multilateral interests of the European partner states. The ambiguity was well characterized by Hanrieder as 'tendencies towards divergence and tendencies toward integration'.[12] Ambiguity is also pronounced within the grouping of EC states that are more similar in size. After two decades of cooperation, the degree of supranational integration in the EC remains minimal, though consultations have muffled all-out divergencies in some economic fields. Most of the governments recognize that interdependence compels cooperative relations; but these are much easier to achieve in periods of economic growth than in situations of instability and insecurity. While economic vulnerability emphasizes the underlying interdependence, it raises postures of nationalistic self-defence because national autonomy is 'the most secure framework for control'.[13] No state gives all: its general willingness to coordinate policies is tempered by the reserve of seeking competitive advantage where possible and by its anxiety to minimize its vulnerability to unpredictable changes in the external world. A finger is given, the hand held back.

When some grand vision emerges from an American or a French president, the kind of political consultation it inspires among the partner governments is, not surprisingly, accompanied by scepticism and enquiry into motives.

From the point of view of the individual state, membership in the various organizations is valued for the dual purposes already considered, that is, coordination of policies and protection of one's own interests. The option of falling back on national autonomy (at least in certain spheres) is always possible because an important limiting characteristic of international organizations is their lack of sanctions over member states. Thus France withdrew its territory and military forces from NATO, but chose to remain a member of the political alliance. There were no sanctions that could be applied to modify France's behaviour. Sanctions may be applied against a smaller state, but often with uncertain results. Turkey, for example, was not deterred by arms sanctions after its invasion and occupation of Cyprus, and the American ban was eventually lifted despite Greece's strong protests. Sanctions are usually limited in value because international organizations are associations of common interests, and it is difficult to apply sanctions without inflicting deep wounds on the organization itself. The experience is not confined to NATO; the agreed rules of the International Monetary Fund (IMF), General Agreement on Tariffs and Trade (GATT), International Energy Agency (IEA), European Community (EC), as well as of a host of lesser organizations, have been breached on many occasions without serious consequences for the undisciplined member states.

It is advantageous for the individual states to belong to several organizations, each specializing in a policy field, rather than to belong to one large political community that would permanently curtail the autonomy of the member states and perhaps reduce them to the level of provinces. In fear of such restraints Britain chose to stand clear of the early phases of European integration in the 1950s, while participating fully in the western military alliance. France reversed that choice in the 1960s and 1970s. Hence the idea of a Western European political bloc gradually achieving equality with the United States was severely unrealistic. It was not possible either to consider incorporating defence concerns into the EC or to achieve common policies in sensitive matters such as energy and foreign affairs. In any case, most of the issues stretch across the Atlantic, and usually across the Pacific too. While it is all too obvious that defence is inconceivable without the USA, it is no less true that the domestic and foreign economic policies of America are vital determinants of European financial, economic and energy problems too. In these spheres, bilateral interest relations (e.g. USA—Germany, USA—Britain) have not in the slightest diminished in importance. These are among the many reasons why the EC is so very far removed from becoming a European government, which implies *one* executive/legislative authority, *one* currency, *one* army and, above all, *one* sense of political community that surpasses the established orders of Britain, France, Germany, Italy, and the rest.

In fact, the diversity of international organizations corresponds with the *diversity of interests* of the nation-states and with the *scope of those interests,* ranging far beyond Western Europe to the other continents. The game has changed since the Second World War in that the conflict of national interests, backed by armed forces, no longer rules. The game has become that of seeking competitive advantage within coordinating organizations. Instead of old-fashioned trench warfare and civilian destruction, the present order is typified by bloody noses on the faces of apparently bloodless civil servants on away days in Brussels, and by ministerial managed-smiles after all-night conferences. Boring, but a decided improvement.

The game is not without its paradoxes and dangers. The international networks (including those with supranational elements) represent little more than extensions of the existing states. Policy formulation, as well as implementation, still derives in the main from the central governments. The discussions are on a government-to-government level for the purpose of seeking coordination rather than to attempt common policies. Therefore, in its role as coordinator and mediator of policies at both national and transnational levels, central government remains in a key strategic position. The diffusion of its sovereignty rather paradoxically serves to strengthen its power of decision. Similarly at the sub-state level, where regional units exist in non-federal systems, the same tendency prevails. The central administration alone possesses the capacity and information necessary to oversee the entire scope of the governmental process. A further paradox in the game is that the introduction of additional democratic institutions (regional assemblies, the directly elected European Parliament) does not necessarily lead to more democracy. Since the process of decision-making has become so firmly on an executive-to-executive basis, involving primarily ministers, higher civil servants and representatives of organized interest groups, parliamentary bodies have suffered a long-term decline in their relevance. Parliaments may not be marginal institutions, but they are at a remove from the centres of policy formulation and implementation. What occurs in the national context is all the more likely to be repeated in newly emergent contexts. Where regional assemblies exist, their powers are narrowly circumscribed by central government, which moreover jealously protects its traditional prerogative of exclusive right of representation abroad (i.e. prohibits formal relations between a region and the Commission). The directly elected European Parliament is less easily manageable, but is handicapped by restricted powers and has to operate in an ill-defined situation of an embryonic political community. These paradoxes give rise to the danger that national parliaments, already weakened by a reduced capacity to control and scrutinize legislation and budgets, are forced to cope with complex systems of decision-making in which responsibility is much more elusive than the traditional doctrine of ministerial responsibility would suggest. The loss of capacity is not compensated by transfer of powers to the European Parliament or to regional assemblies. The emergent situation of new circuits of consultation and decision-making increases parliamentary weakness because power lost on the national level does not accrue elsewhere. It simply disappears, leaving central government with its bureaucracy freer of constraint. The danger is by no means that of impending dictatorship, but the ease with which responsibilities may be blurred. Public uncertainty as to where both power and responsibility lie can diminish the vitality of democracy if more effective controls over central government activity, appropriate to the changing circumstances, are not found.

NOTES AND REFERENCES

1. See Helen Wallace 'National bulls in the Community china shop' in H. Wallace, W. Wallace and C. Webb (eds) *Policy-Making in the European Communities* (London: Wiley, 1977); and her 'Problems of government and administration' in M. Kolinsky (ed.) *Divided Loyalties* (Manchester: Manchester University Press, 1978).
2. See A. W. Orridge 'Uneven development and nationalism' *Political Studies* (forthcoming, late 1980).
3. See *Royal Commission on the Constitution 1969–1973* (Kilbrandon Report) 2 vols, Cmnd. 5460 (October 1973).
4. Kurt Sontheimer *The Government and Politics of West Germany* (London: Hutchinson, 1972) p. 154.
5. See Hugh Berrington 'Dangerous corner' in Kolinsky, *op. cit.*
6. See H. Machin 'All Jacobins now?' *West European Politics* (October 1978).
7. For more details, see Peter Gourevitch 'Reforming the Napoleonic state' in S. Tarrow, P. J. Katzenstein and L. Graziano (eds) *Territorial Politics in Industrial Nations* (New York: Praeger, 1978). See also Michalina Vaughan, Martin Kolinsky and Peta Sheriff *Social Change in France* (Oxford: Martin Robertson, 1980).
8. See A. Mughan 'Modernization and ethnic conflict in Belgium' *Political Studies* (March 1979) p. 25.
9. Werner Link and Werner J. Feld (eds) *The New Nationalism* (New York/Oxford: Pergamon, 1979).
10. See John Newhouse *Collision in Brussels* (London: Faber and Faber, 1967) and *De Gaulle and the Anglo-Saxons* (London: Andre Deutsch, 1970).
11. *NATO Facts and Figures,* NATO Information Service (1971) p. 80.
12. Wolfram F. Hanrieder 'Co-ordinating foreign policies' in Link and Feld, *op. cit.* See also Walter Goldstein's discussion of Hanrieder's classification of systemic constraints on nation-state behaviour, in Link and Feld, *op. cit.,* p. 143.
13. Edward L. Morse 'The new economic nationalism and the coordination of economic policies' in Link and Feld, *op. cit.,* p. 66.

FURTHER READING

European Unity: Co-operation and Integration by Michael Palmer, John Lambert, *et al.* (London: PEP/Allen and Unwin, 1968) is an informative survey of the major European organizations. For useful studies of political parties in the member states of the European Community and in the European Parliament, see Stanley Henig (ed.) *Political Parties in the European Community* (London: Policy Studies Institute/Allen and Unwin, 1979).

Analyses of specific policy areas are provided in Helen Wallace, William Wallace and Carole Webb (eds) *Policy-Making in the European Communities* (London: Wiley, 1977). Ghita Ionescu has edited a stimulating collection of essays, entitled *Between Sovereignty and Integration* (London: Croom Helm, 1974) and he has discussed the relationship of government and the new centres of power in Europe in *Centripetal Politics* (London: Hart-Davis, MacGibbon, 1975).

The subsequent development of issues is considered in Martin Kolinsky (ed.) *Divided Loyalties: British Regional Assertion and European Integration* (Manchester: Manchester University Press, 1978). The essays in Sidney Tarrow, Peter J. Katzenstein and Luigi Graziano (eds) *Territorial Politics in Industrial Nations* (New York: Praeger, 1978) analyse the scope of changes in a number of countries. An earlier survey, James Cornford (ed) *The Failure of the State* (London: Croom Helm, 1975), is also useful, despite its misleading title.

Two penetrating and informative collections of papers that focus on transatlantic relations are noteworthy: Werner Link and Werner J. Feld (eds) *The New Nationalism* (New York/Oxford: Pergamon, 1979); and 'Looking for Europe' *Daedalus* Harvard University (Winter 1979).

5

The Nation-State in Asia

Hugh Tinker

India a nation! What an apotheosis! Last comer to the drab nineteenth-century sisterhood! Waddling in at this hour of the world to take her seat! She, whose only peer was the Holy Roman Empire, she shall rank with Guatemala and Belgium perhaps!

So E. M. Forster concluded *A Passage to India* in words revealing his concern that India's future would only be confused and distorted by an anti-colonialist insistence that the alternative to Western colonialism must necessarily be the nation-state. His message was discounted (though many Indians would claim that this novel is the truest statement ever recorded about British-India) and, as the independence epidemic spread across Asia after the Second World War, each repudiation of the colonialists' yoke was followed by the proclamation of a nation-state, whether the new nation was a feudal domain, such as Bhutan, a tiny island, like Singapore, or a subcontinent the size of Europe, as was India.

By a curious paradox, in the hour of their departure, the Western rulers had imposed their ideas more completely upon their erstwhile subjects than during the height of their ascendancy. The Western nation-state has become *de rigeur*; the only form of political association that is recognized as legitimate and the only form to bestow legitimacy upon the successor regimes. Yet it is premature to assume that this pattern will prevail. The strains that have appeared in so many of the emergent nations may lead to a new set of norms. For the present, Asia struggles on, operating the nation-state system with all its difficulties and disadvantages. However, the nation-state rests upon the assumption of popular sovereignty. The notion of 'government by the people' is very much open to question in many new states today. Additionally, the concept of nationality as the supreme factor of loyalty is under question — particularly in the Islamic countries and also in the communist bloc: both in the People's Republic of China and in the Soviet Union, nationality is secondary to the dominance of the Socialist State and Party.

NATION-STATES IN QUESTION?

The Western nation-state has been erected upon certain beliefs that today seem far from sacrosanct:

> Peoples with a homogeneous culture, living together in close association on a given territory, and sharing a belief in a distinctive existence and a common destiny . . . Nationalism connotes a loyalty to the group entity superior to all other loyalties, a pride in its achievements, and a belief in its excellence, or even superiority over all other similar entities . . . While its greatest impulsion has come from intellectual circles, it makes its greatest appeal to the masses.[1]

This American definition of the nature of the nation-state is recent (1963) and yet it already appears to lack conviction in the Western, or European, context: how much less convincing when applied to the ancient cultures of Asia? In many instances, the only factor that applies is that of the 'given territory'. Asian nation-states are really territories: and in most cases the territorial base remains a colonial legacy. Indonesia is Indonesia because it was formerly the Dutch East Indies.

This is not true of a minority of Asian nation-states. Japan, it may be claimed, was a nation — or a national empire — in the fourth century AD, or about a thousand years before England became something like a nation. Burma and Vietnam have about a thousand years of national history — based upon something like their present territory. Cambodia is much older; Thailand somewhat less old. Before his downfall, the last Shah of Iran celebrated two thousand years of Iranian independence and, although the connection between the Parthian Empire and modern Iran is somewhat loose, there is substance in the idea of historical continuity. Each of these national cultures was reinforced by a sense of cultural exclusiveness and superiority. Foreigners impinging upon their borders were regarded as barbarians, or lesser breeds. Just as English nationalism has received an enormous reinforcement from centuries of conflict with France, so Burmese and Thai nationalism has been strengthened by internecine conflict.

In these historical manifestations we find a distinction (as also in Europe) between the nation and nationalism and the *patria* and patriotism. The nation was a term that was associated with a people: the tribe or the 'race'. Patriotism connotes a loyalty to a territory:

> Breathes there a man, with soul so dead,
> Who never to himself hath said,
> This is my own, my native land.

Yes; my native land: but do I also accept that it is the native land of folk who dwell therein but who do not share my tribe or religion or skin colour? It was in the working out of this problem that traditional Asian societies showed their relative capacity to evolve towards the nation-state. Japan was able to become a nation because the autocthonous non-Mongolian inhabitants, the Ainu, were few and the unrecognized Burakumin (untouchables, unknowables), characterized as sub-human, were confined to degraded occupations. Burma was able to move towards nationhood by assimilating the élites, and to some extent the masses, among some non-Burmese minorities (such as Mons, Shans, Arakanese) into a common religion, Buddhism, a common political allegiance (the monarch in his capital) and, to a lesser extent, a common culture (the Burmese language and script).

But minority folk cultures remained distinct; potential rallying points whenever the grip of the central Burmese power weakened. In situations where the minorities could reverse the assimilationist process and reassert their own political strength, the threatened Burmese emphasized an *exclusive* not an *inclusive* identity. From 1740 to about 1755, the Mons succeeded in liquidating Burmese power and imposed their rule upon central Burma. The warrior king Alaungpaya (reigned 1752–60) reasserted Burmese dominance by exploiting the sense of solidarity of his own people, 'the Burmese race' (myan-ma lu-myo), and by excluding the Mons, Shans and other non-Burmese from any leading position in his state.

TRADITIONAL ASIAN EMPIRES

In general, the idea of state—nation—race being the source of political legitimacy was less potent than the idea of empire. Most Asian lands preserved the folk-memory of a universal ruler on the Hindu—Buddhist model of *chakravartin* and on the Perso-Hellenic model created by Alexander the Great, known to Asia as Iskander. In lands where power was disputed between rivals, men looked back (as in Dante's Italy) to the days when a universal empire had united their known world in peace. In India, the ancient empire of Asoka and the empire of the Mughals (which effectively lasted from Akbar to Aurangzeb, 1556—1707) served to unify peoples divided by religion, language and caste. It has been argued that modern Asian nationalism arose from the resistance of subject peoples to Western colonial rule. The concept *civis Romanus sum,* which made the turbulent Jew, Paul of Tarsus, identify with imperial Rome, was not echoed by nineteenth-century Indians asserting *civis Britannicus sum.* Why, then, it may be asked did not the Mughal Empire arouse a spirit of resistance among its Hindu subjects? The answer is that in the end a resistance movement did emerge among the Marathas under their guerrilla leader, Shivaji. But it only emerged at the furthest frontier of the empire, when it was overstretched and reaching exhaustion. Previously, the Mughals were remarkably successful in winning over the martial clans, the Rajputs, to their regime: indeed, the emperors took Rajput princesses as their queens. Collaboration, not resistance, was the main feature of the Mughal Empire. Collaboration, not resistance, was also the dominant feature of the Chinese Empire when the Manchus, the invaders from beyond the Great Wall, defeated the indigenous Ming dynasty in the seventeenth century. The Manchus (the Ch'ing dynasty) ruled until the empire finally collapsed in 1912.

China was not China to those who dwelt throughout its vast plains and mountains: it was an imperial entity — the Middle (or Central) Kingdom, surrounded by feudatories, and beyond them the barbarians.[2] China had no common language, but for official purposes there was a recognized spoken and written language, *Kuan-Hua* (known in the West as 'Mandarin') that was cultivated by the literati. India was not India to those who lived there. In ancient times there were sacred, cosmic names — *Bharatvarsha, Jambudvipa* — but no recognized political term for the land and even less for its people. The Muslim conquerors applied the term *Hindu* to all their non-Muslim subjects. They took the name from the great river Sind (which is now in Pakistan). Greek and Latin geographers also applied their rendering of the river's name, *Indus,* to the sub-continent, and it was the Europeans who started giving the name 'Indian' to all the peoples of the sub-continent.[3] Those peoples did not themselves recognize the term. The Muslim conquerors used Persian as the language of their administration, and for a time Persian became a medium of communication for all in authority — Mughal officials and Hindu princes and chiefs.

For some future Asian nation-states there was no imperial unifying process and no significant formation of unifying myths and unifying media. Before the Dutch conquered the islands that they called the Dutch East Indies the region had been divided among local rulers whose area of control was limited. Java was the one large unit that had a common sense of history and a common language. Attempts were made to create a unifying past out of the empires of Sri-Vijaya and Majapahit, but in reality the sway of these maritime powers did not extend over more than a fraction of what was to become Indonesia. The very name 'Indonesia' was an artefact, being employed for the first time in 1884 by a German geographer who wished to differentiate the 13,000 islands he so named from the sub-continent also called the Indies.

Perhaps the Asian country that most lacks a unifying past is the Philippines. An archipelago of 7,000 islands, the islands of the south were within the Islamic orbit of South Asia, but the main group were beyond external cultural influences: almost without a political framework greater than that of village and tribe. Named after a Spanish king, given a cultural superstructure by Dominican and Jesuit missionaries, the Philippines passed three centuries searching for an identity.

THE IMPACT OF THE WEST

Whether the countries of Asia had become proto-nations, or whether they were inspired by imperial memories, or whether they were congeries of tribal or feudal fiefs, they offered only sporadic opposition to the Western invaders. Significantly, there was much fiercer resistance in those countries that did have a sense of ethnic nationalism — notably Burma and Vietnam — than in others where divided peoples had become reconciled to one alien ruler after another. The impact of Western colonial rule was deeper in Asia than in Africa, largely because the process was of much longer duration in key areas. We may reckon that the Philippines, Indonesia and Ceylon endured three centuries of Western rule (though this did not extend to the whole territory) while India was ruled by the British for two centuries. British Malaya and French Indo-China were under the Western grip for less than a century. China, Thailand, Japan and Iran all remained formally independent, yet each in different ways had to accept measures of Western control and extensive Western penetration. The Western impact was greatest in the port cities like Calcutta, Bombay, Singapore, Shanghai, Batavia (Djakarta). In these cities an Asian commercial middle class emerged that assimilated Western education, institutions and concepts. Many of these *evolués* (lawyers, merchants, journalists, educationists) were willing collaborators with the colonial power. But increasingly they demanded representation in assemblies and a share of bureaucratic control. The argument they invoked to justify their claims was that of nationalism.

Probably no other movement attracted greater attention than that of Mazzini, who created the idea of Young Italy (*Giovine Italia*) through hundreds of semi-secret revolutionary societies. Although it was not Mazzini, the intellectual, but Cavour, the political operator, and Garibaldi, the romantic activist, who secured Italy's freedom, Mazzini first popularized the idea of one nation arising out of a dozen political systems. This key idea captured the imagination of political pioneers outside Europe. The 'Young Turks' have become part of our common terminology but beside them we must put Young India (Gandhi took this as the name for his newspaper), Young China, Young Burma, and similarly named movements and societies.

THE GOAL OF INDEPENDENCE

The mobilization of educated middle-class youth did indeed popularize the idea of national unity in India, Indonesia and the Philippines where previously it had been absent. However, these 'Young' manifestations lacked a broad base of popular support, and when populist movements began to emerge they appealed not to an imaginative ideal of national unity but to a more earthy combination of historical tradition and grassroots economic discontent. The Western colonial regimes introduced reforms that cut across cherished traditions; they also shook up the established order of rural society, lowering the status of sections of the peasantry. Protest might be given shape by a modernizing populist politician (as Tilak orchestrated the memories of the Marathas who had resisted the Mughals) or sometimes it might be taken over by a millenarian traditionalist (as Saya San did in Burma, assuring his followers that his magic made them immune to British bullets). All these movements pointed to the same goal — independence — though paths might be very different. In seeking to exploit the idea of nationalism, the goal was a short-term one: expel the foreigners. Very few nationalist leaders actually explored the meaning of nationalism; it was just accepted as a natural phenomenon. In large part this was a reaction against the Western imperialists' insistence that these were not nations. The pretensions of the political middle class were dismissed: they were a 'microscopic minority', they had no following among the peasant masses. Moreover, the Westerners emphasized the differences among their subjects: differences of language, religion, interest. It often appeared as though these divisions were deliberately created. The Westerners encouraged the settlement of foreigners, especially Chinese and Indians, in their South East Asian posessions, in order to create a market economy as the basis of their own worldwide export economy. The Westerners recruited their security forces — military and sometimes police — from minorities or from immigrants. The argument was that these were martial peoples; usually they were from hill and borderland, unaffected by the new spirit of nationalist politics. In Burma, the British depended upon the mainly Christian Karens; in the Dutch East Indies, the Protestant, pro-Dutch inhabitants of Ambon in the South Moluccas were recruited. In Ceylon, the British employed a regiment of Malays; in India they relied heavily upon the Gurkhas from neighbouring Nepal. No wonder that Asian nationalists constantly compared colonial policy with that of imperial Rome: *divide et impera,* or Divide and Rule. From asserting that the Western powers were dividing them it was but one step to asserting that there were actually no divisions between them.

The great example for Asian nationalists was Japan. Japan defeated the might of Russia in 1905. Japan overthrew the combined strength of Britain, the Netherlands, France and the United States in 1942 (or so it seemed). Japan was unquestionably a nation. They had assimilated all the strengths of the West and had overcome the West by exploiting its own techniques and beliefs. Why should not other

Asians also become strong by (as it were) beating the West at its own game?

Western dominance in Asia and Africa was largely based upon bluff. So long as Western superiority was not challenged and Asian collaborators could be recruited to implement Western rule, all would be well. How else could Britain have governed India's hundreds of millions with only 28,000 British troops?[4] As soon as the bluff began to be in doubt the days of Western dominance were numbered. In India, it began to appear that the British were preparing to go — though they might try to drag their feet — after the First World War. The main pressure was exerted by the Indian National Congress, which Gandhi succeeded in welding into a mass movement combining the secular political aspirations of 'Young India', the political middle class, with semi-religious, semi-traditional support that the peasant masses felt for their venerated Mother India.

One section of the population was noticeably aloof: the Indian Muslims. They feared that Gandhi's idea of nationalism was a reassertion of Hinduism and they began to make separate political demands. When a Round Table Conference was convened in London in 1931, one Muslim politician, Mohammad Ali, addressed the British chairman in these words: 'My Lord, Divide and Rule is the order of the day: we divide, and you rule.' The assertion of minority rights was a feature of every struggle for independence — as in Ceylon, Burma, Malaya, Indonesia, the Philippines — but only in the Indian sub-continent was minority pressure strong enough to alter the independence settlement. Significantly, the Muslims only won their demands by asserting, not that they were a minority, but that they were a separate nation! The separation of Pakistan from India left half the Indian Muslims within the new Indian Republic, and this created uncertainty in the minds of non-Muslim Indians; were their Muslim neighbours really committed citizens of the new republic, or were they, mentally at any rate, committed to the new Pakistan? As relations between the two states deteriorated, the Muslims left in India were seen by many as little more than a fifth column, an underground agency of Pakistan.

COMPARTMENTALIZED SOCIETIES

In so many of the new states, despite lip service to the idea of a new unity — symbolized in such national mottoes as 'Unity in Diversity', 'Out of Many, One Nation' — some citizens were less equal than others. The problem arose out of the multiple nature of society in almost every Asian state except Japan. There exists what J. S. Furnivall called the 'plural society':

> It is in the strictest sense a medley, for they mix but do not combine. Each group holds by its own religion, its own culture and language . . . As individuals they meet, but only in the market place, in buying and selling. There is a plural society, with different sections of the community living side by side, but separately, within the same political unit.[5]

As one American writer puts it: 'The plural society is a characteristic phenomenon of great stretches of the world: "the crazy quilt of the Balkans" is generally more typical than the model nations of England and France.'[6] Asian exponents of nationalism may have forgotten that whereas in Italy and Germany the national principle was a unifying force, bringing together peoples previously divided between petty states, within the Ottoman and Austro-Hungarian empires nationalism had been a disintegrating force, dividing up large political units into small ones, some of which were politically and economically not viable.

For most of the new states the problem was that of incorporating minorities into the system. India is unique in being a land where there really is no majority; for it is deceptive to regard Hinduism as a corporate entity. The traditional divisions that have placed Hindus within thousands of separate caste categories may have diminished, but at least, present-day Hinduism contains within it several distinct social, economic and political groupings: the Brahmans, the upper agricultural castes (Rajputs, Jats, etc.), the lower castes, and those who before independence were Untouchables.[7] In addition, there are the Muslims, Sikhs, Christians, Buddhists and Animists with varying degrees of minority consciousness. However, a more potent sense of identity — separate identity — is provided by the linguistic groupings. The Indian constitution recognizes fifteen languages as the country's main regional languages (the list also includes the classical language, Sanskrit). In response to pressures from the regional language lobbies, the political map of India has had to be redrawn.

The Philippines is another Asian country in which there is no definable majority, while in Malaysia also there is no arithmetical majority, though the Malays (constituting 45.9 per cent of total population) have a majority mentality. East Asia (Japan, China, Korea) has minority problems that thus far are quiescent. The remaining countries have massive majority/minority difficulties that inhibit the formation of a sense of national identity. The situation may be roughly tabulated as in Table 5.1.

TABLE 5.1

Country	Majority community	Minorities	Differences
Sri Lanka	Sinhalese	Tamils, Moors, Indians	R/L
Pakistan	Punjabis	Pathans, Sindhis, Baluchis	L
Afghanistan	Afghans	Baluchis, Persians	L
Iran	Persian-Shias	Baluchis, Kurds, Bahasi	R/L
Bangladesh	Bengali Muslims	Hindus, Buddhists, Animists	R/L
Burma	Burmese	Karens, Shans, Kachins, Chins and others	L/R
Thailand	Thais	Malays, hill tribes, Chinese	R/L
Kampuchea	Khmers	Vietnamese, Chinese	L
Vietnam	Vietnamese	Chinese, hill tribes	L/R
Indonesia	Javanese-Sumatrans	South Moluccans, Chinese Papuans, etc.	L/R

L = linguistic differences   R = religious differences

POLITICAL FORMULAE FOR NATION-BUILDING

Constitutionally, different Asian countries have approached the problem from two different angles: one may be called the assimilationist approach, the other the position of majority dominance. Influenced by what seemed to be the success of the American 'melting-pot' philosophy, India began by heavy reliance upon the capacity of a detailed written constitution to ameliorate differences. The constitution incorporated directive principles of state policy designed to create a secular society, to safeguard minorities and to promote the growth of national consciousness. Thus, in designating Hindi as the official language, the constitution declares: 'It shall be the duty of the Union . . . to develop it so that it may serve as a medium of expression of all the elements of the composite culture of India and to secure its enrichment by assimilating . . . the forms, style and expressions used in Hindustani and in other languages of India' (article 351). This noble sentiment remains almost entirely unfulfilled. The Hindi fanatics have attempted to impose a narrow, exclusive form of the language upon all other elements in India. Fearing that the Hindi-speakers would become dominant (particularly by securing a monopoly of posts in the public services), the other linguistic elements have fought to retain the use of English in central government and to promote their own languages as the medium for regional government. If this controversy has not torn India apart it is because of the accommodationist, bargaining, 'bazaar' character of Indian politics. Trade-offs have been negotiated in all directions and a more or less acceptable balance preserved between different interests.

The alternative strategy to assimilation is to require minorities to conform to the norms of the majority. This course has been followed in Sri Lanka since the mid-1950s. Sinhalese has been adopted as the language of government, education (including university education), the law and all other spheres of public life. Similarly, Buddhism has been emphasized as the cultural expression of national life and the claims of Christians and Hindus have been ignored.[8] Much the same policy has been adopted in Malaysia, where Malay has been imposed upon the Chinese and Indian minorities as the national language and Islam has become the dominant religion: proselytization by other religions among Muslims is prohibited, while the conversion of non-Muslims to Islam is vigorously encouraged. Yet, in both these countries, after twenty years of majority dominance the minorities remain unconverted and alienated.

The Union of Burma first attempted to dissolve the differences between its peoples by promulgating a constitution that gave assurances to minorities while at the same time the leaders appealed for a new spirit. Thus spoke Bogyoke Aung San, the architect of independence:

A Nation is a collective term applied to a people, irrespective of their ethnic origin, living in close contact with one another, for such historic periods as have acquired a sense of oneness. Though race, religion and language are important factors, it is only their traditional desire and will to live in unity through weal and woe that binds a people together and makes them a nation and their spirit a patriotism.[9]

Unhappily, subsequent governments did not match these words by deeds. The minorities almost all formed resistance movements and challenged the central government. After three decades of independence, about half the territory of Burma is held by the rebels.

Despite the strains imposed by centrifugal forces, almost all Asian nation-states have managed to resist break-up — though Western commentators have been prophesying the disintegration of India, Indonesia and other new nations for the last two decades. Thus far, there have been only two disruptions. Singapore was excluded from the Malaysian Federation after only two years (1963–5) because the Malays believed that its inclusion meant the threat of a Chinese takeover. More traumatically, East Bengal struggled bloodily out of Pakistan to become Bangladesh in 1971; but this separation could never have been achieved but for the massive military intervention of India.[10] Among the other secessionist movements, only one appears likely to succeed. This is the guerrilla war waged by the Muslims of the southern archipeligo of the Philippines against the central government. There are two million Filipino Muslims or 'Moros'. Their long resistance has received only minor clandestine support from outside, but if ever the oil-rich Arabs should decide to support their fellow Muslims the effort to hold the Moros down might prove too much for Manila.

STATES BEFORE NATIONS

The successful maintenance of the nation-state system depends far more upon the development of the apparatus of the state than the development of a national consciousness. During the first era of independence, a time of aspiration, much emphasis was placed upon symbols and on charismatic leadership. The symbolic emphasis concentrated upon creating new names for the state and its capital. Siam was renamed Thailand; Ceylon became Sri Lanka.[11] Indonesia's capital resumed its ancient name, Djakarta; Pakistan's new capital was named Islamabad; communist Vietnam renamed Saigon, Ho Chi Minh City. Perhaps even more weight was given to the magnetic influence that a larger-than-life national leader would provide. Pakistan's M. A. Jinnah, *Qaid-i-Axam* (known as 'great leader', though his title means 'the nation's magistrate'); Bung Sukarno, 'Great Leader of the Revolution' 'Lifetime President' of Indonesia;

Bogyoke Aung San, 'generalissimo' of Burma; and most genuinely nation-making of them (though without honorifics), Jawaharlal Nehru, prime minister of India, 1946 – 64.

Subsequent presidents and prime ministers have been unable to generate this charismatic influence (though Z. A. Bhutto in Pakistan and Indira Gandhi in India have aroused widespread appeal) and nation-building has depended more upon the development of institutions. Among these, parliamentary assemblies have played a disappointingly small part, often splitting into factions and cliques that demonstrate division, not unity. Similarly, the parties that in most countries emerged at independence, or before, as broad-based 'fronts' — 'freedom movements', in their own terms — splintered apart in subsequent years; although the prestige of the original name is often jealously preserved by what has become a much more limited party. Alternatively, the Marxist regimes have eliminated all opposition parties and formed 'rally' type parties that serve to mobilize the workers in support of the regime. In what has become the Socialist Republic of Burma, the only political expression permitted is through the *Lanzin* or Socialist Programme. In China, Vietnam and Kampuchea, the only organization is, of course, the Communist Party. Malaysia has endeavoured to create the politics of communal cooperation by means of an all-embracing dominant government coalition: first of the Alliance, and then in preparation for the 1974 election through the *Barisan Nasional* (National Front).

However, even in the one-party states, parliament and party are of lesser importance in holding the nation-state together than the army. All Asian states have expanded their armed forces considerably since independence and (except, perhaps, in Sri Lanka) these forces are the biggest sector of state power, absorbing the largest share of the budget. These armies have come to see themselves as guardians and protectors of the nation, particularly as the politicians have demonstrated their incapacity to rise above faction. The officer corps has a strong sense of professional solidarity. Any attempt at interference by politicians will be repulsed and may cause a pre-emptive strike against them. At the beginning of the 1980s the military are effectively in power in Pakistan, Bangladesh, Indonesia, Burma, Thailand and, arguably, in Kampuchea. They form the essential foundation for civil government in Malaysia, the Philippines, Vietnam, Korea and China (where the People's Liberation Army is recognized as a key political component). Only in India, Sri Lanka,

Singapore and Japan is the army definitely subordinate to the control of the politicians.

Second in importance in structural support of the nation-state is the bureaucracy. The professional civil servants of the Western colonial powers were the undisputed rulers; their successors have a slightly diminished prestige, but their power is increased by the much greater extent of government participation in the economy and in society in post-colonial times. A web of regulations stretches out to every part of the country, penetrating trade, industry, the communications network, education, health, and almost every aspect of life except religion. Even in the free enterprise economies, which still continue in Singapore, Malaysia, Pakistan and Sri Lanka, national planning has become an essential component of development; and the bureaucracy of the plans is a key factor in promoting or vitiating national unity. In the former Pakistan, East Bengal was convinced that planning and policy favoured the West wing at their expense: this was a considerable factor in the Bangladesh demand. In the other direction, the capacity of India and its five year plans to move away from a rigid, centralized concept of planning towards a system of trade-offs between the various states has helped to make the states feel that they have a stake in the formulation of central policy.

Overall, the emphasis upon institutional structure in the maintenance and preservation of the new states represents something like a return to the colonial pattern of the administrative state.[12] Political mobilization was only partial in the 'freedom struggle' phase, and in many countries there has been something like demobilization. How else are we to describe political conditions in Singapore where, periodically, elections are held but invariably every seat in the legislature is won by the ruling People's Action Party? In several states we see echoes of pre-colonial dynastic formation. General Ne Win in Burma, General Suharto in Indonesia and Lee Kuan Yew in Singapore have monopolized power for twenty years or so, and seem likely to hand on power upon their own terms. The dynastic pattern seems most potent in India, where Nehru was succeeded (after an interval of less than two years) by his daughter, Indira Gandhi, whose triumphant return to power in 1980 appeared to be orchestrated by her son, Sanjay Gandhi.

NATIONALISM IN DECLINE?

In these circumstances, the appeal of nationalism is less strident. Asian regimes are aware that their task is actually that of survival.[13] Having downgraded democratic participation by the masses as the principal means of nation-building, the leaders look in other directions. The concept of development is still emphasized, but after twenty or thirty years of frustration most Asian states have not achieved the much-heralded 'take-off into sustained growth'. The only exceptions are the private enterprise regimes of Japan, Singapore and Taiwan. Religion represents a potent force. But it is a force that, once released, can acquire its own momentum, as in Iran where the 'revolution' appears to have substituted for the Shah's authoritarianism a directionless populist tyranny. Hence, even the Islamic leader of Pakistan, Field Marshall Zia-al-Haq, hesitates to commit himself to the demands made for a fully religious system. The idea of nationalism remains, then, as the cement that holds together the state: even though it is increasingly clear that the cement is mainly sand.

Only in Japan, in the devastating aftermath of Hiroshima, has there been a serious revision of the previous exaltation of nationalism and the role of Japan as the liberator of the subjugated nations of Asia.[14] Perhaps this is partly because Japan *is* a nation and does not have to try to create a reality out of contradictory materials. The other great states of Asia have produced no important revisionist ideas, though long before independence Rabindranath Tagore questioned the too-easily accepted concept of Indian nationalism: 'We, the famished, ragged ragamuffins of the East are to win freedom for all humanity! We have no word for 'Nation' in our language. When we borrow this word from other people it never fits.' Tagore perceived that 'patriotism dissociates itself from the higher ideal of humanity'.[15] His fears have proved justified.

Even in the form of pan-Asianism, the new states have been unable to realize the idea of humanity. The *Panch Shila* ('five principles') that were meant to unite India and China in brotherhood ended in a border war (1962). The Bandung Conference of 1955, which sought to unite the Afro-Asian countries — declaring 'friendly co-operation . . . would effectively contribute to the maintenance and promotion of international peace and security' — was followed by decades of squabbling and conflict. Yet, why should Asia have succeeded where Europe and the West have so signally failed? The British people seem unable to identify with Western Europe (the EEC), a community in which they have been members (even if reluctant members) for a thousand years.

In Asia, the nation-state continues to be the largest unit that the mind of the ordinary man can conceptualize. He does not really identify with it. It does not do anything for him, and he is not prepared to do anything for it — unless he is pitched into action as a fighter in the armed services, or much more selectively selected to represent his country at table tennis, cricket or volley ball.

The nation-state served a genuine purpose in Europe in the shift from the traditional society to modernity. In Asia, it proved to be an invaluable instrument in getting rid of Western colonialism. It still has an important function in affording membership of the United Nations, the one real hope of a supranational tomorrow. It does little or nothing to help Asians solve their most immediate problem: that of institutionalizing the relations of communities and groups, whom geography has made neighbours but who possess no real feeling of a common identity.

NOTES AND REFERENCES

1. 'Nationalism and Internationalism' by J. B. Whitton *Encyclopedia Americana, 19,* (1963 edn) p. 749.
2. The term *I* is usually translated 'barbarian'; there was also the opprobrious *Yang-Kuei-Tzu* ('foreign devil') used in the nineteenth century. The Latin West knew the Middle Kingdom as *Sinae,* hence China. What the West calls 'the People's Republic of China' is actually 'the People's Republic of the Central Land' in Chinese.
3. In European usage, the name 'Indian' was transported West, as well as East, being applied to the indigenous inhabitants of the entire western hemisphere from the Eskimos of the north to the Patagonians of the south.
4. At the start of the First World War India demonstrated a remarkable support for Britain's cause and the number of British troops was reduced to 15,000.
5. J. S. Furnivall *Colonial Policy and Practice* (Cambridge: Cambridge University Press, 1948) p. 304.
6. Rupert Emerson *From Empire to Nation* (Cambridge, Mass.: Harvard University Press, 1960) p. 122.

7. The Indian constitution 'abolished' untouchability, but in reality the Untouchables are still treated as semi-human by all other castes.

8. The 1978 constitution of Sri Lanka, while not acceding to Tamil demands for a federal state, did go some way towards recognizing minority rights. The constitution actually speaks of 'the Tamil community as a distinct nationality' thus appearing to distinguish between *nationality* and *citizenship*.

9. Quoted in Hugh Tinker *Ballot Box and Bayonet* (London: Oxford University Press, 1964) p. 47.

10. Cyprus (which cultivates its Third World membership) is the extreme example of a territorial state in which ethnic differences could not be contained by the state. The Greeks attempted to enforce the majority dominance policy leading to a complete break with the Turkish minority and the partition of the island. As with the emergence of Bangladesh, this relied upon massive intervention by an outside power, Turkey.

11. Another reminder of Japan's almost unique nationhood lies in the historic refusal ever to depart from the traditional name, *Nippon* or *Nihon*. Most Japanese dislike the word 'Japan' as being *gaijin-kusai* ('smelling of foreigners').

12. Rajni Kothari, *Politics in India* (Boston: Little, 1970), describes this trend as 'governmentalism'.

13. I have suggested elsewhere (*Reorientations: Studies on Asia in Transition* London: Pall Mall, 1965) that instead of 'development' many Asian regimes would end in the 'broken backed state'. Lee Kuan Yew was sufficiently impressed to make this the subject of warnings to the people of Singapore.

14. See Saburo Ienga *Japan's Last War* (English translation; Oxford: Blackwell, 1979). 'It is true that Japanese military occupation severed Western control and weakened the former rulers. But this was merely an incidental consequence: Japan did not liberate Asia. The Asian struggle for independence unfolded through the rigours of the Japanese occupation . . . To call Japan's disgraceful and bloody rampage a crusade for liberation is to stand truth and history on their heads.'

15. *Letters to a Friend* (ed. C. F. Andrews; London: Allen and Unwin, 1928) pp. 128, 123. Tagore's astringent study, *Nationalism* (London: Macmillan, 1917), warned: 'The advent of another people into the arena of nationality makes another evil which contradicts all that is highest in Man.' Paradoxically, Tagore's poetry has provided two countries with their national anthems: India and Bangladesh.

FURTHER READING

Two short books that consider most aspects of the nation-state in Asia are Michael Brecher *The New States of Asia: a political analysis* (London: Oxford University Press, 1963) and Hugh Tinker *Ballot Box and Bayonet: people and government in emergent Asian countries* (London: Oxford University Press, 1964). At rather greater length, Dick Wilson *Asia Awakes:*

a continent in transition (London: Weidenfeld and Nicolson, 1970) also provides an overall introductory survey. Probably the most perceptive full-length study is still (though a little dated) Rupert Emerson *From Empire to Nation: the rise to self-assertion of Asian and African peoples* (Cambridge, Mass.: Harvard University Press, 1960), while Elie Kedourie in *Nationalism in Asia and Africa* (London: Weidenfeld and Nicolson, 1971) has brought together selected writings by political leaders and thinkers.

Special problems of the new states are discussed by John Badgley *Asian Development: problems and prognosis* (New York: Free Press, 1971) and by E. I. J. Rosenthal *Islam in the Modern National State* (Cambridge: Cambridge University Press, 1965), while W. F. Wertheim *East-West Parallels: sociological approaches to modern Asia* (The Hague: Institute of Pacific Relations, 1964) provides sensitive Marxian and Weberian perspectives. Clifford Geertz in *Old Societies and New States* (New York: Free Press, 1963) has brought together a symposium that discusses the tradition—modernity syndrome.

Most readers will want to assess general ideas and theories about the nation-state by studying specific examples of what independence has meant to about half the population of the world. The literature on India is particularly varied, and among many significant works are Selig S. Harrison *India: the most dangerous decades* (Princeton, NJ: Princeton University Press, 1960); Philip Mason (ed.) *India and Ceylon: unity and diversity* (London: Oxford University Press, 1967); and Paul Brass *Language, Religion and Politics in North India* (Cambridge: Cambridge University Press, 1974). Among the other major Asian countries, the nation-state is so firmly rooted in East Asia that one considers their history rather than the contemporary scene: but consult Edwin O. Reischauer *The Japanese* (Cambridge, Mass.: Harvard University Press, 1977). Nationality problems are briskly analysed by Guy Hunter *South-East Asia: race culture and nation* (London: Oxford University Press, 1966).

One should not neglect Asian views of their own condition. Two perceptive though polemical works by political leaders may be cited: Z. A. Bhutto *The Myth of Independence* (London: Oxford University Press, 1969) and Mahathir Bin Mohamad *The Malay Dilemma* (Singapore: Asia Pacific Press, 1970).

Finally, a useful insight into nationality problems from the angle of those who do not fit into the accepted framework can be obtained through the booklets issued by the Minority Rights Group, London, all cheaply priced, for example: *The Kurds, The Palestinians, The Tamils of Sri Lanka, India and the Nagas, The Chinese in Indonesia, the Philippines and Malaysia*, and many more.

6

The Nation-State in Black Africa

Arnold Hughes

Black Africa presents a great challenge to the nation-state concept of political community. Though we loosely refer to the recently created countries of that part of Africa as 'nation-states', and their peoples as 'new nations', it is by no means certain that such formal appelations have any substance. During the run-up to independence, people in the West grew accustomed to regard the anti-colonial movements than coming to power in Africa as variants of the global phenomenon of nationalism; the rhetoric of their leaders and sympathetic accounts of their organizations by liberal academics helped to create such an impression.[1] However, after some two decades of formal independence, it is not at all clear how far these earlier expressions of nationalistic sentiments have survived to become the basis of state formation. Numerous students of political change in black Africa today dispute the existence of nation-states in much of the continent, preferring instead to describe these young countries at best as 'state-nations', where a state system derived from the colonial era survives uncertainly, and at worst as client-states of their former colonial metropoles or of new external powers, or the personal fiefs of despotic rulers and their followers. Clearly, twenty years is far too short a period to attempt a definitive assessment of the transplantation of the nation-state principle to African soil, but at the same time it does enable us both to review the realities of post-colonial African states and to examine changes in the way scholars view these countries.

PRE-COLONIAL AFRICA

Describing black Africa prior to its annexation by European colonial powers, Elizabeth Colson observed that 'nineteenth century Africa supported a greater variety of political and social institutions than Europe'.[2] This is not surprising when we consider that there were some estimated 6,000 distinct cultural—linguistic groups spread across this vast sub-continent from the Atlantic to the Indian Ocean and from the fringes of the Sahara to the Cape. These political communities comprised bands, statelets, states, principalities and empires at different stages of evolution. Of relevance to our discussion is her observation that in many societies the state as such did not exist. Regulatory functions in these kinship communities were carried out instead by age-sets, secret societies and representatives of lineages operating without formal bureaucratic institutions. Although she notes the existence of quite large and long-lived empires, particularly in parts of West Africa, whose political boundaries did not coincide with ethnic ones, nowhere does she claim that nation-states existed in the period before contact with the West.

The presence or absence of national communities similar to those to be found in Western Europe at this time is an unresolved issue among Africanists.[3] Perhaps it is nothing more than a semantic exercise, for the divide between fully fledged nation-states and proto-nations possessing some degree of common identity and institutions is a grey one, but in the absence of significant levels of modernization[4] it is difficult to press home too far claims for indigenous nation-states. What would seem to be the case though, following initial contact with Europe, is that some African societies sought consciously (interestingly, at the same time as Meiji Japan was successfully undergoing similar change) to emulate European nation-states through the modernization of their economies and administrative institutions. In West Africa attempts at political modernization along nation-state lines were undertaken by the Fanti of the Gold Coast (now Ghana) and the Egba section of the Yoruba people of south west Nigeria. The Basutos of Southern Africa, one of the few ethnically homogeneous political communities in present-day Africa, preserved their national autonomy from Afrikaner encroachment (though not from eventual incorporation into the British Empire) by similar means. In the old empire of Abyssinia in East Africa, the most celebrated example of resistance to European rule took place as a result of the modernizing policies aimed at creating a greater sense of solidarity among the dominant ethnic groups and a more efficient military and administrative capacity. Here an Italian army was routed in 1896 by the forces of Menelik II, so earning the Abyssinians a prestige among African nationalists of the kind enjoyed by the Japanese among Asian nationalists. These were rare exceptions though and eventually all succumbed to the superior military and economic resources of the invading Europeans. Domestic evolution of nation-states, of the kind found in Asia, was thus prematurely prevented so that the process of nation formation was to be delayed and significantly modified by the effects of colonial conquest.

NATIONALISM IN COLONIAL AFRICA

The most apparent effect of the European partition of black Africa was the arbitrary redesignation of political boundaries, mainly with little concern for the indigenous political communities. These new colonial boundaries have survived almost unchanged to the present day. (There were some alterations during the colonial period itself, either to resolve differences between colonial powers, as in the case of Germany and France in the Cameroons area or Britain and Italy in respect of the north-eastern boundary of Kenya Colony, or for the administrative convenience of a particular colonial power, as was the case in parts of West Africa.) Despite their initial novelty and artificiality, they are now firmly defended by post-colonial governments, notwithstanding protestations of allegiance to regional and continental unification. This monumental transformation of the political map of Africa created a new focus for nascent nationalism — the colonial state.

Territorial nationalism was slow to evolve in black Africa for it was not until the early twentieth century that stable boundaries emerged. But the ideology of nationalism, it must be stressed, despite accounts to the contrary,[5] entered parts of Africa long before colonialism had carved out future colony-states. Hair[6] has shown that as early as the end of the eighteenth century black settlers from North America and the Caribbean in Freetown, Sierre Leone, were advocating rights to self-determination and displaying a form of racial nationalism, described as 'Africanism', at about the same time as nationalism was becoming a significant political force in Europe. A similar process was taking place in neighbouring Liberia where other repatriates, freed blacks, were carving out a country of their own and describing their enclaves as a nation. From these small beginnings modern forms of nationalism developed in West Africa, the first part of black Africa to take up these new ideas.

Yet theirs was not a straightforward nationalism. The coastal pockets where they lived hardly merited the description of 'country', so that the nationalism that emerged here combined parish-pump issues with the promotion of the interests of the Negro race as a whole. Lacking a sufficiently large homeland and, in the case of Freetown and later British colonial acquisitions further along the West African coast, an autonomous territory, these pioneer nationalists took up a racial patriotism. Langley[7] has shown that this defence of the black race against the increasing attacks of pseudo-anthropological European racism constituted an important element in early black political consciousness. Not content to attack the shortcomings of colonial rule, these racial nationalists gave birth to *Pan-Africanism,* a movement of ideas and later, political organiza-tions, that advocated the unity of all persons of Negro-African descent and eulogized their culture and past achievements. This racial category of nationalism, spanning the Atlantic Ocean as well as extending across the whole of sub-Saharan Africa, would appear to be unique among colonial peoples; certainly no pan-Asian movement of similar extent and persistence seems to have existed.[8] The principal reason for this dimension of African nationalism was the confraternity of blood and suffering that drew blacks together wherever they might dwell. Although Pan-Africanism continues to arouse strong passions in radical and intellectual black circles in particular, so far it has not provided a sufficient impetus to alter the boundaries inherited from colonial Africa.

It should not be overlooked that up to around the turn of the twentieth century African nationalism could strongly identify with the imperial mission in Africa. In West Africa, leading racial patriots such as Dr James Horton or Dr Edward Blyden, readily accepted employment in the British colonial service and achieved important positions, as indeed did a number of Africans in the late nineteenth century, and saw the advance of their race in terms of a partnership with imperialism. Kedourie[9] rightly reminds us that imperialism was not always a term of abuse and, certainly until the emergence of a racially intolerant version of it in Africa at the beginning of this century, educated Africans considered it to be a beneficial and progressive force that would prepare African societies for eventual nationhood. *Assimilationist nationalism* — identification with the imperial metropole — survived well into this century. Among French and Portuguese Africans any political advancement could only be expressed in terms of equal citizenship with metropolitan nationals. In French black Africa, territorial self-determination only became a major demand in the mid-1950s; and the failure of the Portuguese to grant citizenship rights to their African subjects turned the latter to armed national liberation struggles in the 1960s. Perhaps the most effusive demonstration of this imperial nationalism is that of Blaise Diagne, the first black deputy from French Africa to sit in the imperial parliament in Paris. Rejecting the Pan-Africanist blandishments of Marcus Garvey in 1920 he proudly stated:

> We French natives wish to remain French, since France has given us every liberty and since she has unreservedly accepted us upon the same basis as her own European children. None of us desires to see French Africa delivered exclusively to the Africans.[10]

Both imperial nationalism and Pan-African nationalism gradually gave way to *territorial nationalism* as the colony-states began to acquire a political character of their own. This was initially more noticeable in the British dependencies, where each colony advanced separately (though there were inter-colony functional organizations both in West and East Africa, such as common currency boards and airlines). It was less evident in the French possessions most of which were amalgamated in two vast Governments-General for West and Equatorial Africa and, additionally, came to acquire direct political representation in the metropolitan parliament.[11] In the Portuguese and Belgian territories, political activity was discouraged and suppressed for most of the colonial period and they contributed little to the advancement of African nationalism; on the contrary, their African subjects responded tardily to political advance in neighbouring British and French colonies.

Over time each colony began to produce its own class of educated Africans, generally regarded as the recipient and transmitter of nationalist ideas.[12] Inter-colony racial solidarity had to compete with a nationalist sentiment towards creating national communities within the confines of the colonial state. Nationalism has rightly been seen as a product of modernity,[13] if not necessarily an inevitable response to it, and a reaction to colonial rule.[14] As the colonial powers opened up Africa to the forces of modernization — literacy, a monetary economy, wage employment, improved communications, urbanization, common official language, and modern legal and administrative systems — it helped bring into being a new stratum of African society, not divorced, as colonial officials were to insist, from traditional society, but a link group between local communities and the wider world. Where Africans were allowed to acquire advanced education and professional training, largely in the British and French colonies, and where freedom to organize politically was permitted (initially confined to the older coastal footholds of West Africa, or on a restricted basis in the Cape Province of South Africa), new political ideas deriving from liberal European political philosophy and constitutional history began to gain currency.

This phase of African nationalism has been termed *élite* or *proto-nationalism,*[15] in contradistinction to the *mass* or *populist nationalism* that supplanted it after the second World War. Elite nationalism was dominated by a constitutionalist and generally conservative body of professionals and merchants. Their political claims were usually moderate, although their polemical newspapers frequently goaded colonial officials. Principally, they sought the gradual extension of African political rights in keeping with the political ideals of the metropolitan powers, with dominion status or full assimilation as the main objectives of British and French subjects respectively. Their other main preoccupation was racial equality in terms of employment and social acceptance. By the beginning of the twentieth century, opportunities for Africans in public employment narrowed considerably as more and more Europeans sought work in the colonies, and racial segregation, of the kind found in East and Southern Africa, spread to the West. Thus African nationalism took on a defensive as much as an assertive character, quite different from the aggressive radical nationalism of the 1940s. While minor concessions were obtained, in the main the élite nationalists had to wait until after the second World War before any significant move towards constitutional change was conceded. Even so, the élite nationalists were more than proto-nationalists. In retrospect, their nationalism seemed to have been of a much higher intellectual calibre than what was to follow: their newspapers and political publications remain unsurpassed in their erudition and familiarity with contemporary political philosophy (Edward Blyden, the leading West African poliltical thinker in the late nineteenth century, corresponded with numerous European intellectuals, including Herbert Spencer); their contributions to debates in colonial legislatures were equally of a high order, though rather verbose to the contemporary ear; and they pioneered an interest in African *cultural nationalism.*

While we should stress the role of early nationalists as spokesmen for racial equality and modernity, their contribution to the rediscovery and reinterpretation of African history must not be forgotten. A Gold Coast 'nationalist school' flourished in the 1890s, emphasizing traditional African values and encouraging scholarly research into indigenous laws and customs and local history. Similar intellectual pursuits took place in Lagos and Freetown as members of the educated élite came to reject excessive or uncritical emulation of European dress and manners. Some prominent individuals discarded their European names and took to wearing African dress, thereby anticipating by several decades similar practices among populist nationalists. Their efforts to establish nationalist educational establishments also anticipated more recent attempts at 'cultural' and 'mental' decolonization.

Educated Africans of this earlier generation of nationalists also promoted ecclesiastical nationalism, usually referred to as *Ethiopianism.* Ethiopian churches sought a measure of autonomy of organization and worship from mission control and independent churchmen were often active in secular politics as well. Independent churches were very important in colonial societies such as the white settler dominated territories of East and Southern Africa where open political activity among Africans was outlawed. The more extreme forms of religious separatism, often called Nativism, actually engaged in armed rebellion against the colonial powers in order to obtain political as well as religious freedom. They were particularly troublesome to the Belgians in their Congo colony, where they went by the general name of 'Ngunzism' (prophetism). Such movements passed into the hands of the non-élite and often acquired a vast following, which contributed indirectly to modern nationalism.

Despite their pionering role, the élite nationalists were to be overshadowed in the years after the second World War by a new generation and stratum of African society. The war undoubtedly contributed to the political advance of colonial Africans, in that it led to important constitutional concessions that enabled African political organization and representation to expand rapidly in West Africa, which then served (particularly Gold Coast nationalism under Kwame Nkrumah) as a beacon for the less politically advanced colonies of East and Central Africa. More so than the First World War, it exposed many Africans, through military service (603,000 men were mobilized by Britain and France) and wartime propaganda, to a range of radical opinions from Soviet communism to Asian nationalism; these found ready acceptance among the growing number of partly educated, socially mobile and aspiring persons created by the colonial presence. These people constituted an economically and politically dissatisfied stratum of society — frequently referred to as a petty bourgeoisie as opposed to the middle class of more successful colonial Africans — that pursued broadly egalitarian objectives aimed at undermining the position of established African social élites as well as that of the colonial powers. Not that their 'genteel' predecessors were entirely eclipsed, for a number of leading post-war political leaders still came from established families; but increasingly the leadership and support for the new mass parties that sprang up across Africa in the late 1940s came from lower middle-class and provincial backgrounds. The popularity of these new mass movements owed much to their ability to act as umbrella organizations for a variety of disaffected groups, nursing old grievances, and ones derived from wartime political and economic restrictions.

The shift in the tenor of African nationalism is indicated not so much by the kinds of change desired, for the older ideals of self-determination, racial equality and socioeconomic advancement were common to both sets of nationalists, but by the manner in which they were articulated. No longer was the colonial government 'humbly and loyally' petitioned; the new nationalists demanded, not requested, constitutional change and insisted on it immediately — 'self-government now!' to cite Nkrumah's most famous slogan — not at some vague future date. The domestic and international circumstances were fortuitous and British and French West Africa set the pace for other parts of black Africa.

The speed and relatively amicable nature of the decolonization of most of black Africa is widely recognized, but the very success of mass nationalism brought difficulties in its train. Two problems merit mention here. In order to obtain rapid self-government nearly all nationalist movements had to abandon their most extreme claims and come to terms with the important European interests in their countries. These accommodations were of immediate advantage, both politically and economically, but in future years were to cast doubts about the 'real' independence, as opposed to the 'formal' sovereignty, enjoyed by these new states. The other disadvantage of rapid success related to the changing composition of the mass parties. In order to overcome problems of resources and organizations, it was common for these parties to recruit a variety of existing organizations and interests with little in common with each other and sharing only the desire for autonomy with the party itself. Heeger has described such movements as 'segmented' nationalism,[16] within which tensions existed between modern secular nationalists and various kinds of particularist partisans.

Sub-territorial allegiances persisted during the colonial era and in several important ways were nurtured by the colonial powers. 'Divide and rule' is a familiar accusation hurled at imperialists and certainly in the ethnically fragmented African dependencies it was frequently resorted to as an administrative convenience. Thus, though the colonial state contributed to the growth of territorial nationalism in a number of anticipated and unexpected ways, it also gave a new lease of life to primordial and more recent forms of communal loyalties. The British practice of 'indirect rule' (governing local communities through modified forms of traditional rule) existed in less codified forms among the other European powers as well, and deliberately encouraged Africans to think in terms of local rather than territorial affiliation. It went with the policy of mistrusting educated Africans and idealizing the 'unspoilt native'. By the late 1940s, when the new mass parties were seeking a territorial following, communalism, based on ancient polities or on 'new' peoples created by colonial reorganization or the activities of Christian missions,[17] was a force to be contended with. There was a tradition of rural opposition to colonial rule in many parts of the African continent, principally in French and Belgian Central Africa, and it could be tapped by the new mass parties. But much of this opposition fed on communal or politico-religious (millenarian) sentiment that objected to the secular and centralized state, be it European or African controlled. This Janus-like aspect of African nationalism remains a problem for nation-building. On the one hand, nationalists take pride in traditional African culture and resistance to European rule, but, on the other hand, these collective memories may fuel particularist movements opposed to the nation-state. The possibility of rival forms of nationalist allegiances within the colonial state became increasingly apparent during the closing years of colonial rule as minority groups or rival dominant groups battled for political succession, exposing the incomplete and fragile nature of African nationalism.[18]

TRANSPLANTING THE NATION-STATE: PROBLEMS AND APPROACHES

We have seen that persons speaking the language of nationalism came to power in black Africa as the colonial empires receded, but belief in their intentions and ability to translate that language into the concrete achievement of the nation-state has waned since independence. No longer do scholars subscribe to a belief in a unilinear progression from 'tribe-to-nation' or colony to sovereign state.[19] Rather, scholarly attention is more readily engaged by the inadequacies of a segmented anti-colonial nationalism in coping with the problems of a plural society, or by the restrictions placed on territorial autonomy by a scarcity of resources and a continuing dependence on external powers. Yet despite this pessimism and doubt, African countries continue to exist, claiming to be sovereign nation-states and receiving the customary diplomatic courtesies granted such entities. What are these obstacles to nation-statehood and what approaches have been adopted to overcome them?

The plural society

With the qualified exception of Somalia, Lesotho and Swaziland, the states of black Africa are made up of a mosaic of peoples, each with distinct linguistic and cultural features, separate histories and frequently different and opposed political values and institutions. Furnivall,[20] describing broadly similar societies in colonial South East Asia, labelled them 'plural societies': territories lacking a national identity and in which distinct racial (or cultural) groups coexisted economically but did not integrate socially or politically under alien colonial rule. Some indication of this diversity of sub-territorial groups in black Africa may be obtained from these random figures: Nigeria has in excess of 250 distinct sub-groups, though the three largest groups may comprise about 60 per cent of the population; Tanzania has 120 groups; Ivory Coast about 60; there are 9 in Kenya; and even tiny Gambia, with a population of little over 600,000, has 8 distinct ethnic groups.

The existence of many sub-national groups need not of itself present a problem, but when accompanied by an uneven access to resources or by historical rivalries or wide differences in values such diversity can place enormous strain on the state and hinder the emergence of a common identity. Too frequently, natural and state resources pass under the control of some groups only because of their greater numbers, earlier access to modern skills or superior organization. In such cases the nation-state is seen as the instrument of one sub-nationality, leading to bitter rivalry and even open conflict. It may also be that better-off groups, who consider their prosperity to be hard-earned, resent having to 'subsidise' others they may despise for their lack of enterprise. The following are only a few examples of the challenge to a frail national consciousness. The most dramatic examples are Zaire (formerly the Belgian Congo), Nigeria, the Sudan and Chad, four of Africa's largest and most fragmented countries. Each has undergone lengthy internal break-up because of regional—ethnic hostility and in each case lengthy military operations were needed to bring the secessionists to heel. In the case of Chad the struggle continues. The non-Muslim and non-Arab minorities of Southern Sudan rebelled against the central government soon after independence and held out for nearly two decades until a new constitution granting a form of local autonomy was conceded by the Khartoum government. In Zaire, provincial interests based on the wealthy Katanga province attempted to create a separate state in 1960, again at the time of independence. Although the United Nations sent in troops to help the central government restore unity, other, and more serious, regional revolts broke out elsewhere in Zaire in the mid-1960s and, up to the present day, this vast country is threatened by provincial secession or attempts to topple the national government from regional centres of power. Regional—ethnic hostility, aided by economic disparities, led to the dismemberment of Nigeria between 1967 and 1970. Arguing the case for their own national homeland (Biafra), the mainly Ibo secessionists won a measure of external support. In Chad, regional and cultural differences have been exacerbated by personal rivalries and ideological cleavages. Each of these examples also illustrates how domestic upheavals led to outside intervention: Israeli support for the southern Sudanese; Belgian and international capitalist backing for Katanga, and Eastern bloc support for the quasi-Marxist dissidents of the mid-1960s; a variety of international assistance for both protagonists in the Biafran War; and French and Libyan intervention in Chad. In all four, mercenaries have also made their unwelcome presence, exposing the vulnerability of indigenous state institutions and their inability to exercise control over allegedly national territory.

Somalia offers an example of another kind of nationalism — what has been termed *irredentist nationalism.* The bulk of the Somali people live in their own national state, but perhaps as many as a third of all Somalis live in neighbouring countries — Ethiopia, Kenya and Djibouti. Despite a recent mauling at the hands of the Ethiopians, reinforced by the Soviet Union and its allies, the Somali cling to their dream of a unified national homeland. At the same time the Ethiopians have been waging a war against Eritrean *ethnic nationalism,* which militarily resists incorporation in the plural but Amhara-dominated Ethiopian state. Less violent illustrations of colonial boundaries cutting across ethnic—historical communities are widespread: in West Africa, the Ewes straddle the Ghana—Togo boundary and have maintained a fitful campaign for their reunification (even taking an advertisement in the London *Times*); and in Central Africa, the Bakongo people, who are found in Congo, Zaire and Angola, previously sought to recreate the ancient Kongo kingdom.

In the plural society 'the government cannot assume a residual loyalty to the state among the majority of its citizens' and territorial nationalism ('statism', to use Smith's term) has to contend with ethnic or regional nationalism, often led by educated elements rather than illiterate traditionalists (the Asantehene, paramount ruler of the powerful Asante people of central Ghana, is a barrister and the late Kabaka (king) of Buganda, in Uganda, was a Cambridge graduate and served in the British Brigade of Guards). Self-determination, that universal panacea of nationalism, may seem less than satisfactory in a plural society once independence is obtained, for, as Kautsky observes, 'Why does one tribe in the Congo think of a government dominated by another tribe as less "alien" than a government of Belgians?'[21]

Territorial limitations

Virtually all black African states suffer from one or several territorial limitations. Some of the forty-seven countries surveyed (Sudan and Mauritania are included because of demographic and historical connections with black Africa) are truly enormous. The largest, Sudan, is over 1,500,000 square kilometres and Zaire is only a little less extensive, and there are several other very large countries as well — making it extremely difficult to create a communications network that effectively draws their scattered peoples together. At the other extreme, no fewer than thirteen states are under 30,000 square kilometres in area. By comparison, the United Kingdom is 230,000 square kilometres, Wales is larger than the seven smallest black African countries, and the American state of Rhode Island has a larger area than the four smallest. The West Midland Metropolitan County in England is twice the area of Africa's smallest country, the island group of the Seychelles! The geographical configuration as well as the size of some of these countries causes difficulties: Equatorial Guinea consists of a small slice of the Central African mainland and several islands in the South Atlantic; fourteen countries have no coastline; Angola is divided into two sections; and The Gambia is only some fifteen kilometres wide in parts and effectively cuts off the lower reaches of the river Gambia from its hinterland.

This contrast in extremes is also found among the populations of black African countries. The total population of this vast sub-continent (though growing fast) is much less than that of India, and only Nigeria has a substantial population. Black Africa is largely made up of small states, many qualifying for the description 'micro-states': twenty-nine states have less than 5,000,000 inhabitants; thirteen (28 per cent of the total) have less than 1,000,000 people. To refer once more to our comparators: the small American state of Rhode Island (population 3,000,000) is more populous than the smallest twenty black African states; and the West Midlands (population 2,730,000) exceeds nineteen of these countries. While a small territory and population need not prevent a strong national consciousness from developing (indeed, it may encourage it), they do present problems of political and economic autonomy. Leaving aside great or middle power intervention, fifty mercenaries and a dog were able to take over the 'independent' state of the Comoros in May 1978, and other mercenaries nearly succeeded in taking over Benin the previous year.

Additionally, many of these countries have extremely limited resources, further contributing to fears about their independence. Their ability to raise revenues is often hindered by economic poverty as much as by dishonest public servants and politicians. Table 6.1 demonstrates their financial vulnerability. In 1976/77 only Nigeria and South Africa had GNPs in excess of US$5 billion. Twenty countries had GNPs of less than US$500 million. Comparison with other types of organizations can be misleading, but some striking contrasts are not out of place. For instance, the *total* annual governmental revenues (recurrent and development budgets) of the forty-seven countries for 1976/77 were less than those of the world's largest multinational corporation, Exxon (formerly Esso) (US$47,019 million to US$49,491 million). The 1978 income of the University of Birmingham (US$65,500,000) puts it ahead of the nine poorest black African states; similarly the City of Birmingham (US$763,000,000 in 1979/80) has an income exceeded only by nine black African states. Persistent fears of economic subversion on the part of African political leaders must be viewed against such a backcloth of inequality. When Exxon's *profits* exceed the GNP of the fifteen poorest of these states together, there is legitimate reason for concern. Neo-Marxist students of African politics frequently cite such economic inequalities as a basis of economic manipulation, but their arguments find support from conservative political scientists as well. Bretton claims that 'independence varies in direct proportion to ability to generate capital resources on a sustained basis'.[22] In the case of many black African states their inability to generate capital, now and in the future, bodes badly for any future autonomy. He further notes the challenge presented to autonomous regulatory capacity by various kinds of dependence on international technologies and value systems that leave the nation-state in nominal control only of its economic affairs. Cobban shares his gloom:

> while the traditional theory of national self-determination looks forward to the establishment of independent and sovereign nation states, unfettered by external influences, or internal divisions, the smaller communities are often too small to aspire to such complete independence . . . economic sovereignty for small states is a thing of the past.[23]

Undoubtedly the 'economic smallness' of large as well as small black African states and their reliance on other countries and

Table 6.1

Resources of Black African States

	Population (millions)	Gross National Product (US$m)	Gross National Product per capita (US$m)	Total Government Revenues (US$m)
Angola	6.05	4,290	710	108
Benin	3.02	370	120	83
Botswana	0.65	190	290	92
Burundi	3.65	330	90	67
Cameroun	7.12	1,760	250	662
Cape Verde	0.29	140	470	39
Central African Republic	1.75	370	210	113
Chad	3.95	410	100	83
Comoros	0.26	60	230	16
Congo	1.30	610	470	317
Djibouti	0.13	180	1,720	37
Equatorial Guinea	0.32	90	290	64
Ethiopia	27.24	2,660	100	805
Gabon	0.53	1,030	1,960	1,323
Gambia	0.53	90	170	30
Ghana	9.61	4,130	430	340
Guinea	5.39	630	120	246
Guinea-Bissau	0.52	210	390	14
Ivory Coast	6.38	2,930	460	2,523
Kenya	12.91	2,610	200	1,136
Lesotho	1.19	170	140	39
Liberia	1.50	580	390	159
Malagasy	8.56	1,570	180	455
Malawi	4.96	660	130	115
Mali	5.56	450	80	290
Mauritania	1.29	380	290	196
Mauritius	0.87	510	580	145
Mozambique	9.03	3,030	340	219
Namibia	0.86	690	800	170
Niger	4.48	540	120	232
Nigeria	73.00	20,810	280	21,208
Rwanda	4.06	310	80	85
Sao Tome	0.08	40	570	3
Senegal	4.87	1,590	330	614
Seychelles	0.06	30	520	23

Sierra Leone	2.91	540	190	159
Somalia	3.10	290	90	216
South Africa	24.94	30,180	1,210	9,674
Sudan	15.23	3,460	230	1,515
Swaziland	0.48	190	390	108
Tanzania	14.35	2,320	160	966
Togo	2.17	370	250	285
Uganda	11.18	2,700	240	216
Upper Volta	5.76	520	90	120
Zaire	24.07	3,530	150	315
Zambia	4.78	2,470	520	522
Zimbabwe	6.10	3,200	520	872

Compiled from *Africa Contemporary Record 1977—78* (New York: Africana Publishing Corporation, 1978).

Data mainly for 1976/77.

organizations for budgetary support, development, aid, technological know-how, military assistance and even administrative personnel, as well as for markets for their predominantly raw material exports, hampers, if not rules out, national autonomy to a much greater extent than with economically advanced states. Given these severe domestic divisions to be overcome in order to create a national community and an effective set of state institutions, and given the difficulties of reconciling national sovereignty with a heavy dependence on outside forces, how have these new countries tried to surmount these obstacles?

Surmounting the obstacles

Initially, the emphasis was on *political* approaches involving the alleged charisma of national leaders, the claimed ability of the mass ruling party to transform society (often a single-party regime), and the use of nationalist—collectivist ideology. These approaches still find favour in a number of African states, but frequently they have proved unsuccessful. The elevation of the national leader into the 'father of the nation' or 'national saviour' is a familiar enough device in established nation-states as well as in aspiring ones, but such a stratagem runs the risk of abuse without any real gains. Africa today can list several fallen heroes, civilian and military, who courted a kind of deification in the name of nation-building but were later exposed or denounced as corrupt tyrants. Although Africans often claim to foreigners that circumstances 'require' a strong leader, such *duces* or *caudillos* quickly earn public hatred or fear. It is doubtful if any person, however altruistic, can, singled-handed, fashion a nation out of the polyglot peoples of an African state.

'Mass mobilizing' single-party regimes also have an uneven record in creating national identity and economic development. Much was claimed twenty years ago, by academics as well as politicians, in respect of the ability of mass nationalist parties to provide an alternative organizational structure, imbued with patriotic values, to the bureaucratic institutions inherited from colonial days. Some of the more celebrated of these party regimes, notably Kwame Nkrumah's Convention People's Party, visibly failed to undertake their self-declared tasks and degenerated into faction-ridden, corrupt and ineffective political machines, more concerned with the gratification of their operatives than with transforming African or Ghanaian society. After independence it is doubtful if the CPP contributed much either to Ghanaian nationhood or state sovereignty. Its lack of popular dynamism was matched only by its economic mismanagement, which left the country hopelessly in debt to outside financiers by 1966. While Ghana under the CPP may be an extreme case, it is by no means the only example of the failure of so-called mass parties (which in reality had far fewer supporters than originally credited) to fulfil nation-building objectives. Today, the search for an effective left-collectivist party system in black Africa takes us to the former Portuguese colonies where familiar claims are made. Here, the experience of liberation through armed struggle, rather than by constitutional accommodation, is singled out as a crucial factor in creating a powerful national sentiment and effective institutional base.[24] But as these countries only became independent in 1974–75, and have still not recovered from decades of colonial neglect and years of war, any judgement must be premature and uninformed.

Allied to national hero and the mass party is nationalist ideology. In the absence of any convincing research it is hard to say just how effective any brand of national ideology is in black Africa. The air-waves reverberate with revolutionary slogans; newspapers graphically proclaim patriotic aims; and party cadres stump the constituencies to reassure the faithful and convert the sceptics by word of mouth; but to what effect? Here, as well, we find considerable evidence of 'consumer resistance' or sheer incomprehension, for if ideological claims are not backed up by practical benefits many Africans remain cautiously unimpressed. The personal shortcomings of political leaders all too often undermine their ideological credibility.

Allied to the use of ideology are the manipulation of 'patriotic' symbols and rituals and the use of history. The changing of colonial names — Gold Coast to Ghana; French Soudan to Mali; Congo to Zaire; or Rhodesia to Zimbabwe — may offer symbolic gratification, but it is questionable if this achieves much more. Both in Mobutu's Zaire and Tombalbaye's Chad, widely publicised 'authenticity' campaigns were undertaken in order to eliminate European and colonial influences. Today Tombalbaye is dead, his policies having done much to offend and drive to armed resistance the non-Negro populace of northern Chad, while little is heard of Zaire's 'cultural revolution' as the need for Western loans and military support increases dependence on Europeans. Often such displays of cultural chauvinism (perhaps more African than national) are nothing more than harmless and entertaining pageants, but they may, as in Chad, arouse widespread hostility. One people's noble traditions may fail to inspire brotherly sentiments among other groups, and too flagrant a recourse to often ethnic—regional—historical symbols may encourage ethnic nationalism in plural societies.

Regardless of regime and ideology, territorial nationalism has had to come to terms with ethnic pluralism and even the most stridently secular and unitarist of states usually practises what is termed 'ethnic arithmetic' (that is, ensuring that political offices and public investments are distributed in proportion to the importance of ethnic groups in the country; an expedient familiar to students of American urban politics). A form of 'consociational democracy'[25] is also practised in some states, whereby potential ethnic conflict is avoided through élite consensus. Such arrangements ensure the survival of governments; they may also encourage inter-ethnic accommodation and, over time, may produce the kind of 'social transactions' Karl Deutsch[26] regards as essential to create some kind of interdependence among peoples not yet welded into a common nationality. They do however require considerable political finesse and an ability to generate economic rewards broadly in line with popular aspirations. Too often, such arrangements are obtained only by a sacrifice of economic efficiency, as the distribution of modern skills may be concentrated among a few ethnic groups but all groups must share in the hand-out of jobs in the modern sector.

The assimilationist approach to national unit, observed in the essay on the nation-state in Asia, is less easily available in black Africa because of the absence of a 'core' or 'projected' group around which others may cohere. Ancient and recent animosities, or the existence of several 'core' groups, may frustrate exercises of this kind. The Swahili language has been utilized with some effect in East Africa to create an overarching linguistic unity but its position is somewhat unusual in that it is not the language of a dominant ethnic group and is consequently more acceptable to others. Hausa or Mandinka dialects in West Africa are widely spoken but suffer from over-identification with particular ethnic—cultural groups. In Mauritania, with a largely Moorish populace, the use of Arabic has aroused the ire of French-speaking blacks, who form a racial minority.

Likewise, religion has only limited utility in creating national consciousness in black Africa. In the Sudan, Islam proved to be a stumbling block. Some millenarian religious cults may be elevated to the status of state religions, as in the case of Kimbanguism in Zaire or the Yondo cult in Chad, but traditional African religions are extremely varied and may oppose the secular nation-state, as they once resisted colonialism. The Kwilu rebellion in the Congo in the mid-1960s combined cultism with vulgarized Marxism, and a little after that the Sudanese had a major and violent show-down with the Mahdist Islamic brotherhood, which threatened to become a rival state within the state. Black African states have sought to operate secular constitutions lest they exacerbate religious divisions and sensibilities. 'Anti-state' religious organizations, such as the Watch Tower Movement, have suffered persecution under independent African as well as colonial governments, despite their anti-colonial record.

In spite of their ethnic pluralism, most black African states have avoided federal political arrangements, though an informal 'federalism' may exist in practice. Zaire and Nigeria are unusual in having adopted this arrangement. The conventional attitude is that this would only encourage ethnic particularism. The new Nigerian constitution, a revised and reformed federal arrangement, will undoubtedly prove instructive in supporting or refuting this widely held view.

National educational programmes also comprise a familiar

technique of nation-building.[27] The Nigerian Universal Free Primary Education programme is an ambitious step in this direction, aimed towards removing gross regional imbalances in the provision of education. It is not only the more equitable distribution of education facilities that is advocated; attempts have also been made to give the educational curriculum a 'national' content, so as to encourage the emergence of common citizenship. Free and widely available education may well prove to be a great national denominator but, again, it must be handled with sensitivity lest the better-educated groups feel threatened by the rapid advancement of less-educated groups (through African variants of 'positive affirmation' policies — that is, deliberate favouring of the deprived to promote social and economic equality).

Finally, economic nationalism has also been encouraged in most new states with the aim of reducing external control over their economies and encouraging economic development. In as much as this approach encourages the growth of economic interdependence among a polyglot populace it may be said to promote national consciousness. The gross deprivation found in most of these states and their economic dependence on external forces makes it difficult, if not impossible, to promote a kind of economic autarky. Economic self-sufficiency must clash with a policy of rapid growth, fuelled largely by outside sources of capital, markets, goods and services, and expertise. As noted earlier, uneven distribution of resources and growth during the colonial period poses the problem of 'internal colonialism' as the better-endowed parts of a new state 'take off' at the expense of their impoverished peripheries, which may be reduced to cheap labour reserves.

ALTERNATIVES TO THE NATION-STATE

Given that the new states of black Africa are at best only embryonic national communities, will the measures reviewed above eventually foster an overarching common allegiance among such varied peoples? For the moment we have states rather than nation-states, though an intermittent national sentiment can be promoted, often unfortunately, through xenophobic attacks on aliens living within the community. The expulsion of Asians from Uganda or Nigerians from Ghana provided examples of 'patriotism' of this kind. The possibility of insecure leaders resorting to this kind of chauvinistic nationalism remains, particularly if economic power remains in the hands of aliens. 'Neo-colonialism', however merited the accusation, often provides a convenient scapegoat for domestic incompetence and a justification for coercion.

Conventional wisdom argues that the new states need time more than anything to enable a sense of common purpose and identity to emerge; that over a number of years group similarities increase as a result of living together in the same state, and differences between neighbouring states increase. However, the passing of time may increase rather than reduce tensions previously concealed by the euphoria of independence. What might be claimed is that if new states survive the years of disillusionment that follows the collapse of post-independence euphoria, then the long-term prospect for inter-ethnic accommodation is enhanced. In the short run what we have seen in Africa is state consolidation by means other than the nationality principle. Although Pan-Africanism continues to be viewed as the ultimate form of political community, at best this can only be regarded as a long-term prospect. Various kinds of inter-state cooperation have been practised from colonial times and continue today. Their record to date is mixed: premature political unions such as the Union of African States (Ghana—Guinea—Mali) in 1960 or the Mali Federation (Senegal—Mali) in 1959—60, and the collapse of common services bodies, as in former British East and West Africa, suggest caution in predicting a rapid growth in inter-state integration. A number of functional and diplomatic organizations, which may or may not lead to closer political and economic ties in future, undoubtedly exist — the Organization of African Unity itself or the Economic Community of West African States (ECOWAS), one of the more promising comprehensive regional associations at present. Ironically, the suppression of Africans in southern Africa by white settler regimes has been one of the most powerful incentives for African unity. What would be the effect on this of the achievement of black majority rule in Namibia and South Africa as well as Zimbabwe? The submergence of existing African states, however inadequate their national territory, into wider unities seems unlikely given the territorial and personal interests attached to them.

For the moment the break-up of existing states into smaller, more truly ethnic national states seems to have been checked. Eritrea may yet break away from Ethiopia, but unassuaged sub-state national feelings are more likely to seek and obtain redress through accommodation within existing frontiers than by altering them. It would appear from the history of Katangese and Biafran secession that the international community and African political leaders as a whole are opposed to what is regarded as the 'balkanization' of Africa. Paradoxically, we may find domestic instability continuing but territorial boundaries remaining largely unchanged.

If nationality at present fails to bind people together in the new states, what else might? *Dynastic* states of the traditional kind have no prospects in Africa. Swaziland alone is ruled by a traditional monarch; elsewhere, republicanism prevails. So far, no modern African ruler (excepting the pathetic attempt to create a Bonapartist dynasty by 'Emperor' Bokassa of the Central African Republic) has sought to create a family state, though *personalist* states are a common derivative of the failed *party* states of the early 1960s.[28] The atrophy of party regimes has led to the strengthening of personal rule, which, when combined with external support, amounts to what Gellar[29] calls *neo-patrimonial* states in which loyalty rests on reciprocity between ruler and clients rather than on dynastic or national sentiment. Such states may well prove unstable and be prone to degeneration into *client*-states, where independence is very much a facade, behind which external economic and political interests manipulate the policies of the new state. The exact effect clientism has on the nation-building capacities of new states is yet to be ascertained: in their different ways Angola and Senegal defend conspicuous external assistance as helping not endangering national development. Given the passion surrounding this debate and an absence of concrete information, no hard and fast conclusion can be arrived at.

The other major political trend in post-colonial Africa (and one observed in Asia as well) is towards the *neo-administrative* state, in which the two most important state institutions, the armed forces and the bureaucracy, determine and implement national policy. The frequent seizure of power by soldiers — nearly half the countries of black Africa have succumbed to them at some time or other — and the reliance of most regimes on bureaucracies inherited from the colonial period indicate their importance. One school of thought considers them as the only agents capable of holding together ethnically divided societies and transforming them into national communities. A contrary view regards their internal rivalries and economic exactions as a source of disunity and an obstacle to economic progress. As the main beneficiaries of the modern state system their interest lies in upholding rather than undermining the nation-state principle.

African nationalism in the main has sought not so much to restore historical states or ancient national communities as to create new ones out of the welter of peoples thrust together as a result of colonial conquest. Its uncertain and future-oriented nature has earned it the label of 'artificial', but it is no more unreal than the nationalism of Belgians or Yugoslavs, who have also sought to create new nations from among the ruins of earlier empires. Given the diversity of black Africa, there is no single or certain path to nationhood, though Seton-Watson's speculation that this may come about through *pluralist empires* — 'multi-lingual empires ruled by centralising despots, perhaps nearer the ancient Iranian or Indian [or ancient African?] models than to any modern European example'[30] — merits closer examination. The eclectic fusion of personalist rule and military-bureaucratic institutions of colonial origins, noted by Roth and Gellar as being widespread in the new Africa, may yet succeed where earlier imitators of the Western European model have failed.

NOTES AND REFERENCES

1. Notable among the latter are David Apter *The Gold Coast in Transition* (Princeton, NJ: Princeton University Press, 1955); Thomas Hodgkin *Nationalism in Colonial Africa* (London: Muller, 1956); and James Coleman 'Nationalism in tropical Africa' *American Political Science Review, 48,* no. 2 (June 1954) pp. 404—26, and *Nigeria: Background to Nationalism* (Berkeley and Los Angeles: University of California Press, 1958).

2. E. Colson 'African society at the time of the scramble' in L. H. Gann and P. Duignan (eds) *Colonialism in Africa* vol. 1 (Cambridge: Cambridge University Press, 1969) p. 27.

3. Some adopt Coleman's distinction ('Nationalism in tropical Africa' *op. cit.*) between initial opposition to colonialism — 'primary resistance' — and modern nationalism seeking nation-statehood. Others, such as Ranger ('Connexions between "primary resistance" movements and modern mass nationalism in East and Central Africa' *Journal of African History, 9,* nos 3—4, 1968, pp. 437—53, 631—41) , stress the affinities and continuities between these two phases.

4. Nationalism is widely regarded as the ideology of modernization: a political response to wider social and economic changes taking place in

traditional societies. See the chapters by Cornelia Navari and Andrew Orridge above.

5. e.g. E. Kedourie, *Nationalism in Asia and Africa* (New York: Meridian Books, 1970) p. 107, incorrectly asserts that African nationalism 'appears only after World War II'.

6. Paul Hair 'Africanism: the Freetown contribution' *Journal of Modern African Studies, 5,* no. 4 (1967) pp. 521–39. These black émigrés returned to their ancestral continent to avoid discrimination in the New World and to be reunited with their kinsfolk. Sensitive to racial indignities and steeped in Anglo-American notions of political equality, they formed a cultural and political élite and fashioned the views of some 70,000 tribal Africans released from slavery at Freetown by the Royal Navy. Their common descendants, the Creoles, were very prominent during the nineteenth century both in serving and criticizing British colonialism throughout West Africa.

7. J. Ayo Langley *Ideologies of Liberation in Black Africa* (London: Rex Collings, 1979) Introduction Part III.

8. Pan-Africanism has certain affinities with other 'pan' movements: Pan-Slavism and Pan-Teutonism n Europe and Pan-Turanianism among Turkish-speaking peoples in the Middle East. Unlike these others though, it had no linguistic basis. There are also parallels with Zionism.

9. Kedourie, *op. cit.,* p. 4.

10. Cited in translation by R. L. Buell *The Native Problem in Africa* vol. 2 (London: Macmillan, 1928) p. 81.

11. Initially there was only one deputy for the whole of French black Africa, but after the Second World War each colony acquired separate representation in the metropolitan parliament.

12. The primacy of educated colonials in the development and transmission of nationalist ideology is widely recognized. Kedourie (*op. cit.,* p. 106) describes nationalism as the ideology of the disaffected élite — the 'visionary malcontents'.

13. Again there is common agreement on the importance of socioeconomic and psychological changes brought about by exposure to Western values and practices. In Coleman's words: 'African nationalism . . . is the inevitable end product of the impact of Western imperialism and modernity upon African societies' ('Nationalism in tropical Africa', *op. cit.,* p. 426).

14. Self-determination, as opposed to national consciousness, as the main ingredient of 'anti-colonial nationalism', again is widely noted. Rotberg goes as far as to claim that 'Without the partition and subsequent colonial rule of tropical Africa by the powers of Europe, there might have been no African nationalism' R. I. Rotberg 'African nationalism: concept or confusion?' *Journal of Modern African Studies, 4,* no. 1 (1966) p. 37.

15. This distinction is found in P. Worsley *The Third World* (London: Weidenfeld and Nicolson, 1964) Ch. 2. Other writers have used broadly similar categories to distinguish between these two phases or stages in nationalist development.

16. G. A. Heeger *The Politics of Under-development* (London: Macmillan, 1974) p. 23: 'The nationalist movement . . . has been not so much a cohesive mass movement as a collection of movements in a society segmented by region, community, kinship, and the pace of social change.'

17. The regrouping of peoples in new colonial administrative units and the creation by European missionaries of a common written language among groups divided by dialects, helped create wider communal awareness. The Ibo of Nigeria and Tonga of Zambia are good examples of such changes. Colson, *op. cit.*, pp. 28–30.

18. Rival sub-territorial ethnic nationalism was a feature of Gold Coast and Nigerian politics during the terminal stages of colonial rule, and numerous other examples of this phenomenon can be cited.

19. For an excellent survey and criticism of the earlier evolutionary approach see Sheldon Gellar 'State-building and nation-building in West Africa' in S. Eisenstadt and S. Rokkan (eds) *Building States and Nations* vol. 2 (Beverly Hills, Calif./London: Sage, 1973).

20 J. S. Furnivall *Colonial Policy and Practice* (Cambridge: Cambridge University Press, 1948).

21. J. H. Kautsky (ed.) *Political Change in Underdeveloped Countries: Nationalism and Communism* (London: Wiley, 1962) p. 37.

22. H. L. Bretton *Power and Politics in Africa* (London: Longman, 1973) p. 20.

23. Alfred Cobban *The Nation State and National Self-Determination* (London: Collins/Fontana, 1969) p. 242. In similar vein he claims that 'Backward small states have had in effect the choice between poverty and independence, or economic development at the price of political subjection' (p. 278).

24. The case for regarding wars of liberation as a positive contribution to nation-building is considered in F. Popper 'Internal war as a stimulant to political development' *Comparative Political Studies, 3* (January 1971) pp. 413–23.

25. A term popularized by Arend Lijphart in 'Consociational democracy' *World Politics, 21* (January 1969).

26. K. Deutsch *Nationalism and Social Communication* (Cambridge, Mass.: MIT Press, 1953).

27. On the political aspects of education in new states see J. S. Coleman (ed.) *Education and Political Development* (Princeton, NJ: Princeton University Press, 1965) pp. 3–32.

28. Gunther Roth observes: 'some of these new states may not be states at all but merely private governments of those powerful enough to rule' 'Personal rulership, patrimonialism, and empire-building in the new states' *World Politics, 20,* March 1968, p. 196.

29. Gellar, *op. cit.*

30. H. Seton-Watson *Nations and States* (London: Methuen, 1977) p. 353.

FURTHER READING

There is a substantial literature on the subject of nationalism in Africa, much of it repetitive or fragmentary. Nearly all the general studies of nationalism offer some discussion of non-European nationalism; there are a number of general accounts of African nationalism combining a historical survey with attempts at classification; a number of readers containing a selection of speeches and writings together with introductory surveys may be found; and there are numerous monographs on the political history of individual territories or groups of colonies not detailed here.

General surveys of nationalism:
R. Emerson *From Empire to Nation* (Cambridge, Mass.: Harvard University Press, 1960); P. Worsley *The Third World* (London: Weidenfeld and Nicolson, 1964); J. H. Kautsky (ed.) *Political Change in Underdeveloped Countries* (London: Wiley, 1962, Ch. 2; K. Minogue *Nationalism* (London: Methuen, 1967); A. Cobban *The Nation State and National Self-Determination* (London: Collins/Fontana, 1969); A. D. Smith *Theories of Nationalism* (London: Methuen, 1977).

Specific accounts of African nationalism:
J. Coleman 'Nationalism in tropical Africa' *American Political Science Review, 48,* no. 2 (June 1954); T. Hodgkin *Nationalism in Colonial Africa* (London: Muller, 1956); Lord Hailey *An African Survey* (London: Oxford University Press, 1957) pp. 251–60; R. Emerson 'Africa' in K. Deutsch and W. J. Foltz (eds) *Nation-Building* (Englewood Cliffs, NJ: Prentice-Hall, 1963); R. I. Rotberg 'African nationalism: concept or confusion?' *Journal of Modern African Studies, 4,* no. 1 (1966); S. Gellar 'State-building and nation-building in West Africa' in S. Eisenstadt and S. Rokkan (eds) *Building States and Nations* vol. 2 (Beverly Hills, Calif./London: Sage, 1973); and I. L. Markovitz *Power and Class in Africa* (Englewood Cliffs, NJ: Prentice-Hall, 1977).

Readers on African nationalism:
R. Emerson and M. Kilson (eds) *The Political Awakening of Africa* (Englewood Cliffs, NJ: Prentice-Hall, 1965); H. Kohn and W. Sokolsky *African Nationalism in the Twentieth Century* (New York: Anvil Original, 1965); E. Kedourie ·*Nationalism in Asia and Africa* (New York: Meridian Books, 1970); and J. Ayo Langley *Ideologies of Liberation in Black Africa 1856–1970* (London: Rex Collings, 1979).

7

Socialism and Nationalism

A. W. Wright

> Socialists must be internationalists even if their working classes are not;
> socialists must also understand the nationalism of the masses, but only
> in the way in which a doctor understands the weakness or the illness of
> his patient. Socialists should be aware of that nationalism, but, like
> nurses, they should wash their hands twenty times over whenever they
> approach an area of the labour movement infected by it.

Thus Isaac Deutscher in 1971.[1] His picture of the international
socialist constantly disinfecting himself against the nationalism of
the working class points attention to the continuing difficulty of
socialism in coming to terms, either theoretically or actually, with the
'national question'. Indeed, not merely does this difficulty continue
but it intensifies; so that while Deutscher prescribes a sanitary
dissociation of socialism from nationalism there are now to be found
other Marxists who recommend a contagious embrace. The
relationship has certainly come a long way since both movements
announced their arrival on the European stage in 1848. In that year
the founders of Marxism could confidently predict the socialization
of the nation; but a century later it seemed more plausible to record
(in E. H. Carr's phrase) the 'nationalization of socialism'.

It is only necessary to recall some relevant features of recent world
history to understand why the 'national question' has remained
unresolved and contentious as far as socialism is concerned. The
international expansion of capitalism has led not to the erosion of
national frontiers but to a new fragmentation occasioned by the
nationalist demand for statehood. Even within the 'old' capitalist
states of Europe peripheral nationalism has intensified. Socialist
internationalism has shown itself to be fragile and unreliable,
classically so in August 1914, when compared with national loyalties

148

and the deeply rooted nationalisms of the European working class. The centre of gravity of socialism has passed from Europe to the underdeveloped world, not merely confounding the class analysis of classical Marxism but also bringing socialism and nationalism into an intimacy of contact that has spawned varieties of 'national communism'. Within Europe, there was the appearance of a fascism ('national socialism') that could bring to heel a working class that had been regarded as the most promising socialist material in Europe. Finally, of course, there was the development after 1917 of 'socialism in one country' with all its international implications and, later still, the unfolding international relationships between socialist states.

There is more than enough here, then, to explain why the problem of nationalism has not merely persisted within socialism but has been elevated to the centre of socialist discussion. It is interesting to note that whereas only 2−3 per cent of the writings of Marx and Engels touch on the national question, the percentage is ten times higher with Lenin and becomes more than 50 per cent with Stalin.[2] It has continued to rise, for there is now wide agreement that this whole issue has been 'a permanent, unsolved theoretical difficulty of Marxism and a practical difficulty of socialist movements'.[3]

THE MARXIST TRADITION

Let us begin with the Marxist theory before turning to the socialist practice. If the focus here is on Marxism at the expense of other varieties of socialism, it is because it was within Marxism that theoretical discussion of the national question overwhelmingly took place. In its classical period before 1917 there developed within Marxism an important discussion on the nation-state and nationalism, beginning with the original (but undeveloped) formulations of Marx and Engels, taking in the culturalist approach of Austro-Marxists like Otto Bauer and the 'radical left' position of Rosa Luxemburg, before culminating in the authoritative statements of Lenin and their mechanical transcription by Stalin. This period of discussion, which reached its intellectual peak in the Second International in the years before 1914, served to identify a number of approaches to the national question that claimed to be securely anchored to the Marxist tradition.[4] The arrival of international war and a national revolution soon curtailed and transformed the discussion itself.

If the work of Marx and Engels served to open this period of debate, it was too sketchy and insubstantial to guarantee the future shape and direction that the debate would take. There was little in the writings of the founders of Marxism to suggest that the national question would loom large in, let alone subvert, the development of socialism. Instead, there were only the global pronouncements to be found in the *Communist Manifesto* about the international nature of the class struggle and its destined resolution, coupled with contemporary reflections on particular national struggles and evidence of a set of attitudes towards certain nations and races. This scarcely amounted to a developed theory of nationalism, as all studies of the thought of Marx and Engels on the national question agree.[5]

The thrust of the *Manifesto* is familiar but important. It firmly establishes the modern national state as the creation of capitalism, for 'independent, or but loosely connected provinces, with separate interests, laws, governments and systems of taxation, became lumped together into one nation, with one government, one code of laws, one national class interest, one frontier, and one customs tariff. However, just as capitalism has eroded local particularisms and created the national state, its need for new markets 'chases the bourgeoisie over the whole surface of the globe' and gives 'a cosmopolitan character to production and consumption in every country', which has 'drawn from under the feet of industry the national ground on which it stood'. Having created the national state, capitalism thus also created the conditions for its abolition. In Marx's view, 'national differences and antagonisms between peoples are daily more and more vanishing, owing to the development of the bourgeoisie, to freedom of commerce, to the world market, to uniformity in the mode of production and in the conditions of life corresponding thereto'. Moreover, the victory of the proletariat would hasten the disappearance of national differences and antagonisms, for 'in proportion as the antagonism between classes within the nation vanishes, the hostility of one nation to another will come to an end'.

This analysis in turn provided the basis for understanding the position of the proletariat in relation to the nation. Answering the reproach that communists sought to abolish nations, Marx and Engels declared that 'the working men have no country', which meant that 'we cannot take from them what they have not got'.

However, they went on to say that 'since the proletariat must first of all acquire political supremacy, must rise to be the leading class of the nation, must constitute itself *the* nation, it is, so far, itself national, though not in the bourgeois sense of the word'. United national struggles by the proletariat of the leading countries was the road to general emancipation and harmony. The famous clarion call at the end of the *Manifesto* ('Workingmen of All Countries, Unite!') thus became the cornerstone of the doctrine of 'proletarian internationalism'.

These few pages of the *Manifesto,* with their grand historical sweep, were to provide the theoretical framework within which revolutionary socialists approached the national question. Yet the theory was unsystematic and incomplete, a deficiency that Marx never remedied despite some of his own later observations on national struggles that suggested the need for a richer analysis, more precise definitions and a more concrete political strategy. In the *Manifesto* Marx revealed himself as a characteristic product of his age, with his easy anticipations of the beneficent international effects of contemporary economic developments. This mode of thought had to be abandoned when it became clear that the spread of a bourgeois world order did not resolve international antagonisms; and when socialists had to construct a theory of imperialism to explain their continuance. Similarly, the mechanical way in which Marx made national differences dependent upon (and abolished by) changing material conditions scarcely did justice to contemporary experience. However, the argument of the *Manifesto* did point attention to the global character of the economy; just as it revealed in striking form Marx's conception of a universal socialist humanism, with all the implications this has for the future organization of international society.[6] Finally, there is more than a touch of irony in the fact that Marx announced the resolution of the national question in class terms at the very moment in European history at which nationalism gave notice that it was unlikely to be content with such subordinate and derivative status.

In the absence of further systematic theory, those seeking guidance from the work of Marx and Engels in this area have to excavate amongst their *obiter dicta* and their commentaries on particular national struggles. The result of such excavation is a curious mixture of suggestive interpretation and contradictory judgements, rooted in a set of national and racial stereotypes (more pronounced with

Engels but seemingly shared by Marx) and decisively influenced by strategic considerations. Thus Marx's support for the national struggle in Poland was a product of his desire to see a damaging blow struck against Russia as the heartland of European reaction; and he made no attempt to generalize such support into a wider theory of national self-determination. So too with Marx's mature position on Ireland, often cited as the most important part of his work as far as the construction of a socialist theory of nationalism is concerned, for here nationalism is supported because of its revolutionary implications for the class struggle in England — 'the English working class will never accomplish anything before it has got rid of Ireland'. Thus support for nationalist movements was always specific not general, strategic nor theoretical; and always a product of Marx's conception of the balance of advantage in the international class struggle.

In general, Marx's approach was rooted in a progressive view of historical development, linked to a belief in large-scale economic units. For Engels, it also included a Hegelian distinction between 'historic' and 'non-historic' nations, the former being progressive and revolutionary, the latter essentially counter-revolutionary throwbacks. This distinction had the effect of consigning southern Slavs, Bretons, Basques, Scots, etc. to the dustbin of history, for in Engels' words these 'remnants of a nation, mercilessly crushed, as Hegel said, by the course of history, this *national refuse,* is always the fanatical representative of counter-revolution and remains so until it is completely exterminated or de-nationalized, as its whole existence is in itself a protest against a great historical revolution'. This is Engels not Marx of course, but they shared a belief in large 'progressive' nations, a dismissive view of peasant societies outside Europe, a considerable contempt for small 'unhistorical' peoples and a general conception of the merits of higher civilizations over lower ones. Thus Poles, Hungarians, Italians and Irish were supported in their national struggles, while the claims of the many ethnic groups within the multinational Russian, Prussian and Austrian empires were rejected. It was right also that Germany should be unified at the expense of Danish self-determination in Schleswig. It was possible to support the conquest of Mexican territory by the United States and the colonization of Algeria by the French. The progressive impact of British rule in India could be stressed, even while pointing to its barbarities. All this provided an ambivalent legacy for the Marxist tradition in its increasing preoccupation with the national question.

The tradition contested

This preoccupation was apparent during the period of the Second International, before the cataclysm of 1914. This period saw the development of powerful socialist parties in continental Europe, united in their allegiance to Marxism and in their belief in a forthcoming social revolution of international dimension. Yet this same period also saw a quickening of old national struggles and the emergence of new ones, ensuring that the national question became central to socialist argument. The question seemed particularly important to Russian, Polish and Austrian socialists, confronted as they were with the problem of multinational empires, and this produced a series of major attempts to develop a socialist theory of nationalism consistent with the canons of Marxism.

One interesting and significant fact to emerge from the debates on the national question within the Second International during this period was that positions adopted on the issue did not simply reflect the more general 'left' or 'right' locations of the protagonists. Characteristically, nationalism confounded routine theoretical positions and political demarcations. The clearest example of this was the opposition to national separatism and the endorsement of a policy of cultural autonomy shared both by the ultra-left Rosa Luxemburg and the centrist Austro-Marxists. This latter school of undogmatic Marxists, neglected but important, did pioneering work on nationalities, nationalism and the nation.[7] Its most notable product was Otto Bauer's study of *The National Question and Social Democracy* (1907), described by Kolakowski as 'the best treatise on nationality problems to be found in Marxist literature and one of the most significant products of Marxist theory in general'.[8]

Confronted by the particular problem of how to guarantee national rights within the framework of the multinational Austro-Hungarian state, Bauer developed a general Marxist analysis of the national question that was historical, psychological and sociological. The nation was a historically and culturally determined national character: it was 'the totality of men bound together through a common destiny into a community of character'. In a class society, participation in the 'national cultural community' was the preserve of the ruling class, whereas 'only socialism will give the whole people a share in the national culture'. The doubtful Marxist credentials of this approach became even more doubtful when it was extended by Bauer into an argument that socialism, far from producing an international socialist culture, would enhance the differentiations and diversities among national cultural communities, although without the national antagonisms associated with capitalism. There was thus no conflict between proletarian internationalism and national cultural diversity. Socialism would realise nationality, not abolish it.

When applied to the political and territorial problem of multinational states, Bauer's approach (like that of another Austro-Marxist, Karl Renner) involved a rejection of separate statehood for each nation but an assertion of cultural autonomy and of the constitutional arrangements necessary to secure such self-determination. It also involved an acceptance of the need for international political organizations above the level of national states in future socialist society, corresponding to the necessary development of larger economic regions, but linked to this was the parallel need to ensure a secure status for national communities in all their rich diversity. Bauer summed it up thus:

> The transformation of men by the socialist mode of production leads necessarily to the organization of humanity in national communities. The international division of labour leads necessarily to the unification of the national communities in a social structure of a higher order. All nations will be united for the common domination of nature, but the totality will be organized in national communities which will be encouraged to develop autonomously and to enjoy freely their national culture — that is the socialist principle of nationality.

Much of this, not least what seemed its cultural metaphysics, aroused the wrath of the Marxist establishment; and, more generally, Bauer's approach has been criticized for its alleged failure to come to terms with the political and territorial dimensions of nationalism — the demand for statehood often regarded as its *raison d'être*. Nonetheless, Austro-Marxism was important for its concern with the national question in itself and not (like Lenin) merely for its strategic connection with the class struggle; for its view of the valuable richness and diversity of national communities; and for its understanding that socialism would not abolish national differences. It can fairly claim to represent the most substantial and suggestive of the classical Marxist attempts to grapple with the national question.

Another attempt, of a rather different kind, came from the Polish socialist, Rosa Luxemburg, who elaborated a doctrine of thorough-going proletarian internationalism in opposition to the notion of national self-determination. In the words of her biographer, Luxemburg 'stands at the apex of the attempt to make operational the Marxist concept of class as the primary social referent, and to break once and for all the old alternative stranglehold of nation'.[9] She declared war on Polish nationalism in the name of a dynamic interpretation of Marxism, undeterred by Marx's own earlier support for an independent Poland, and generalized this position into a comprehensive internationalism hostile to national movements. In the case of Poland, she argued that nationalism was a distraction from the real business of the forthcoming social revolution in Russia itself, a position further buttressed by an economism that made the alleged economic integration of Poland with Russia into the decisive political fact (described by Löwy as an example of her 'unmediated assimilation of politics to economics'[10]). More generally (and most notably in her 1908 work on *The National Question and Autonomy*), Rosa Luxemburg developed a systematic case against national self-determination and invoked the authority of scientific socialism: 'Social Democracy, which has based its entire policy on the scientific method of historical materialism and the class war, cannot make exceptions in the question of nationality.'

In Luxemburg's view, Marxists should reject the notion of a 'right' of nations to self-determination as hopelessly abstract, utopian and unscientific. Moreover, the whole concept of 'nation' was essentially transitory, the creation of the bourgeois epoch, and destined to wither away in the socialist world order. The 'nation' also suggested a unity of interest across classes, confirming nationalism as a bourgeois phenomenon that was reactionary from the point of view of the international class struggle. Finally, Luxemburg poured scorn on the aspirations to statehood of small nationalities in the face of the inexorable logic of history. In all this, then, there was the statement of an extreme and doctrinaire internationalism, heroic in personal terms but rigid and schematic in its failure to understand the political dimension of nationalism or its radical potential for the wider process of social change. When nation triumphed over class in 1914 and the International collapsed, Rosa Luxemburg found the 'subjective' explanation in the opportunism of revisionist social democratic leaders; 'objective' internationalism remained intact.

Together, Luxemburg's internationalism and Austro-Marxist cultural autonomy set the framework for the debate on the national question out of which a Bolshevik nationality policy was to be forged. Thus Bauer's work elicited a response in the form of Stalin's tract on 'Marxism and the National Question' (1913), written at Lenin's request by his 'wonderful Georgian' and destined to become (like Stalin himself) an official source of authority on Bolshevik nationality policy. Stalin's particular task was to attack the Austro-Marxist idea of cultural autonomy for its encouragement of nationalist and separatist tendencies, as revealed in its adoption by the Jewish Bund and the Caucusus movement. At the same time, he sought to set this particular attack within the framework of a general statement on the national question. Hence his attempt to list the factors that definitionally comprised a nation ('a historically constituted, stable community of people, formed on the basis of a common language, territory, economic life, and psychological make-up manifested in a common culture') and his denial of national status where these factors were not all present. In organizational terms, socialists (committed to proletarian internationalism and repudiating the bourgeois character of nationalism) could only contemplate a form of regional autonomy that enshrined the principle of multinational class solidarity. Stalin's essay hardly deserved to be 'elevated . . . into the role of a textbook on nationality problems for the world communist movement'.[11] Its definitional approach to the nation was rigid and schematic (hence earning the wrath of some contemporary Marxists for an empiricism characteristic of bourgeois social science), and could not accommodate historical experience. Moreover, his failure to understand the ambiguous, dynamic (dialectical?) character of nationalism gave it a purely negative status in relation to socialism, which closed the door to any strategic accommodation.

It was Lenin who made sure that this door remained open; and in doing so laid the basis for the 'correct' development of Marxism in this area. Obliged to give increasing attention to the theory of the national question between 1913 and 1916 (as in his article on 'The Right of Nations to Self-Determination' (1914), directed against Rosa Luxemburg), Lenin sought to define the relationship between socialist internationalism and national rights. Rejecting both Luxemburg's anti-nationalism and Bauer's national cultural autonomy, Lenin advanced the slogan of 'national self-determination'. However, its simplicity concealed its theoretical and strategic complexity, for the slogan 'epitomises all the problems which it was designed to settle'.[12] In strategic terms, it reflected Lenin's understanding of the need for socialists to participate in and lead 'progressive' national movements and to ally themselves with oppressed nations against their oppressors. In the Russian context in particular, it was important that socialists should avoid the taint of Great Russian chauvinism by a scrupulous regard for national rights. At the same time, however, to proclaim a 'right' to self-determination did not mean support for the exercise of that right in concrete situations. Lenin denied any contradiction here; to support the legalization of divorce did not also mean support for the break-up of marriages. Indeed, it was the duty of socialists to oppose secessionism in their own countries and to uphold the principle of international proletarian solidarity, for socialists 'are enemies of all nationalism and for democratic centralism . . . [and] are against particularism, being convinced that, other conditions being equal, large states can solve the tasks of economic progress and the tasks of the proletariat's struggle with the bourgeoisie much more successfully than small states'.

Hence there is clearly some truth in the suggestion that these reservations 'nullified the right of self-determination and turned it into a purely tactical weapon'.[13] Certainly the theoretical controversy between Luxemburg and Lenin narrowed down considerably on concrete issues. Equally, Lenin's adoption of self-determination as a tactical weapon was never allowed to interfere with his unitary and centralist conception of party structure. At the same time, however, Lenin's treatment of the national question located it firmly in the political domain (for it 'belongs wholly and exclusively to the sphere of political democracy') and this acknowledgment of the relative autonomy of politics was an important part of Lenin's enduring contribution to Marxism. Yet his specific legacy on the national question was pragmatism — the need for correct revolutionary judgements in concrete cases. Lenin himself displayed this approach until the very end of his life; and his famous 'last struggle' had the national question at its centre, as he criticized Stalin's treatment of the Georgians and warned against a nationality policy rooted in Great Russian chauvinism. After Lenin's death, however, the fate of the revolution in Russia meant that 'the Leninist view of the national question was hypostatized, and treated as a largely ritual formula for consecrating judgements convenient to Moscow'.[14]

FROM THEORY TO PRACTICE

It is evident from this brief survey of the major contours within classical Marxist thought on the national question both that, by the time of Lenin's death in 1924, the issue had come to assume increasing importance for Marxism and also that no comprehensive theory had been developed. Leninist pragmatism left open the question of whether particular national movements should be supported. The Marxist attribution of nationalism to the bourgeoisie (a position duly fossilized by Stalin) was a Eurocentric approach, limited in time and space, that was ill-prepared to grapple with the social complexity of twentieth-century nationalism. Even within Europe it became clear that the question of the genesis of national states required a richer analysis than that provided by classical Marxism, though it was still possible to conclude that 'the growth and consolidation of the nation state is intimately connected, in all its phases, with the rise to power of the bourgeoisie'.[15] More generally, Marxism's reduction of nationalism to a function of class struggles, both traditionally and in the era of capitalist imperialism, linked to the expectation that national struggles and antagonisms would subside as socialism developed, hardly anticipated the variety or virulence of nationalism in the modern world. However, it might be pointed out that the theoretical deficiencies of Marxism in relation to nationalism have been amply matched by theorists of other persuasions.

The collapse of the Second International in 1914 effectively pricked one theoretical balloon, that of proletarian internationalism. 'Do you know what the proletariat is?' asked the French socialist leader Jaurès in July 1914: 'Masses of men who collectively love peace and abhor war'. Here was the summation of half a century of international socialist orthodoxy. Yet when war came nation triumphed over class. The German Social Democrats voted for war credits; the president of the International joined the Belgian government; and the 'Union sacrée' was consecrated in France. It was a traumatic moment for European socialism, with enduring consequences. An incredulous Lenin attacked the betrayal by reformist and opportunist leaders of their working classes, but the story was really one of 'their helplessness in the face of reality'.[16] Moreover, it is now possible to see the failure of the Second International as one episode in the general history of failure of organized socialist internationalism.[17] It may be recalled, for example, that the First International was initially convened, paradoxically, to express support for the Polish national movement; and even that the event that occasioned the disintegration of the International — the Paris Commune and its defeat — had a strong nationalist dimension (overlooked by Marx). The rhetoric of the Second International concealed an ingrained nationalism; and the organization was effectively dominated by one national party, the German Social Democrats. The Third International, formed by Lenin in the wake of the Russian Revolution to provide the headquarters staff for the forthcoming international revolution, was even more dominated by a single national party — and one that soon developed a nationalist ideology of its own. As for Trotsky's Fourth International, it was (and is) a theory in search of a movement.

All this points attention to 'one of the most striking paradoxes in the history of the Internationals'.[18] This is the fact that all the great social revolutionary upheavals of our time have taken place independently of, in the absence of, or even against, any existing international revolutionary organization. From Russia to China, from Cuba to Vietnam, this has uniformly been the case. Such revolutions have not depended upon the existence of an international general staff; and their success has always been linked to their ability to fuse with national movements (even in Russia, where it was the great national defensive struggles of 1919 and 1941 against foreign intervention that were crucial in mobilizing mass support for the regime). When combined with the evidence about the greater strength of national identity over that of class, certainly at moments of national crisis, there has seemed ample reason to revise both the theory and practice of socialist internationalism. It has also seemed necessary to incorporate the fact that in many modern revolutionary situations there is no significant working class at all, as well as the fact that many sections of the working class are not socialist. It is hardly surprising, therefore, to find a contemporary Marxist writer on nationalism declaring that: 'it is time to drop altogether the idea that the "international working class" will bring about the revolution'.[19]

The debacle of 1914 also threw much light on the real nature of European socialism. Behind the Marxist rhetoric there had developed a socialism that was both national and reformist. Little wonder, then, that Rosa Luxemburg regarded 1914 as the end of an illusion. The European Marxist establishment had been dismissive about the sort of reformism represented by British socialism of course. British Marxism, notably in the shape of Hyndman, was heavily imbued with nationalism; the Fabians embraced imperialism and flirted with racism; Blatchford's *Merrie England,* British socialism's best seller, was openly chauvinistic; and even Keir Hardie's legendary internationalism 'stemmed from belief in the value of co-operation between national labour movements and not from either a deep sentiment in favour of the brotherhood of man or from the doctrine that the workers have no country'.[20] Yet British socialism was the authentic product of a particular, national, historical experience and struck deep roots in the working class because of that. Moreover, its commitment was to 'state' as well as to 'nation', for it saw a democratic state as the key agency for the achievement of socialism. Its belief in 'nationalization' thus well summarized its philosophy on the matter. On the continent, Bernstein's 'revision' of Marxism also carried with it an explicit embrace of state and nation, for in his view the extension of political rights had turned workers into citizens by the last quarter of the nineteenth century, giving them a stake in the national 'property' and thus good reason to defend it. Bernstein's revisionism occasioned some virulent polemics and a closing of orthodox Marxist ranks, but his claim to have only described at the theoretical level what was already the socialist pratice seemed vindicated from the vantage point of 1914. Had not Jaurès asserted the proletariat's membership of the *patrie* and the inseparability of the national and socialist ideals? Had not the leaders of German socialism like Bebel announced their loyalty to the fatherland and compatibility of national and class interests? In a more general sense, was it not clear that the German Social Democratic Party had become integrated into the German state? Even more generally, were not the socialist parties revealed as the essentially national products of the pre-existing national states in which they had grown and developed? It was indeed the end of an illusion, producing the historic rupture within international socialism.

As for 'democratic socialism', it has continued to earn Marxist wrath for its embrace of state and nation, and its recourse to a 'national' socialism reflected in Orwell's impish judgement that 'no real revolutionary has ever been an internationalist'.[21] Hence, for example, Nairn's powerful polemic against the British Labour Party (in the context of the debate about the Common Market) for being 'national to the core' and having presided over 'the nationalization of class'.[22] However, it might also be remembered that many anti-war democratic socialists went to prison in 1914 while many Marxist internationalists went to war; that Orwell's life and work did represent a conspicuously honest and courageous engagement with socialism on an international terrain; and that many democratic socialists (those 'social fascists' of Comintern demonology) did have a surer grasp of fascist 'national socialism' than those schematic Marxist internationalists who were content to regard it as the death agony of capitalism.

If the experience of 1914 pricked one theoretical balloon, then the experience of 1917 and its aftermath punctured several others. As 'defeat of the fatherland' was replaced by 'defense of the fatherland', as international revolution shrivelled into 'socialism in one country', events in Russia further illuminated the developing relationship between socialism and the nation. The failure of the Russian 'spark' to ignite an international conflagration undermined the theoretical foundations of the Bolshevik revolution and threw it back on its own resources, with consequences relevant to the concern of this essay. Some of these may be mentioned briefly. One immediate issue was the practical application of 'self-determination' in the multinational Soviet state. At a theoretical level, Stalin soon transmuted the slogan into the self-determination of the proletariat, while the practical need to save the revolution, rather than any application of Leninist theory, determined the handling of the nationality question. In the event, secession took place only where it could not be prevented (in Poland, Finland and the Baltic states); while the formal recognition of national rights and autonomy of the constituent republics was overlaid by the monolithic centralism of the party. Incipient nationalism and demands for party federalism (as in the 'muslim socialism' of Sultan-Galiev) were suppressed. The early warnings about Great Russian chauvinism were replaced by denunciations of local nationalisms. In the 1930s Stalin played the nationalist card in earnest, with all its invocations of Russian history and its policy of forced Russification. When, after 1945, communist governments were established in Eastern Europe, the ideology of the unitary nation was extended into the conception of the unitary *bloc,* culminating in Brezhnev's doctrine of 'limited sovereignty' in the context of the Soviet invasion of Czechoslavakia in 1968. Yet it is clear that communism has not solved its national problem; just as it is clear that, in terms of the reform movement in Eastern Europe, 'more "nationalism" and less "internationalism" is part of the reform'.[23]

The 'nationalization of socialism' in the Soviet Union has had other dimensions too. For example, it is relevant here to notice the way in which Stalin had 'stumbled on a major discovery'[24] in his forced march of the Soviet economy and social order. The discovery — novel enough in Marxist terms — was of the capacity of the state machine (and of the political sphere generally) to make social change from above. This had immense implications for the status of the national state throughout the world, as well as raising important theoretical questions (further highlighted by fascism) about Marxism's treatment of the political 'superstructure'. The world's first party-state was to provide a powerful model for emulation and imitation. The Soviet state became national in another sense too. The failure of international revolution to take place in the wake of 1917 meant that the Soviet Union had to become a national state like any other, defining its territory and engaging in the business of international relations. Moreover, when the world's first socialist state was later joined by others, the whole problem of the relations between socialist states had to be accommodated to Marxist theory. Where these relations were antagonistic (as in the Sino-Soviet dispute) and reflected in opposing attitudes to independence struggles (as with Biafra and Bangla Desh), this problem became even more acute. As H. B. Davis writes, 'when the Chinese workers consider that the Russian workers are their principal enemies, it is surely time to reappraise the early blind faith in proletarian internationalism'.[25]

Indeed, there was good reason to reappraise such faith in proletarian internationalism much earlier in view of the way in which it was interpreted by the Soviet state. As the vanguard socialist state, the Soviet Union claimed an international allegiance as the fatherland of workers everywhere. It formed and dominated the Third International, with the result that national communist parties were merely outposts of Moscow (hence Léon Blum's description of the French Communist Party as 'un parti nationaliste étranger'). At the same time, Soviet foreign policy showed itself to be less interested in the application of principles of socialist internationalism than in the self-interest of the Soviet national state. The most telling demonstration of this was provided by the Nazi—Soviet pact, which thus represented the end of yet another illusion. Since 1945 the shell of socialist internationalism has been further cracked by Soviet armed intervention in Poland, Hungary and Czechoslovakia; by the rupture from Moscow of Yugoslavia and China (significantly, both regimes rooted in their own successful national struggles); and by the demonstrable nationalism of the foreign policies of the two leading (and rival) socialist states. It is against this background that the contemporary national assertiveness and embrace of domestic, national political traditions by the communist parties of Western Europe should be seen — 'even if as a first stage towards *their* variety of national communism they had to use a pseudo-internationalist figleaf like "Eurocommunism" '.[26]

To complete this brief account of some of the arenas in which nationalism and socialism have encountered each other, it is necessary to notice the crucial contemporary importance of the Third World. In this century (and especially since 1945) the centres of gravity of both nationalism and socialism have shifted away from their European base to Asia, Africa and Latin America; and in doing so the two ideologies have combined to produce 'a proliferation of Marxist nationalisms and highly nationalist Marxisms'.[27] Such a conjunction may seem surprising in terms of traditional Marxist theory, but it is rendered less surprising in view of the crucial role of the theory of imperialism in building a bridge between Marxism and modern nationalism. This bridge was originally constructed at the beginning of this century in the context of the imperial rivalries of the great European powers; and it was used (notably by the Austro-Marxist, Hilferding) to show how nationalism had become the ideology of capitalism in its imperialist phase. More significantly, however, the theory of capitalist imperialism was used by Lenin to suggest a process of uneven development in the world economy that had the effect of generating movements of resistance and emulation in the exploited countries, thus giving these countries a decisive role in the international class struggle. In this way Lenin managed to link nationalism and socialism through 'the dialectics of backwardness'.[28] This is not the place to explore the Marxist theory (or theories) of imperialism,[29] but it is necessary to understand just how important this developing theoretical tradition has been in facilitating an ideological and practical accommodation between socialism and nationalism.

The effects of this accommodation are now part of the history of our times. The rollcall of victorious 'national communisms' (China,

Cuba, Yugoslavia, Algeria, Vietnam, Angola, Mozambique, Somalia . . .) is long and impressive. Its hybrid ideology has enabled a popular mobilization against colonialism and dependency, with nationalism contributing its accessible appeal to socialism's materialist explanations and organizational *élan*. However, despite the mediating role of the theory of imperialism, this has also entailed a considerable revision (even dissolution) of traditional Marxist categories. As 'class' has fused with 'people', diverse social movements have equipped themselves with motley ideologies for national wars with alien imperialisms. It often seems that Marxism has been nationalized down into national populism, spawning the ideological assortment of Maoism, Castroism, African socialism and all the rest. Some theorists of socialist nationalism (such as Fanon and Cabral) have explicitly discarded Marxism as part of their wider rejection of the Western cultural tradition. 'We looked for the working class', wrote Cabral, 'and did not find it.' When this type of revolutionary nationalism is integrated into a contemporary theory of imperialism, it can provoke the despair of an exponent of classical Marxism:

> thus nationalism is identified with socialism, the peasantry with the proletariat, anti-imperialism with anti-capitalism, until all the distinctions painfully elaborated in Marxist literature for a century are cast overboard in favour of a simple dichotomy: Western imperialism versus the starving masses of the Third World.[30]

However, this may of course tell us as much about the relevance of Marxism's painful distinctions as it does about the nature of the relationship between socialism and nationalism in contemporary struggles around the globe.

NATION, STATE AND SOCIALISM

What, finally, may be safely concluded on the matter of socialism and the national question? Perhaps only that both theoretically and practically the relationship between socialism and nationalism has developed from cool hostility to warm liaison, even to proposals of marriage. This has presented few problems for a congenitally promiscuous nationalism, but it has been a source of increasing difficulty for a socialism anxious about its fidelity to its founding fathers. Indeed, the whole question has now become a major controversy within the socialist household.

The seriousness of this controversy is revealed by the recent work of Tom Nairn,[31] with its assertion that 'the theory of nationalism represents Marxism's great historical failure'. From within the Marxist tradition, Nairn mounts both a particular case for the role of neo-nationalism in breaking up an archaic British state and a general case for a revised Marxist understanding of the phenomenon of nationalism. Situating this general argument in a familiar analysis of capitalist uneven development, Nairn draws unfamiliar conclusions about the necessarily nationalist response to this process rather than a response in class terms: 'As capitalism spread, and smashed the ancient social formations surrounding it', writes Nairn, 'these always tended to fall apart along the fault-lines contained inside them. It is a matter of elementary truth that these lines of fissure were nearly always ones of nationality . . . They were never ones of class'. So the story is of an uneven development of the capitalist world economy producing disruption instead of diffusion, fragmentation instead of unity, nation instead of class. Marxism's failure to anticipate this process is seen as an expression of the limitations of the whole rational, optimistic and Eurocentric tradition to which classical Marxism belonged. Nairn's argument is rich and suggestive, even if ultimately it has to be regarded as evidence of the lack of a general Marxist theory of nationalism rather than the construction of such a theory (if only because of its difficulty in showing why the processes it describes should be mediated through nationalism and national statehoods, let alone why this should prove favourable to socialism). However, Nairn's work (like Hechter's on 'internal colonialism',[32] situated outside the Marxist tradition) reveals the accommodation between nationalism and socialism in the 'peripheral' movements within the heartland of capitalism no less than in its global periphery. It should, perhaps, be noted that Nairn has been duly rebuked by orthodox Marxism for his subordination of socialism to nationalism, for being a symptom of the sickness rather than its cure.[33]

Yet there are enough other voices to be heard within European Marxism on the side of an accommodation with nationalism to prevent such an easy dismissal. There is the insistence on the national state as the historical and spatial terrain of working-class struggle;[34] and there is even the suggestion that the national question represents the crucial gap in the whole Marxist system, so that:

> In this small gap, everything not said in Marxism is concentrated and crystallized. And when the unsaid is said, it explodes all the rest. In this sense . . . the nation is like the atomic nucleus in a general conflagration of Marxism as theory and socialism as practice.[35]

Even in England the works of cultural and social history by such figures as Raymond Williams and E. P. Thompson may be seen as a sort of rescue archaeology directed towards the discovery of a national popular tradition.

Debray's remarks on the general failure of Marxism revealed by its particular failure on the national question raise fundamental issues. These go beyond the familiar observations about Marxism's failure to make elementary distinctions (between nations, nationalities, nationalisms) in discussing the national question, or its historical and sociological errors in giving a particular account of the development of nationalism and imperialism.[36] More fundamentally, it is suggested that these specific deficiencies are an expression of an economic determinism that neglected the crucial determining role of the political realm and the political process; and that this is the arena in which nationalism has operated, with consequences central to the history of our time. Moreover, Marxism's theoretical failure in this respect may be directly linked to its political difficulty in comprehending the nature of such phenomena as fascism.[37]

One or two further reflections suggest themselves on the material reviewed in this essay. In the first place, the impact of class in the modern world did not operate upon a *tabula rasa,* but upon social formations already rooted in such basic units as family, religion and ethnicity. These units gained strength from their primacy and it was to be expected that social change would be mediated through them. Class did not act as a universal solvent and it was improbable that it would. The socialist movement confronted a world of nation-states in Western Europe and it seemed necessary to accommodate itself to this framework, while outside Europe it has accommodated itself to a diversity of social formations and their political expression. In the second place, socialism has had to come to terms with the durability of the state and the force of the demand for national statehood. In Western Europe the state, increasingly interventionist and regulatory, has become the prize pursued both by Marxists and social democrats (which helps to explain the fate of non-state versions of socialism). Elsewhere in the world the demand for statehood has been stimulated by the visible evidence of the modernizing and mobilizing potential of the state machine, as well as by the historical experience of the successful national states of Europe. In short, the national state — with its claims to sovereignty and independence — remains the central political reality of the contemporary world, notwithstanding those accounts of an internationalized economy dominated by multinational corporations that suggest its transcendence. Both 'nation' and 'state' have proved to be (*contra* Marx) more than transitional categories; and socialism has had to live with (and within) the resultant 'nation-state'.

Finally, what can socialism still contribute to the sane development of a world order now rooted in the potential destructiveness of national states? Much of this essay suggests a gloomy conclusion. Nationalism and socialism have dominated the history of the past century, yet it cannot be denied that nationalism has fared better in this encounter. There have been wars rather than social revolutions, national struggles rather than class struggles. Far from providing an effective alternative ideology to nationalism, socialism has had to 'nationalize' itself to buy political influence. Socialist internationalism has acquired a hollow ring after its uses and abuses in this century. Leninist pragmatism (despite its sensible recognition of the need for good judgement about an essentially Janus-faced phenomenon) has come to seem an inadequate response to the challenge of nationalism.

Yet there is, fortunately, another side to this picture, capable of relieving at least some of the gloom. Marx's vision of a 'global species community'[38] remains a challenging contribution to social thought and human imagination. Socialism still provides the materials for a rejection of national chauvinism and for an affirmation of wider loyalties, despite its ideological perversions in this century. If one of our tasks is to be the development of new forms of organization above the level of the nation-state, capable of handling the global problems of economic inequality, resource depletion and nuclear proliferation, then socialism would seem to be well placed to sustain this new supra-nationalism. At the same time, however, if another task is to be the development of new loyalties and forms of organization below the level of the nation-state, then socialism will have to revive some of its neglected traditions of pluralism and decentralization at the expense of the statism that has hitherto dominated the politics of both Marxism and social democracy. If socialism cannot effect such a dual transformation in the ordering of

the world (and perhaps it cannot), it seems unlikely that any other
theoretical tradition can. In that case the prospect for the human
condition is gloomy indeed.

NOTES AND REFERENCES

1. I. Deutscher 'On internationals and internationalism' in his *Marxism in Our Time* (Berkeley: Ramparts Press, 1971) pp. 110−111.
2. Cited in E. Cahm and V. C. Fisera (eds) *Socialism and Nationalism* (Nottingham: Spokesman, 1978) vol. I.
3. L. Kolakowski *Main Currents of Marxism* (Oxford: Oxford University Press, 1978) vol. II, p. 88.
4. A useful summary of these approaches is provided by M. Löwy 'Marxism and the national question' in R. Blackburn (ed.) *Revolution and Class Struggle* (London: Fontana, 1977).
5. For example, H. B. Davis *Nationalism and Socialism* (New York: Monthly Review Press, 1967); S. F. Bloom *The World of Nations* (New York: Columbia University Press, 1941, 1961); N. A. Martin 'Marxism, nationalism and Russia' *Journal of the History of Ideas, 29* (1968) pp. 231−52; J. A. Petrus 'Marx and Engels on the national question' *Journal of Politics, 33* (1971) pp. 797−824.
6. On this, see R. N. Berki 'On Marxian thought and the problem of international relations' *World Politics, 24* (1971) pp. 80−105.
7. A recent anthology is T. Bottomore and P. Goode (eds) *Austro-Marxism* (Oxford: Oxford University Press, 1978), from which the following quotations from Bauer are taken.
8. Kolakowski, *op. cit.,* p. 255.
9. J. P. Nettl *Rosa Luxemburg* (London: Oxford University Press, 1966) p. 862.
10. Löwy, *op. cit.,* p. 143.
11. Davis, *op. cit.,* p. 164.
12. A. G. Meyer *Leninism* (Cambridge, Mass.: Harvard University Press, 1957) p. 150.
13. Kolakowski, *op. cit.,* p. 401.
14. T. Nairn *The Break-up of Britain* (London: New Left Books, 1977) p. 85.
15. T. Bottomore *Political Sociology* (London: Hutchinson, 1979) p. 113. See V. G. Kiernan 'Nationalist movements and social classes' in A. D. Smith (ed.) *Nationalist Movements* (London: Macmillan, 1976).
16. G. Haupt *Socialism and the Great War* (London: Oxford University Press, 1972) p. 7.
17. Deutscher, *op. cit.,* and R. Debray 'Marxism and the national question' *New Left Review, 105* (1977).
18. Deutscher, *op. cit.,* p. 108.
19. H. B. Davis *Toward a Marxist Theory of Nationalism* (New York: Monthly Review Press, 1978) p. 245.

20. F. Reid *Keir Hardie* (London: Croom Helm, 1978) pp. 123—4.
21. G. Orwell *The Lion and the Unicorn: Socialism and the English Genius* (London: Secker and Warburg, 1941).
22. T. Nairn *The Left Against Europe?* (Harmondsworth, Middx: Penguin, 1973).
23. V. V. Kusin 'Socialism and nationalism' in L. Kolakowski and S. Hampshire (eds) *The Socialist Idea* (London: Quartet, 1977) p. 146.
24. G. Lichtheim *A Short History of Socialism* (London: Weidenfeld and Nicholson, 1970) p. 263.
25. Davis *Toward a Marxist Theory of Nationalism, op. cit.,* p. 52.
26. N. McInnes 'From Comintern to polycentrism: the first fifty years of West European communism' in P. F. della Torre, E. Mortimer and J. Story (eds) *Eurocommunism: Myth or Reality?* (Harmondsworth, Middx: Penguin, 1979) p. 61.
27. A. D Smith *Nationalism in the Twentieth Century* (Oxford: Martin Robertson, 1979) p. 115.
28. Meyer, *op. cit.,* Ch. 12.
29. See V. G. Kiernan *Marxism and Imperialism* (London: Edward Arnold, 1974); R. Owen and B. Sutcliffe (eds) *Studies in the Theory of Imperialism* (London: Longman, 1972); M. Barratt Brown *The Economics of Imperialism* (Harmondsworth, Middx: Penguin, 1974).
30. G. Lichtheim *Imperialism* (Harmondsworth, Middx: Penguin, 1974) p. 139.
31. Nairn, *op. cit.*
32. M. Hechter *Internal Colonialism* (London: Routledge and Kegan Paul, 1975).
33. E. Hobsbawn 'Some reflections on *'The Break-up of Britain'* New Left Review, 105* (1977).
34. N. Poulantzas *State, Power, Socialism* (London: New Left Books, 1978).
35. Debray, *op. cit.*
36. These criticisms are set out in A. D. Smith *Theories of Nationalism* (London: Duckworth, 1971), and in his 'Nationalism: a trend report and bibliography' *Current Sociology, 21* (1973).
37. This link is made, for example, by Isaiah Berlin *Against The Current* (London: Hogarth, 1979).
38. J. Dunn *Western Political Theory in the Face of the Future* (Cambridge: Cambridge University Press, 1979) p. 94.

FURTHER READING

Reference has been made in the text to some of the most accessible and relevant literature in English on this topic. The best sources for Marx's own observations on the national question are two volumes in the Penguin series of his *Political Writings:* these are Vol. 1, *The Revolutions of 1848* (Harmondsworth, Middx. 1973) and vol. 3, *The First International and After* (1974). A useful selection of Austro-Marxist literature on nationalism is contained in the anthology *Austro-Marxism* (ed. T. Bottomore and P. Goode; Oxford: Oxford University Press, 1978); and an important collection of Rosa Luxemburg's work in *The National Question: Selected Writings by Rosa Luxemburg* (edited and introduced by H. B. Davis; New York: Monthly Review Press, 1976). Most of Lenin's most important writings on the national question are to be found in Vols 20—23 of his *Collected Works,* and Stalin's in J. Stalin *Marxism and the National and Colonial Question* (London: Lawrence and Wishart, 1936). The standard account of Marx's thought in this area is S. F. Bloom *The World of Nations* (New York: Columbia University Press, 1941). That account now has to be supplemented by two works by H. B. Davis: these are *Nationalism and Socialism* (New York: Monthly Review Press, 1967), dealing with the pre-1917 period, and *Toward a Marxist Theory of Nationalism* (New York: Monthly Review Press, 1978), although this latter work — despite containing much useful material — hardly lives up to the promise of its title. Tom Nairn's analysis of *The Break-up of Britain* (London: New Left Books, 1977) is indispensable, although it might usefully be read in conjunction with Eric Hobsbawm's critique (*New Left Review, 105,* 1977). Finally, the collection of essays contained in *Socialism and Nationalism* (ed. E. Cahm and V. C. Fisera; Nottingham: Spokesman, 1978) provides some useful material, and two further volumes are promised from this same source.

8

Resisting the Nation-State: the Pacifist and Anarchist Traditions

Geoffrey Ostergaard

> The nation-state [writes A. D. Smith] is the norm of modern political organization . . . [I]t is the almost unquestioned foundation of world order, the main object of individual loyalties, the chief definer of a man's identity . . . It permeates our outlook so much that we hardly question its legitimacy today.[1]

To most readers Smith's generalizations may appear to be statements of the obvious. But it would be a mistake to suppose that the legitimacy of the nation-state has never been seriously questioned or even that it is not so questioned today. The strong tide that has flowed in the direction of the nation-state has been resisted from the start, and this essay looks at two traditions of political thought and action that have been 'against the current'.

The first, pacifism, may be seen as the ideology and movement that has resisted an institution closely related to the development of the nation-state; it challenges the right of the state to engage in, and conscript its citizens for, war. The nature of this challenge is exemplified in the statement issued by the No Conscription Fellowship, the British organization of Conscientious Objectors to military service in the First World War. Affirming their belief in the sacredness of human life, its members 'deny the right of Governments to say, "You shall bear arms". . . [T]hey will, whatever the consequences, obey their conscientious convictions rather than the commands of Governments.'[2]

The second, anarchism, is even more radical: it challenges not merely the nation-state's right to make war but also its very right to

171

exist. The central negative thrust of anarchism is directed against all the core elements that make up the nation-state: its territoriality with the accompanying notion of frontiers; its sovereignty, implying exclusive jurisdiction over all people and property within those frontiers; its monopolistic control of the major means of physical force by which it upholds that sovereignty, both internally and externally; its system of positive law, which overrides all other law and custom and which implies that rights exist only if sanctioned by the state; and, finally — the element that was added last — the idea of the nation as the paramount political community.

PACIFISM, PACIFICISM AND ANTI-MILITARISM

In discussing pacifism some clarification of terms is necessary. The word 'pacifist' was coined (as recently as 1901) to refer to all who oppose war and work to create or maintain peace between nations. This broad sense of the term is still current, but in Anglo-American usage 'pacifist' normally has the narrower meaning in which it refers to those whose opposition to war takes the form of refusing personally to take part in it or support it. Such persons, for reasons that will become clear, have also usually opposed all overt violence between human beings, though not necessarily covert violence, commonly called 'force', the kind used by police. 'Pacificist' is perhaps the more appropriate term to convey the broader meaning. Paci*fi*cists may support the use of military forces in 'peace-keeping' operations, whereas pacifists are generally 'anti-militarist'. However, not all anti-militarists are pacifists. Historically, anti-militarism is associated with the belief that most modern wars are fought in the interests of ruling classes, such as feudal lords or capitalists. In the late nineteenth and early twentieth centuries, before socialist parties controlled any states, many socialists were anti-militarists and some socialist leaders, such as Keir Hardie, were also pacifists. The socialist anti-militarist, if he were not a pacifist, might, when war broke out, join the army in the hope that thereby he could speed the downfall of capitalism, perhaps by spreading disaffection among the troops and persuading them, if a revolutionary situtation arose, to use their weapons against their class enemies. In practice, 'paci*fi*cism', 'pacifism' and 'anti-militarism' often overlap, but the terms do stand for fairly distinct orientations.

Sectarian origins of pacifism

The intellectual origins of Western pacifism are firmly rooted in the beliefs of religious sects. The first of these sects were the followers of Jesus who, in the Sermon on the Mount, preached a new message:

> Ye have heard that it hath been said, An eye for an eye, and a tooth for a tooth: But I say unto you, That ye resist not evil: but whosoever shall smite thee on thy right cheek, turn to him the other also . . . Love your enemies, bless them that curse you, do good to them that hate you, and pray for them that despitefully use you, and persecute you.[3]

These words express the doctrine of 'non-resistance to evil', and for nearly two centuries, while awaiting the Second Coming of Christ, his followers accepted the plain implications of the message. They refused military service while, otherwise, in St Paul's words, rendering unto Caesar his due. The eclipse of early Christian pacifism came with the conversion in 312 AD of Constantine who made Christianity the official religion of the Roman Empire. With the sect transformed into a church allied to the state, St Augustine enunciated a new doctrine: the *clergy* were to be totally dedicated to God and to live accordingly, but the *laity* were to fulfil the normal obligations of subjects. He also developed the doctrine of 'the just war', which later, in the thirteenth century, St Aquinas elaborated.

In the late middle ages several heretical sects, notably the Waldensians, the Cathari and the Czech Brethren of the Law of Christ, challenged the new orthodoxy and espoused pacifist ideas. But the real beginning of modern pacifism dates from the Reformation of the sixteenth century, which marked a victory for the nascent modern state over the Catholic Church. Unlike Luther, various radical supporters of the Reformation in Switzerland, Germany and the Netherlands, who came to be known as the Anabaptists, called for an unqualified return to the teachings of Jesus. In the 'Schleitheim Confession of Faith' (1527) they argued that it was not possible to reconcile the way of Christ with the way of the world. Until the coming of Christ's Kingdom, a true Christian must be a 'non-conformist'. The sword, symbolizing state power, was indeed ordained by God but 'ordained outside the perfection of Christ'. The secular political authorities formed part of the unregenerate world and existed only because people did not follow Christ's teachings and needed to be coerced. True Christians needed no coercion, should not coerce others, and should, as far as possible, effect 'a separation from the abomination'.[4]

Accordingly — except for one group who attempted by force to establish the Kingdom of God on earth in the city of Münster in 1534, and who, for their pains, were bloodily repressed — the Anabaptists abstained from politics, refused to bear arms or serve as policemen, refrained from lawsuits and the taking of oaths, and declined to recognize the existing laws of property. One group, the Hutterites, proceeded to establish communist communities, 150 of which continue to exist to this day in the USA and Canada.[5] Subjected to severe persecution for heresy, many other groups rallied under the leadership of Menno Simons (1496 — 1561), and it is as 'Mennonites' that they are now generally known.

The Anabaptist strategy of withdrawal from the unregenerate world was not followed by the Puritans who gathered round George Fox in the England of the 1650s to form the Society of Friends, or Quakers. They aimed to Christianize the world and to establish 'the realm of the saints'. Believing that God exists in every person, they stressed the importance of the Inner Light as the guide for living. After some initial uncertainty about the use of violence, in 1661 they issued the Declaration that became the basis of their 'peace testimony'. It stated firmly: 'All bloody Principles and practices we (as to our own particular) do utterly deny, with all outward wars and strife and fightings with outward weapons, for any end or under any pretext whatsoever . . . .'[6] Pacifism was only one of the peculiarities of the Quakers but it became their most distinguishing mark. It was in America, where some had gone in search of religious freedom, that Quakers were given the first opportunity to apply their principles in politics — 'the ˚Holy Experiment' in non-violent government in Pennsylvania, which lasted from 1662 to 1756.

Early in the eighteenth century, the radical wing of German Pietism gave birth to two new pacifist sects, the Dunkers and the Inspirationists, both of which emigrated to America. The Dunkers, now known as the Church of the Brethren, constitute one of the three 'historic peace churches' of the USA. They were followed later by the Shakers who, like the Hutterites, combined pacifism with voluntary communism. The pacifism of these sects was 'separational', not 'integrational' like that of the Quakers.[7] A rather different kind of pacifism — 'eschatological' — was displayed by several sects formed in the nineteenth century whose doctrines centre on a belief in the imminence of the Day of Judgment when the godless will be destroyed, after which Christ will reign as King over the faithful in the new world. These sects include the Plymouth Brethren, the Christadelphians, the Seventh Day Adventists, and Jehovah's Witnesses. Eschatological pacifism does not reject warfare as such. Wars may be seen as God's way of punishing the wicked and, while adherents should not take part in earthly wars, they may, when the time comes, take up arms in the final battle of Armageddon.

The pacifism of the sects has undergone attrition over the years. Thus, the majority of American Quakers and Brethren of military age served in the Second World War.[8] But, until the twentieth century, the pacifist ethic of Jesus was largely preserved by these fundamentalists. Christian pacifists are now represented in other churches. In the present century there has been a significant growth of pacifist sentiment among Methodists in Britain and Baptists in the USA and, more recently, among Catholics. The Fellowship of Reconciliation, founded in 1914, seeks to unite all who base their pacifism on Christian grounds.

Pacificism and the peace movement

From the sixteenth century onwards, it is also possible to trace the development of the broader pacif*i*cist tradition that focusses on changing modes of statecraft in order to reduce or eliminate war. Erasmus (1466 – 1536), although a theologian who formally accepted 'the just war' doctrine, roundly condemned war on humanitarian rather than on religious grounds. In the seventeenth and eighteenth centuries this line of thought led to a series of proposals to establish permanent peace between states through some form of international organization: the 'peace plans' of Crucé (1623), Penn (1693), Saint-Pierre (1713), Bentham (1789) and Kant (1795). The motivation of the last two was clearly secular, expressing the conviction shared by many *philosophers* of the Enlightenment that war was irrational and contradicted the ideal of human brotherhood.

Mainly through the efforts of individual Quakers, an organized peace movement came into being on both sides of the Atlantic immediately after the Napoleonic Wars. Its main thrust is indicated in the aims of the American Peace Society:

> to increase and promote the practice already begun of submitting national differences to amicable discussion and arbitration, and . . . of

settling all national controversies by an appeal to reason . . . . [T]his
shall be done by a Congress of Nations . . . . Then wars will cease.[9]

Throughout its chequered course, although it has usually had a
radical wing and pacifists have played a prominent part in it, the
peace movement has been predominantly moderate and liberal in
character. It has accepted the nation-state system but sought to make
it more rational. In the nineteenth century its liberal character was
strengthened by association with the Manchester School, represented
by Cobden and Bright, which held that the solution to the problem of
war lay through the promotion of free trade between nations. In the
twentieth century the paci*fi*cism of the peace movement has
contributed to the thinking that led to the League of Nations and the
United Nations, the Kellogg—Briand Pact of 1928 outlawing war,
and efforts to promote disarmament.

Conscription and the nation state

In one sense paci*fi*cism provides an alternative to the more
uncomfortable pacifism that demands personal witness against war.
After heresy hunting had abated with the growth of religious
toleration, pacifism certainly became a more difficult stance to
maintain as the concept of the *nation*-state developed. In the era of
state-building from the Reformation to the French Revolution, as
distinct from the subsequent era of the nation-state, wars were
fought mainly by professional armies, often composed largely of
mercenaries. There was no universal conscription for military service.
Instead, there was the militia system under which able-bodied men
could be mustered for military training and operations, usually on a
local basis and for limited periods. At the same time, legal privilege
for various communities and estates was a feature of political systems.
In this situation, governments tended to deal with their pacifist
subjects in an *ad hoc* way, applying the notion of legal privilege. In
some instances, as in Rhode Island in 1673, all whose consciences
forbade them to bear arms were exempted from militia service. In
other instances, exemption was given to specified sects, a procedure
adopted by the Empress Catherine in 1776 as an inducement to
Mennonites to settle in Russia. Sometimes exemption was granted in
return for payment of a military tax, or a pacifist called up for militia
service was permitted to provide a hired substitute. More commonly,
failure to perform the required military duties attracted a fine, and

failure to pay led to sequestration of property in lieu or a short jail sentence.

All this began to change when the state came to be seen as based on the nation. Subjects were transformed into citizens, all equal before the law, members of a single national community sharing in its benefits and burdens. One consequence was the introduction of compulsory military service for all adult males, usually in time of peace as well as war. Bayonets were thrust into the hands of citizens often before they were given the ballot. Service in defence of the nation came to be seen as a sacred civic duty and was sometimes explicitly linked to the definition of citizenship. Revolutionary France, 'the first nation in arms', paved the way in 1793. Prussia followed suit in 1808. Since then, compulsory military service has become the norm throughout the world. In 1966, only 7 of 140 states did not impose it.[10]

Conscription laws when first introduced usually made no provision for exempting pacifists. Those refusing military service were treated as deserters, imprisoned and sometimes shot. When conscription was introduced in Russia in 1874, the exemption granted to Mennonites 'in perpetuity' was withdrawn, leading thousands to emigrate to the USA. In 1875 the government relented and allowed them to serve in hospitals as an alternative, but the concession applied to no other sect. When in 1895 some 10,000 Doukhobors announced their refusal to bear arms, they were severely dealt with. Tolstoy then publicized their plight and funds were raised to enable the sect to emigrate to Canada.[11]

The CO formula

As a mode of accommodating pacifists within the nation-state, the 'conscientious objector' formula was gradually evolved and grudgingly applied. In effect, by this formula the state recognizes that pacifists are 'peculiar persons' who, in return for their recognizing the state's right to conscript its citizens for war, may be accorded a special status to which penalties are normally attached. In applying the formula, states have usually insisted that applicants show their objection arises out of religious belief and that they object to war in any form — the latter a condition that Jehovah's Witnesses, who also claim exemption as ministers, have found hard to meet. If applicants pass the tests, then they may be directed to perform either noncombatant service in the army or alternative civilian work 'of national importance'. The formula has resulted in dividing pacifists between 'absolutists' — those who refuse all compromise — and 'registrants' (and, among the latter, between those willing to accept noncombatant service and those willing to accept only alternative civilian service). It has also led to confusion between conscientious objection as a moral and as a legal category. From the state's point of view, absolutists are not COs but lawbreakers. It is, of course, absolutists who have posed the most direct challenge to the state's authority, and it is significant that draft evaders have usually been treated more leniently. Those pacifists, relatively few, who have accepted noncombatant service and the larger number who have accepted alternative civilian service seem often to have wished to show that, in every respect save willingness to kill at the state's behest, they were loyal citizens.

The statistics of conscientious objection during the two World Wars in Britain and the USA — the countries where pacifism has been strongest — show how much it has been a minority movement. In the First World War, the number of COs in Britain is estimated to have been 16,100, while in the USA there were 64,693 applications for noncombatant service.[12] In the Second World War, some 60,000 men and 1,000 women applied for CO registration in Britain, while in the USA the total number of COs is estimated to have been about 100,000 — the latter figure representing 0.3 per cent of the 34 million who registered for military service.[13] In both countries, the clash between conscience and the law was less dramatic in the Second than in the First World War, when absolutists were often harshly treated. In part, this reflected greater toleration of COs but also a greater willingness of COs to cooperate with the authorities — as did the historic peace churches in the USA who sponsored and managed Civilian Public Service camps for the 'alternativists'.

The CO formula has been liberalized since it was first adopted. Thus, in the USA the religious test has been dropped and ethical, as distinct from religious, objection recognized. The issue of 'selective objection', i.e. to particular wars, first raised by socialists in the First World War, became increasingly important in the context of the agitation against the Vietnam War in the 1960s,[14] which was marked also by the burning of draft cards and widespread draft evasion. But in most nation-states the issue is not liberalization of the formula. Rather, it is whether pacifists are recognized at all. Thus, in Russia, where at the turn of the century there were several million sectarian pacifists, officially there is now none, this being the Soviet government's explanation of why the Universal Military Service Law of 1939 contained no provision for COs. The Soviet Union, however, is not alone in this. In 1968 only 16 of 140 states had any such legal provision, although the number has increased slightly since then.

Conscientious objection to military service, whether recognized by the state or not, remains and is likely to remain an important aspect of pacifism. To refuse to bear arms links contemporary pacifists with their forebears and provides a clear expression of their witness to truth. But, as a policy for achieving peace, it has obvious limitations, and as a way of defining pacifism it has come increasingly to be seen by many pacifists as inadequate. The tendency to equate pacifism with conscientious objection was probably most marked in the inter-war years when intellectuals like Einstein argued that war could be prevented if a sufficiently large proportion of the male population pledged itself to refuse to fight. It was in line with this way of thinking that, in Britain, Canon Dick Sheppard founded the Peace Pledge Union, which, by 1939, had enrolled over 100,000 members, each of whom had signed the declaration: 'I renounce war and never again, directly or indirectly, will I support or sanction another.' By that date, however, the menace of fascism and sympathy for the Republican side of the Spanish Civil War had severely tested the consciences of many pacifists and Einstein was only one of a number of prominent leaders who felt compelled to renounce their pacifism.

As a moral stance, at least from the perspective of Christian ethics, pacifism is unassailable. But it can be argued that much pacifist and most pacif*ic*ist thought has been vitiated by a tendency to view war and, more generally, violence in a highly abstract way, divorced from the structures in which they are embedded. Until recently, pacifists have been slow to recognize that modern war is inherent in the system of sovereign nation-states, that war is the use of armed force by states and those who aspire to build or control states, and that war is not an aberration or sickness but, in Randolph Bourne's words, 'the health of the state'. Rousseau, who edited an edition of Saint-Pierre's peace plan, grasped clearly the central point: war is a function of the state and has its origins in 'the social compact' that gives rise to the state. 'If the social compact could be severed, at once there would be no more war. At a stroke the state would be killed, without a single man having to die.'[15] Rousseau did not think that the

social compact could be severed, but there have been those who
thought otherwise.

ANARCHISM

Anarchism as a social movement

One such was Pierre-Joseph Proudhon (1809 — 65), the first man to
use the term 'anarchy' as the defiant, but literal, description of his
ideal of a society without government. The classical anarchist
movement, which he initially inspired and which was further
developed by Michael Bakunin (1814 — 76) and Peter Kropotkin
(1842 — 1921), formed an integral, if contentious, part of the wider
socialist movement from the 1840s to 1939. Classical anarchism can
also be seen as at the centre of one of three broad schools of socialist
thought, distinguished by their attitude to the state: libertarian
socialism, Marxian communism, and social democracy. Whereas the
control of state power is central, in different ways, to the strategy of
the last two, libertarian socialism seeks to achieve its goals by direct
voluntary action of the people themselves. Its thrust is either non-
statist or anti-statist, and the action may be wholly peaceful or
sometimes violent. Historically, in both Britain and France, libertarian socialism was the first to emerge. Thus, the first British
socialists, inspired by Robert Owen (1771 — 1858), sought to
establish by peaceful voluntary action a 'new moral world' that
would completely replace competitive capitalism. They envisaged a
worldwide system — one of Owen's organizations was grandly
called The Association of All Classes of All Nations — made up of
small-scale, self-sufficient communist communities, loosely linked
together for purposes of mutual aid and exchange of surpluses. In the
process of establishing this system, the 'old, immoral world' with its
antagonisms, states and wars, would be sloughed off. In France, the
followers of Fourier shared a similar vision. This kind of communitarian socialism later found substantial expression in nineteenth-
century America and in the Israeli kibbutzim, and has surfaced again
in the recent commune movement. From Owenite socialism also
developed the modern co-operative movement, which, throughout
the nineteenth century, sought to build the Co-operative Common-

wealth. In the twentieth century, lowering its sights and usually in alliance with social democracy, it has settled for the voluntary socialization of a sector of the national economy.

Proudhon's socialism, called mutualism, was essentially co-operative in character, envisaging workers and peasants, either individually or in groups, organizing production in their own workshops and fields, financed by free credit from a people's bank. But, unlike Owen and Fourier, he did not ignore the state. Rather, he insisted that the proletariat could not emancipate itself through the use of state power. Bakunin, who emerged as Marx's main rival in the First International (1864—72), made the point more forcibly:

> I am not a communist, because communism concentrates and swallows up in itself for the benefit of the State all the forces of society. I want the abolition of the State . . . . I want to see collective or social property organized from below upwards, not from above downwards, by means of any kind of authority whatever . . . .'[16]

In its Bakuninist phase, the anarchist movement favoured a revolutionary strategy in which the oppressed classes, peasants as well as industrial workers, would rise in popular insurrections, expropriate the means of production and abolish the state. Kropotkin, who developed the theory of anarchist—communism, also favoured this strategy. In place of the state would emerge the autonomous commune, federally linked with other communes at regional, national and international levels. The uprising of the Paris Commune of 1871 approximated to this anarchist model of revolution. Its crushing strengthened the tendency towards state socialism, whether of the Marxist or social democratic variety. It also led some anarchists to adopt the tactic of 'propaganda by the deed' — acts of assassination of political leaders and terrorism of the bourgeoisie — intended to encourage popular insurrections. 'The dark angels' of anarchism who performed these acts are largely responsible for the popular but misleading stereotype of the anarchist.

The consequent repression of the movement led other anarchists to develop an alternative syndicalist strategy. The idea was to turn trade unions into revolutionary instruments of class struggle and to make them, rather than communes, the basic units of a socialist order. The revolution would take the form of a General Strike in the course of which the unions would take over the means of production and abolish the state. In place of sovereign, territorial nation-states, there would be 'industrial republics' organized on functional lines with sovereignty divided between unions and federations of unions at all levels. It was through syndicalism that anarchism exercised its greatest influence on labour and socialist movements in Europe and the USA in the period 1890 – 1920. The influence lasted longer in Spain where, during the Civil War (1936 – 39), the anarcho-syndicalists, with some short-lived success, attempted to carry through their conception of revolution.

Anarchism as a tradition of political thought

Considered as a tradition of political thought, however, anarchism is more complex than its manifestation in the classical anarchist movement might suggest. From this perspective, anarchism appears to be as closely related to liberalism as it is to socialism. Indeed, one form, individualist anarchism, may be seen as liberalism taken to its extreme — some would say, logical — conclusion. Individualist, as distinct from socialist, anarchism has been particularly strong in the USA from the time of Josiah Warren (1798 – 1874) onwards, and is expressed today by Murray Rothbard and the school of 'anarcho-capitalists'. Individualist anarchism emphasizes individual liberty, conscience, individuality and the uniqueness of each person — the latter brilliantly expressed by Max Stirner (1805 – 56) in *The Ego and His Own*. Often, as with William Godwin (1756 – 1836), it leads to a distrust of any kind of enduring cooperation with others, such relations constraining the exercise of what Godwin called the individual's 'private judgment'. In their economic ideas, individualists have usually insisted on the importance of individual production, private property or possession, praised the free market and condemned the iniquity of all monopolies. Their central political principle is 'the sovereignty of the individual'. Taken seriously, this principle is sufficient to explain their rejection of the state and of any government other than 'voluntary government' based on the consent of each and every individual. Their vision is vividly expressed in Shelley's poetic translation of Godwin's philosophy in *Prometheus Unbound*:

> The loathsome mask has fallen, but man remains
> Sceptreless, free, uncircumscribed, but man
> Equal, unclassed, tribeless and nationless,
> Exempt from awe, worship, degree, the king
> Over himself; just, gentle, wise . . .

However, the differences between individualist and socialist anarchism, though important, should not be exaggerated. The economic proposals of most individualists are intended to secure to each person the fruits of his or her own labour, not the accumulation of possessions through the exploitation of the labour of others. On the other hand, even anarcho-communists are imbued with a strong sense of individuality. And both types of anarchism rest firmly on liberal intellectual foundations.

Society and the state

Fundamental in liberal thought is the distinction between society and the state, which, in turn, is related to the distinction made by ancient Greek philosophers between nature and convention. The distinction is expressed by John Locke (1632–1704), the key figure in modern liberalism, in a contrast between 'the State of Nature' and 'civil' or 'political' society. In the state of nature all Men are free and equal, and no one has authority to command the obedience of others. But the state of nature is not, as Hobbes had argued, a lawless condition of strife; it does constitute a society, since it is regulated by natural law from which derive Men's natural rights. Nevertheless, 'inconveniences', principally the absence of a common judge when disputes arise, do exist; and these lead Men by way of a social contract to set up political societies. In this view, the state is an artificial or conventional device with the strictly limited negative function of safeguarding Men's natural rights. Despotism, Locke insists, is worse than 'the natural condition of mankind'.

Locke's notion that a natural order exists independently of the state provides a theoretical underpinning of the classical liberal defence of laissez-faire and limited government. In *The Rights of Man* (1792) Tom Paine elaborates the notion:

> Great part of that order which reigns among mankind is not the effect of government. It has its origins in the principles of society and the natural constitution of men. It existed prior to government and would exist if the formality of government was abolished. The mutual dependence and reciprocal interest which man has upon man, and all the parts of civilized community upon each other, create that great chain of connexion which holds it together. The landholder, the farmer, the manufacturer, the merchant, the tradesman, and every occupation, prospers by the aid which each receives from the other, and from the

whole. Common interest regulates their concerns and forms their law; and the laws which common usage ordains, have a greater influence than the laws of government.[17]

From Paine's position it is but a short step to Godwin's conclusion in *Political Justice* (1793)[18] that government — deemed by Paine 'a necessary evil' — can be dispensed with. The step is reached by postulating 'the perfectibility of Man', by which Godwin meant, not that Men are perfect or will ever become so, but that they are capable of indefinite moral improvement.

Political Justice is rightly deemed the first systematic exposition of anarchism. But, interestingly, its main conclusion was anticipated in an early, allegedly satirical, work of Edmund Burke, *The Vindication of Natural Society* (1756).[19] Its title splendidly expresses the positive thrust of anarchism and the book introduces several themes taken up by anarchists: the close association between war and the state; the division of mankind into separate states as a major source of hatred and dissension; the inhumanity that flows from national prejudices; the despotic nature of all forms of government; the function of positive law in protecting the rich and the powerful against the poor and the oppressed; and the Machiavellian nature of all statecraft. Burke also poses the great anarchist question: who will guard the guardians themselves? — the question that prompted William Morris later to declare: 'No man is good enough to be another man's master.'

The idea of natural society runs like a golden thread through all anarchist thought. That mankind has always lived in society, is naturally social and sociable, and is endowed with all the attributes necessary to live harmoniously without political regulation is the basic premise of anarchism. The idea is most fully elaborated in Kropotkin's *Mutual Aid* (1902).[20] In another work, *Modern Science and Anarchism* (1913), he describes the anarchist concept of society thus:

> a society in which all the mutual relations of its members are regulated, not by laws, not by authorities, whether self-imposed or elected, but by mutual arrangements between the members of that society, and by a sum of social customs and habits — not petrified by law, routine, or superstition, but continually developing and continually readjusted, in accordance with the ever-growing requirements of a free life . . . No government of man by man; no crystallization and immobility, but a continual evolution — such as we see in Nature.[21]

The phrasing suggests a vision of the future, but Kropotkin makes clear that such a society *in some degree* already exists. The point is vividly made by Colin Ward in *Anarchy in Action* (1973):

> an anarchist society . . . which organizes itself without authority, is always in existence like a seed beneath the snow, buried under the weight of the state and its bureaucracy, capitalism and its waste, privilege and its injustices, nationalism and its suicidal loyalties, religious differences and their superstitious separatism . . . Far from being a speculative vision of a future society, it is a description of a mode of organization, rooted in the experience of everyday life, which operates side by side with, and in spite of, the dominant authoritarian trends of our society.[22]

The anarchist view of the state

Natural society provides the starting point for the anarchist view of the state. For all anarchists, the essence of the state is coercive power — 'organized violence'. Again, it is Kropotkin who provides the best analysis.[23] For him, as for Herder, the state must be explained historically but cannot be justified morally. Distinguishing between state and government — terms often used interchangeably by many anarchists and others — he suggests that 'The State not only includes a power placed above society, but also a territorial concentration and a concentration of many or even all functions of the life of society in the hands of a few.'[24] In this sense, the state is a form of organization that has developed at various times in history. The general pattern of development has been from the tribe — the first form of human society — to the more or less autonomous village commune, based on communal possession of land; then came the free cities,` and finally the state. For Kropotkin, the empires of the ancient world represented the statist phase of separate movements towards civilization in different regions of the world; and each time the phase ended disastrously in collapse of the civilization. In Europe, on the ruins of the Roman Empire, civilization began anew. Barbarian tribes slowly elaborated their institutions and the village commune was developed. European civilization remained at this stage until the twelfth century when rose 'the Republican cities which produced the glorious expansion of the human mind, attested by the monuments of architecture, the grand development of the arts, the discoveries that laid the basis of natural sciences.'[25] Then, in the sixteenth century, the modern state began to develop, destroying in the process the village commune and free federations of cities, such as the Hanseatic

League. At the centre of state-building was the monarch and, around the throne, soldier—lords, lawyers and priests formed a 'triple alliance' to dominate society in the alleged interests of society. This alliance, joined later by the capitalists, proceeded to centralize power, destroying traditional bonds of union among people, obstructing the development of local initiative, crushing existing liberties, and preventing their restoration. The advent of democracy, symbolized by the theoretical relocations of sovereignty from the person of the monarch to the people as a whole, had not halted this trend. On the contrary, centralization had been enhanced by the insistence of modern radicals — from the Jacobins to the state socialists — that only the state can redress the grievances of its subjects. Thus universal suffrage had proved to be what Proudhon had foreseen — the great instrument of counter-revolution. The masses had been persuaded to cooperate in the building of their own prison.

The analysis brings out one difference between liberals and anarchists. While liberals believe in some kind of balance between state and society, anarchists believe that no such balance can be maintained and that the logic of the state, unless resisted, leads to the complete domination of society by the state — to what later writers have called 'the total state' (of which 'the totalitarian state' is simply the most extreme, or pathological, form). Kropotkin's idea that the statist phases of past civilizations have ended disastrously is also suggestive now that, eighty years on, superstates have armed themselves with H-bombs and other weapons of mass destruction.

The anarchist view of the nation and of nationalism

But missing from the analysis are the concepts of the nation and nationalism. In part, this reflects the basic cosmopolitan outlook of anarchism. Natural society is first and foremost a condition of *mankind*, and anarchists, like the ancient Stoics, see themselves primarily as 'citizens of the world'. As such, anarchists have vigorously attacked what Godwin called 'the deceitful principle' of patriotism and have been the staunchest proponents of internationalism or, more strictly, transnationalism.[26] But, living as they did in the century of European nationalism, Proudhon, Bakunin and Kropotkin all addressed themselves seriously to the questions raised by it. In general, they supported national liberation struggles as part of the wider struggle for freedom but opposed the statist aspirations of the nationalists. Thus, Bakunin argued that nationality is 'a natural fact' and each nationality has 'an incontestable right to free existence and development'; but because it lacks 'the power of universality' and is exclusionist in tendency, nationality cannot be accepted as a political principle.[27] Organizing themselves from below upwards, on the federal and functional lines suggested by Proudhon, the masses would decide for themselves any divisions between nationalities; and he was confident that the proletariat, unlike the bourgeoisie, would recognize none of the frontiers associated with the claims of states.

But it is Rudolf Rocker (1873–1958) who, in *Nationalism and Culture* (1937), provides the fullest anarchist discussion of nationalism. To Rocker it is clear that 'The nation is not the cause, but the result of the state. It is the state which creates the nation and not the nation the state.'[28] This assertion becomes more plausible when he proceeds to distinguish between a 'people' — what Proudhon had called a 'folk-group' — and a 'nation'.

> A people is the natural result of social union, a mutual association of men brought about by a certain similarity of external conditions of living, a common language, and special characteristics due to climate and geographic environment. In this manner arise certain common traits, alive in every member of the union and forming a most important part of its social existence. The nation, on the other hand, is the artificial struggle for political power, just as nationalism has never been anything but the political religion of the modern state. Belonging to a nation is never determined, as is belonging to a people, by profound natural causes; it is always subject to political considerations and based on those reasons of state behind which the interests of privileged minorities always reside.

And in a passage relevant to the manifestation in recent years of both 'sub-nationalism' and the nascent 'supra-nationalism' of some ideologists of the EEC, Rocker insists:

> A people is always a community with narrow boundaries. But a nation, as a rule, encompasses a whole array of different peoples and groups of peoples who have by more or less violent means been pressed into the frame of a common state ... National states [he concludes] are political church organizations ... All nationalism is reactionary in nature, for it strives to enforce on the separate parts of the great human family a definite character according to a preconceived idea ... Nationalism creates artificial separations and partitions within that organic unity which finds its expression in the genus Man ...

Anarchism and violence

The concept of natural society also helps to explain the ambiguous and ambivalent attitude towards violence in the anarchist tradition.[29] The state seen as 'organized violence' is the antithesis of natural society, and it would seem logical, therefore, that anarchists should reject all violence. Many anarchists, particularly individualists and those adopting a cooperative or communitarian approach, have drawn this conclusion. But most mainstream anarchists from Bakunin onwards have not. With rare exceptions, such as Kropotkin who supported the Allies in the First World War, they have opposed all wars between states and taken a leading part in anti-militarist agitations; but they have not rejected violence in principle and, on occasions, have participated in civil wars (in Russia and Spain) and even raised anarchist armies, as well as joined insurrections and conducted 'propaganda by the deed'. In part, this may be explained by their association with the revolutionary socialist movement, which took as a truism Marx's dictum that 'Force is the midwife of all revolutions'. But, in part also, anarchist violence is related to the concept of natural society itself. When violence is directed towards the destruction of the state, or when, in a revolutionary situation where central government has broken down, it is used to prevent the establishment of a new government, it can be seen as fulfilling an essentially liberatory role. Natural society then is not being betrayed but, on the contrary, forcibly vindicated.

The ambivalent attitude towards violence of mainstream anarchists was one reason why anarchism and pacifism developed as separate movements in the nineteenth century, despite their common opposition to war and militarism and their shared historical roots. (Kropotkin, not implausibly, claimed the Anabaptists among the precursors of modern anarchism.) But it was not the only reason. Most anarchists were militant atheists, even anti-theists: 'If God really existed, it would be necessary to abolish him!', declared Bakunin. Church was coupled with state, and religion was seen as part of the fraud that, along with force, ruling classes used to maintain their dominance. In addition, most anarchists saw the peace movement as irredeemably bourgeois and liberal, weak in its analysis of the causes of war and absurdly naive in seeking to establish international peace while wishing at the same time to retain the state.[30]

These are some of the reasons why, when Christian anarchism emerged, it was either not seen as anarchism or its adherents rejected the anarchist label. But what could be more anarchist than the Declaration of Principles of the New England Nonresistance Society, founded by William Lloyd Garrison and Adin Ballou in 1828: 'We cannot acknowledge allegiance to any human government; neither can we oppose any such government by a resort to physical force . . . Our country is the world, our countrymen are all mankind.'?[31] This kind of anarchism started, not from an analysis of society and the state but from the doctrine of non-resistance expounded in the Sermon on the Mount. The implications of the doctrine were spelled out with even greater clarity, vigour and effect by Leo Tolstoy (1828 – 1910) in *The Kingdom of God is Within You* (1893)[32] and other 'peace essays' that flowed from his prolific pen.

CONVERGENCE OF PACIFISM AND ANARCHISM

The development of Christian anarchism presaged the increasing convergence (but not, it must be emphasized, the complete merging) of pacifism and anarchism in the twentieth century. The outcome is the school of thought and action — one of its tenets is developing thought through action — known variously as 'pacifist anarchism', 'anarcho-pacifism' or 'nonviolent anarchism'. Experience of the two World Wars encouraged the convergence. But, undoubtedly, the most important single event to do so (although the response of both pacifists and anarchists to it was curiously delayed) was the dropping of the atomic bomb on Hiroshima on 6 August 1945. Ending as it did five years of 'total war', it symbolized dramatically the nature of the modern Moloch that Man has erected in the shape of the state. In the campaign against nuclear weapons in the 1950s and early 1960s, more particularly in the radical wings of it — such as the Committee of 100 in Britain, pacifists and anarchists educated each other.

The single most important intellectual influence helping to shape anarcho-pacifism is that of M. K. Gandhi (1869 – 1948), who began his career as a disciple of Tolstoy. Tolstoy's great weapon for undermining (rather than overthrowing) the state was the refusal by individuals to cooperate with it and obey its immoral demands — the weapon defended by Thoreau in his classic essay on 'Civil Disobedience' (1849)[33] and the one used by pacifist COs. But Gandhi, in the course of the movement for Indian national liberation, showed that there is a whole range of weapons, collective as well as individual, in the armoury of those who are prepared non-violently to resist oppressive structures. In doing so, he shifted the emphasis from passive non-resistance to active non-violent resistance. He also emphasized the theory of power underlying their use: the theory of 'voluntary servitude', originally outlined by Etienne de la Boétie in 1548, namely that structures of power, even when they seem to rely on physical force, depend in the last analysis on the cooperation, however reluctant, of those over whom power is exercised. Further, Gandhi clarified the relationship between means and ends, particularly with reference to the use of violence. Means, he insisted, must not merely be consistent with ends. This principle, though preferable to the Machiavellian principle that 'the end justifies the means', perpetuates a misleading dichotomy. Means *are* ends, never merely instrumental but also always expressive of values; means are end-creating or ends-in-the-making. One implication of this view is that we can, in a sense, forget what are called 'ends' and focus on 'means', confident in the knowledge that if the 'means' are pure then the desired 'ends' will follow. Another is that our conceptions of desirable futures, our 'utopias', are only mental constructs for guiding our actions *here and now*. We realize our utopias, insofar as they are realizable at all, by acting now *as if* utopia had already arrived. Lastly, Gandhi sought to revolutionize revolutionary thought by developing the concept of non-violent revolution, to be seen, not as a programme for the seizure of power but as a programme for transforming relationships. The concept sits neatly with the observation of the German anarchist, Gustav Landauer (1870 – 1919): 'The state is a condition, a certain relationship between human beings, a mode of behaviour; we destroy it by contracting other relationships, by behaving differently.'

Gandhi's ideas were popularized in the West in books such as Richard Gregg's *The Power of Nonviolence* (1935)[34] and Bart de Ligt's *The Conquest of Violence* (1937).[35] The latter is particularly important for anarchists since, as one himself, de Ligt specifically addressed those who lust for revolution. 'The more violence, the less revolution', he declared. He also linked Gandhian principled non-violence with the pragmatic non-violent direct action of the syndicalists. (The General Strike is an expression of total non-cooperation by workers — though it should be added that most syndicalists believed that the revolution should be defended by armed workers.)

In the 1950s and 1960s anarcho-pacifism began to gel, tough-minded anarchists adding to the mixture their critique of the state, and tender-minded pacifists their critique of violence. Its first practical manifestation was at the level of method: non-violent direct action, principled and pragmatic, was widely used in both the civil rights movement in the USA and the campaign against nuclear weapons in Britain and elsewhere. These two movements provided part of the matrix for an emergent New Left, a transnational movement whose mainly youthful constituents moved across frontiers, mentally and often physically, in a way reminiscent of Bakunin in his prime. It soon became clear that what was 'new' about the New Left — hardly surprising since it was triggered by disillusionment among socialists with both Marxian communism (Stalinist variety) and social democracy — was in large part a rediscovery and reassertion of libertarian socialism, which had been submerged for over a generation. In its first decade, several themes, theories and actions, all distinctly libertarian, began to come to the fore and were given intellectual expression by the American anarcho-pacifist, Paul Goodman (1911–72):[36] anti-militarism, the rediscovery of com-munity, community action, radical decentralism, participatory democracy, the organization of the poor and oppressed inter-racially, and the building of counter-culture and counter-institutions (such as new co-ops, collectives and communes). For a brief moment it looked, at least to anarcho-pacifists, as though these might be woven into a grand strategy for non-violent revolution. Then, from 1967, for reasons explored by Nigel Young,[37] the movement (really 'a movement of movements') experienced a failure of nerve. The prospect (or dream) vanished, and by the early 1970s the New Left had disintegrated, the end being marked by, among other things, the bombings carried out by the New Left's 'dark angels', the Weathermen and the Angry Brigade.

The collapse of the New Left coincided with the exhaustion of the less well-publicized *Sarvodaya* (welfare of all) movement for non-violent revolution in India, led by Vinoba Bhave (1895–) and Jayaprakash Narayan (1902–79), which had sought through voluntary villagization of land to realize Gandhi's dream of an India of village republics. The implication of *Sarvodaya* for the nation-state is brought out by the statement of Jayaprakash Narayan: 'In a

Sarvodaya world society the present nation-states have no place.'[38]
In the Indian case the disintegration was disguised by the movement's
venture, sparked off by students in Bihar, into confrontation, and
ultimately conventional, politics — a venture that led to the
declaration of a state of emergency (1975—77) and the three years of
unstable politics that followed.[39]

It would be premature, however, to write off anarcho-pacifism. As
the historical record suggests, the ideas of both pacifism and
anarchism have shown a remarkable ability to survive the demise of
the organizations and movements that have expressed them. As
currents of thought, they may at times disappear from public view,
but only to surface again later. The same is likely to be true of the new
hybrid. In India, Gandhi remains a potent symbol and source of
inspiration. And in the West, since the demise of the New Left,
various groups — such as War Resisters' International, the *Peace
News* constituency in Britain, and the Philadelphia Life Center in the
USA — have sought to give clearer definition to the central concept of
anarcho-pacifism: non-violent revolution.[40] At the same time, the
counter-cultural critique of modern industrial society has been
extended, notably by Theodore Roszak,[41] and links established
between anarcho-pacifism and the ecological and women's liberation
movements. The production and use of nuclear power, an issue being
pressed by anarcho-pacifists (among others), may — just possibly —
become in the 1980s the catalyst for a mass non-violent movement,
comparable to the movement against nuclear weapons twenty or so
years ago.

Meanwhile, the nation-state still stands as 'the norm of modern
political organization'. It is not likely to be abolished in the way
Bakunin envisaged. But it may be subverted and transcended. There
are forces at work in the world — multinationals, supra-nationalism
and sub-nationalism, for example — that are finding it necessary to
use either larger or smaller frames of reference than the nation-state
provides. Anarcho-pacifism is only one of these forces and not, some
may think, the most important. But its continued opposition to war
and preparations for war, its clear transnational orientation and
appeal, and its insistence on the importance of rediscovering
community at all levels from the local to the global — the latter
encapsulated in the counter-culture's vision of mankind coming
home to their 'global village' — make it a potentially significant
source of both subversion and transcendence. These non-violent

revolutionaries, it is clear, do *not* think that the nation-state is 'the foundation of world order'; they think it is the active promoter of disorder, and fear that its various rival agents will one day start throwing nuclear bombs at each other and thus destroy the only civilization we have. The nation-state is *not* 'the chief definer' of their 'identity'; it does *not* 'permeate' their 'outlook'; and even the atheists among them find it blasphemous to regard it as 'the main object of individual loyalties'. These gentle revolutionaries may prattle on about love and peace, but they are our modern Anabaptists and, like their heretical forebears, they can recognize an 'abomination' when they see it.

NOTES AND REFERENCES

1. A.D. Smith *Theories of Nationalism* (London: Duckworth, 1971) p. 2.
2. Quoted in D. Boulton *Objection Overruled* (London: MacGibbon and Kee, 1976) p. 111.
3. St Matthew 5, verses 39 and 44, A.V.
4. See Quentin Skinner *The Foundation of Modern Political Thought* (Cambridge: Cambridge University Press, 1978) vol. 2, p. 78.
5. See Kenneth Rexroth *Communalism* (London: Peter Owen, 1975), which provides a short historical account of the communitarian tradition.
6. Quoted in G. Hubbard *Quaker by Convincement* (Harmondsworth: Penguin, 1974) p. 128.
7. The terms are taken from Peter Brock's typology of pacifism.
8. P. Brock *Twentieth-Century Pacifism* (New York: Van Nostrand Reinhold, 1970) pp. 184 and 186.
9. Quoted in M. Howard *War and the Liberal Conscience* (London: Temple Smith, 1978) pp. 40–1.
10. Not included in the 7 are the USA, which imposed conscription from time to time, and Britain, which imposed it during the years 1915–18 and 1939–57.
11. See Devi Prasad and Tony Smythe (eds) *Conscription* (London: War Resisters' International, 1968).
12. *Ibid.,* pp. 56 and 139.
13. Brock, *op. cit.,* pp. 159 and 177.
14. See David Malament 'Selective conscientious objection and the *Gillette* decision' in M. Cohen, T. Nagel and T. Scanlon (eds) *War and Moral Responsibility* (Princeton, NJ: Princeton University Press, 1974). In Britain during the Second World War the provision for conscientious objection made no mention of religion, nor did it specify that objection must be to all war as distinct from the war actually being waged.
15. Quoted in Howard, *op. cit.,* p. 22.

16. Quoted in E. H. Carr *Michael Bakunin* (London: Macmillan, 1937) p. 341.
17. T. Paine *The Rights of Man* (1792; London: Watts, The Thinker's Library, 1937) Part 2, Ch. 1, p. 134.
18. W. Godwin *Political Justice* 3rd edn (1798; Harmondsworth, Middx: Penguin, 1976).
19. E. Burke *The Vindication of Natural Society* (1756) in *The Works of Edmund Burke* Vol. 1 (London: M'Lean, 1823; London: Bohn, 1854).
20. P. Kropotkin *Mutual Aid* (1902; Harmondsworth, Middx: Penguin, 1939).
21. P. Kropotkin *Modern Science and Anarchism* (1913) in R. N. Baldwin (ed.) *Kropotkin's Revolutionary Pamphlets* (New York: Dover, 1970) p. 157.
22. C. Ward *Anarchy in Action* (London: Allen and Unwin, 1973) p. 11.
23. See especially P. Kropotkin *The State: its historic role* (1903) in P. A. Kropotkin *Selected Writings on Anarchism and Revolution* (Cambridge, Mass.: MIT Press, 1970).
24. *Ibid.,* revised edn (London: Freedom Press, 1943) p. 10.
25. *Ibid.,* p. 44.
26. Since anarchists repudiate the political concept of the nation and direct their appeal to people across national boundaries, their attitude is more properly described as 'transnationalist' than 'internationalist' (favouring cooperation between nations). Bakunin, it should be noted, distinguished three types of patriotism: (i) 'natural', defined as 'an instinctive, mechanical, uncritical attachment to the socially accepted hereditary or traditional pattern of life'. Deriving from the law that determines the separation of all living beings into species, families and groups, it is an expression of social solidarity but exists 'in inverse ratio to the development of civilization, that is, the triumph of humanity in human societies'; (ii) 'bourgeois', whose object is to preserve and maintain 'the power of the national State, that is, the mainstay of all the privileges of the exploiters throughout the nation'; and (iii) 'proletarian', which ignores national differences and state boundaries and embraces the whole world. See G. P. Maximoff *The Political Philosophy of Bakunin* (Glencoe, Ill.: Free Press, 1953) Pt. II, Chs 10 and 11.
27. Quoted in E. Cahm and V. C. Fisera (eds) *Socialism and Nationalism* (Nottingham: Spokesman, 1978) p. 42. The book includes two chapters dealing, respectively, with Bakunin's and Kropotkin's views on the national question.
28. The English edition of Rocker's book was published by Freedom Press, London, and the quotations in this paragraph are taken from pp. 200—13.
29. For an extended discussion of anarchist violence in relation to pacifism, see April Carter 'Anarchism and violence' in J. R. Pennock and J. W. Chapman (eds) *Anarchism* (New York: New York University Press, 1978).
30. See, for example, Bakunin's message in 1868 to the International League of Peace and Freedom, quoted in Carr, *op. cit.,* p. 343.

31. The text is given in the selection of pacifist and pacificist writings edited by Peter May, *The Pacifist Conscience* (Harmondsworth, Middx: Penguin, 1966).

32. L. Tolstoy *The Kingdom of God is Within You* (1893; London: Oxford University Press, The World's Classics, 1936).

33. H. D. Thoreau 'Civil Disobedience' (1849) in H. A. Bedau (ed.) *Civil Disobedience* (New York: Pegasus, 1969).

34. R. Gregg *The Power of Nonviolence* 2nd edn (London: James Clarke, 1960).

35. B de Ligt *The Conquest of Violence* (London: Routledge, 1937).

36. See the collection of Goodman's political essays edited by Taylor Stoehr, *Drawing the Line* (New York: Free Life Editions, 1977). Another mentor of the New Left, Herbert Marcuse, it should be noted, expounded a form of libertarian Marxism and sought to justify 'revolutionary violence'.

37. See Nigel Young *An Infantile Disorder? The Crisis and Decline of the New Left* (London: Routledge and Kegan Paul, 1977).

38. Jayaprakash Narayan *Socialism, Sarvodaya and Democracy* (Bombay: Asia Publishing House, 1964), p. 165.

39. On the *Sarvodaya* movement, see G. Ostergaard and M. Currell *The Gentle Anarchists* (Oxford: Clarendon Press, 1971). The venture into confrontation politics and its sequel are discussed in G. Ostergaard 'JP's total revolution: in retrospect and prospect' *Vigil* (Calcutta) 2, nos 14–17 (November–December 1979).

40. As illustrations of this effort see: *Manifesto for Nonviolent Revolution* (London: War Resisters' International, 1972); Howard Clark *Making Nonviolent Revolution* (London: Housmans, 1978); George Lakey *Strategy for a Living Revolution* (San Francisco: Freeman, 1973); and S. Gowan, G. Lakey, W. Moyer and R. Taylor *Moving Towards a New Society* (Philadelphia: New Society Press, 1976).

41. Roszak's critique is developed in the following books: *The Making of a Counter Culture* (London: Faber, 1969), *Where the Wasteland Ends* (London: Faber, 1972), *Unfinished Animal* (London: Faber, 1976), and *Person/Planet: the Creative Disintegration of Industrial Society* (London: Gollancz, 1979).

FURTHER READING

My own understanding of the ideas and movements discussed in this essay owes much to Nigel Young. His forthcoming sociological study of *The Nation State and War Resistance* (University of California Press) based on his PhD thesis of that title (University of California, Berkeley, 1976) will be the essential reference on the subject.

The best historical introduction to pacifism is Peter Brock's *Twentieth-Century Pacifism* (New York: Van Nostrand Reinhold, 1970). The earlier history is covered in his two large volumes, *Pacifism in the United States* and *Pacifism in Europe to 1914* (Princeton, NJ: Princeton University Press, 1968 and 1972, respectively). The collection of readings edited by Mulford Sibley, *The Quiet Battle* (New York: Doubleday Anchor, 1963), deals with the theory and practice of non-violent resistance. The major work on this topic, however, is Gene Sharp's *The Politics of Nonviolent Action* (Boston, USA: Porter Sargent, 1973). Michael Howard's *War and the Liberal Conscience* (London: Temple Smith, 1978) provides a readable account of what I have called pacif*i*cist thought.

George Woodcock's *Anarchism* (Harmondsworth, Middx: Penguin, 1963) remains the best general introduction to the history of libertarian ideas and movements but should be supplemented with the same author's *The Anarchist Reader* (London: Fontana/Collins, 1977). A short analytical study relating anarchist ideas to the orthodox concerns and concepts of political theory is April Carter's *The Political Theory of Anarchism* (London: Routledge and Kegan Paul, 1971).

See also other works cited in the text and the references.

9

A Future for the Nation-State?

Gordon Smith

It was Mark Twain who once drily observed that reports of his recent death were exaggerated. The same could be said to those who would wish to bury the nation-state; it is more resilient than may sometimes appear. Yet at a time when the nation-state has become the powerful and ubiquitous norm of political organization, it is ironic that there should be signs of its increasing vulnerability and in many respects of its redundancy as well. It is also paradoxical to argue that precisely these weaknesses may be instrumental in securing its continuing survival. That survival is posited not so much on the inherent strength of the nation-state idea — although we should not neglect its positive appeal — but more on the force of inertia, that *faute de mieux* developments are more likely to shore up and buttress the nation-state rather than lead to its imminent collapse.

A necessary starting-point for analysis is the nature of the nation-state itself. Wherein lies its strength? One answer to this question lies in the juxtaposition — the fusion even — of the distinctive concepts of 'nation' and 'state'. They bring together quite conflicting sources of legitimacy. On the one hand, the affinities — cultural and ethnic — that make up the bonds of the nation are essentially non-rational sanctions. On the other hand, the modern state — whatever the nature of particular regimes — embodies the principle of 'legal rationality'. It is a peculiar mixture. Yet we can appreciate that the formula of the nation-state was a powerful force in the transformation of traditional societies to industrialized ones, which required a mass mobilization and the destruction of old social structures. We can see, too, that nationalism — and with it the claim for self-determination in the nation-state — is widely adaptable. In its primary form the nation-state was instrumental in bringing about change chiefly in the European context, but in its later manifestations the nation-state idea became the normative lever to use against the encroachment of worldwide imperialism.

Nationalism has proved to be an extraordinarily potent force, and it also appears to be highly malleable in its formation and expression.[1] This quality allows nationalism to play a key role at different junctures of development — at times quiescent, at others blazing its own trail. Underlying the conventional approach to the subject of nationalism, an implied sequence is discernible: a dormant national spirit is stirred, and the national awakening leads to insistent claims for self-determination and thence to the formation of the nation-state. That paradigm undoubtedly fits many cases, but it by no means exhausts the possibilities. The point is that there is no fixed quantum of 'national' potential awaiting release, nor is it feasible to specify its particular ingredients. A shared culture, race, religion or common language may each be sufficient factors, but none is entirely necessary. In fact, the sequence of the 'sleeping beauty' theory of national progression can just as easily be reversed. A nation may create a state, but a state may forge a nation. Indeed, part of that forging process will involve the subjugation, possibly the eradication, of awkward and deviant 'sub-state' national expressions that could threaten the emerging 'national' unity. This ability of the state to foster an attendant nationhood, to make nationalism a dependent variable, has the natural consequence of enhancing state legitimacy. It is not, of course, a simple recipe that any regime can prepare at will for its own benefit; nonetheless, we have to be on guard against assuming that any apparent decline in national feelings or assertion necessarily represents a permanent weakening of the nation-state.

There is another important sense in which nationalism has a malleable quality. By definition, a national appeal attracts the widest possible following, cutting across social divisions and inviting expressions of popular participation. Nationalist movements are frequently linked with claims for popular sovereignty and demands for democratic institutions. But there is another side to the picture: nationalism is primarily a quest for unity, not for a rationality based on equal rights. The unity may be expressed in terms similar to the German idea of the *Volk,* and the result may be the equivalent of a *völkisch* mysticism, an irrationality that is more compatible with authoritarian styles of government and charismatic leadership than it is with party democracy. Moreover, even if the democratic association is maintained, there is little to prevent a regime from paying lip-service to the democratic ideals whilst at the same time using the national connection as a potent form of social control.

One of the strengths of the modern state has been to harness nationalism to its cause, and that is true irrespective of the nature of the regime or the level of development reached by a society. Even though the roots of nationalism may encourage a backward-looking view of society — its history, its mythology — the overriding effect is towards a modernization of society, and that modernization complements the process of rationalization evident at other levels, particularly the economy. The state itself, demystified, represents an overarching rational force, not just as an expression of legal rationality but as a functioning machine capable of planning and administering on an ever-increasing scale.

On some such basis it is possible to portray the character of a model nation-state, and we should be wary of assuming that nationalism is a spent force or that the 'outmoded' state can be readily supplanted by even more rational forms of political organization. However, it is impossible to skirt the view that a 'crisis of the state' does exist, that the nation-state is a vulnerable entity and ill-suited to perform its traditional functions. Although some states may perform better than others, the kind of weakness displayed can, in principle, be located generally. The incidence of crisis is uneven, and in some types of state regime — notably those with an authoritarian or dictatorial bent — the symptoms can be masked or suppressed, but that reservation merely serves to postpone crisis not eliminate it.

Clearly, the 'crisis' label is much too vague as it stands. There is also a justifiable suspicion of the view that all the ills of contemporary society could be bundled together and laid at the door of the state. Yet it is apparent that the possible points of vulnerability may well be almost unrelated to one another — precisely because the claims of the nation-state have been so far-reaching.

One way of simplifying the problem is to draw a distinction between the external and the internal orientations of the state, for there are quite different considerations involved according to whether we are concerned with the nation-state as a sovereign power or with questions that affect the legitimacy of the state and its regime. It is quite conceivable, too, that a state may suffer in one direction but not another. If, however, its external weaknesses are compounded by internal ones, its future may be bleak.

EXTERNAL PROBLEMS

The notion of a 'sovereign power', recognized as such by other members of the international community, provides the legal basis for a state's external position, but the real situation has been changed by the sheer proliferation of 'nation-states' since the Second World War. The extent of decolonization has led to a variety of states emerging that in other ages would scarcely have been able to gain or maintain an independent existence. In that sense, an almost mechanical application of the nation-state formula has led to a substantial devaluation of its content. It is not only the creation of a number of micro-states that has had this effect, for at any one time there are examples of states that have moved into the 'fictional' category — ones that effectively have no government and have lost all credibility in the outside world, and yet do not disintegrate and vanish. Instead, they are preserved in a kind of nation-state limboland until such time as a competent regime can be re-established.

This devaluation can be expressed as a 'lowering of the threshold requirements' for the nation-state,[2] and it may appear that a difference exists between the old nation-states and those that have been recently created. But the existence of marginal nation-states points to changing conditions for states generally, not just in the granting of new entry permits. The changes may be appreciated by contrasting the requirements of the past with the present. The former conditions can be represented as a 'test of adequacy': could a state fulfil its basic functions? Those functions — vis-à-vis other states — principally related to the state's ability to defend its territory and to provide physical security for its citizens; if it could not, its existence might be short-lived. But the adequacy of a state would also have required it to act as a guarantor in other ways as well, especially in the control of a country's economic destiny. Thus, although the concept of 'legal sovereignty' provided a basis for the relations between states, it was also necessary for them each to present a 'hard shell' to all other states.[3]

It is evident that the contemporary world no longer applies those strict conditions. In place of 'adequacy', the soft-shell state has only to meet the requirement of international recognition: there are no certain penalties for inadequacy. There is no one reason for this fundamental development. Partly, it has resulted from the widespread acceptance of the principle of self-determination: once a state has come into being through the exercise of that principle, then its national status is assured, even though it may prove to be ineffective. However, important as the normative basis is, there are other reasons to consider. One is consequent upon the emergence of the 'super-powers' and their worldwide strategic interests: inevitably, other states are drawn into the network of their alliances and interests, and multilateral defence commitments replace the individual hard shells of physical security. In this vital respect the nation-state shows itself to be obsolescent, and if it were to be the sole consideration the presence of two superpowers would reduce all others to *clientèle* status.

Economic inadequacy may be just as pervasive in its effects, although less overt. Interdependence of trade and national economies means that it is difficult for any state to control its own economic system in isolation from others. Informal multinational links and pressures are supplemented by a host of formal organizations that exist to promote economic cooperation; their resources and their ability to carry out policies that may conflict with the immediate interests of individual members moves beyond simple cooperation towards the realm of 'supra-nationalism' — in its implications a term that at some stage must clash with the pretensions to sovereignty of the nation-state.

These factors all underline the vulnerability of the nation-state towards its external environment. Yet it would be wrong just to extrapolate the tendencies and assume that there is a general movement to superior forms of political organization 'beyond the nation-state',[4] that somehow new supranational entities will inevitably arise to subsume both the states and their partial interests as well as attracting to themselves strong forms of loyalty — literally a supra-nationalism. That could conceivably be the outcome, but a dash of realism is appropriate. After all, the experience of the past thirty years or so scarcely confirms the victory of supranational organization over the nation-state, and the disjunction between the model and reality stems from a neglect of one cardinal motive behind moves towards 'supranational integration': the initiating states have seen the developments as the best way of preserving their own national interests and, ultimately, of maintaining their position, even existence, in the world community. Whatever the motives of idealists may be in seeking to set aside the confining restrictions of the nation-state, the fact remains that the states are the essential building-blocks of any wider organization. Those states are also self-regarding entities, jealously protecting their own prerogatives, not willing their own demise. Furthermore, the states remain the key intermediaries between their respective communities and the new centres of decision-making, and those centres, far from supplanting the role of the states, give them an additional platform from which they can actually move to enhance their position both within the organization and internationally. In this process, some states will benefit more than others, and the imbalances of power and influence that result act as a guarantee that tensions will be maintained between states and not mystically 'subsumed' by the force of common interests.[5] There is thus an inherent ambivalence contained in the integrative pattern: the overcoming of the nation-state proceeds in tandem with its further underpinning. This finding is deliberately couched in general terms, but its applicability to the development of the European Community is fairly obvious, and that experiment is arguably the prototype for future ventures in supranational integration.

INTERNAL PROBLEMS

We should now turn to the other dimension of crisis for the nation-state, that affecting its internal orientation. Are there strains generally evident and comparable with those associated with external inadequacy? A problem immediately arises. Whilst it may appear reasonable to speak generally about nation-states in their external capacities, their internal conditions vary in a critical respect, namely, according to the nature of the prevailing regime. The central question — whether the nation-state is likely to be beset by problems of securing popular legitimacy — remains valid, but the answers may depend to a large extent on the type of state under consideration. In the present context, the differentiation will be kept at a minimum to avoid complexity, but three broad types stand out: liberal-democratic, pragmatic-authoritarian and ideological-authoritarian. In practice, they correspond to the recognizable features of Western democracy, of the developing world and of the family of communist states respectively.

The liberal democracies face problems of legitimacy most directly, since the nature of such systems encourages the expression of dissension by providing channels for the meeting of demands and by insisting on the pluralist nature of their societies. Precisely those attributes enshrine the values that legitimize the political authorities: it is a limitation placed on governments that leads to their acceptability. Yet there appears to be mounting evidence that the liberal democracies are suffering from a malaise of legitimacy, if not quite a central crisis of the state. There is, in fact, a fundamental flaw in the liberal-democratic mode. It is true that the political system is geared to the articulation of demands from society, but ultimately the liberal state faces severe difficulties in coping with the pressures. Those pressures are met initially by the state assuming increasing responsibilities, but, once accepted, they are not easily shed. The nature of political competition — resting on a mass vote that is increasingly volatile — ensures that the parties in government will be subjected to a continuous escalation of demands. The working of the liberal-democratic mechanism is put under further strain by the changing basis of legitimation, away from a sole reliance on the sanction of legal-rational authority to a form that places a moral obligation on the state to promote social welfare: the whole system is judged by its commitment and performance in this respect.

Inevitably, the liberal democracies encounter the problem of an over-extension of the state and its resources, and at the same time the extension of the state's activities brings a resentment from those who are adversely affected and others who feel that their claims have been neglected. Since demands remain unsatisfied and because they continue to be voiced, challenges to governmental authority are rife, but those making the challenge are concerned with their limited aims, not with the violent overthrow of the system. There are accordingly two types of effect. One is that the underlying stability of the system may not be put seriously in jeopardy: no social group wishes to subvert the complete authority of the state for itself. The other effect is summed up by the term 'ungovernability', a description that, although a crass exaggeration if applied as a general description of liberal-democratic societies, neatly captures the helplessness of governments when one group after another acts in defiance of authority on a range of particular issues. The wide incidence of these situations implies that a process of delegitimization is under way,[6] but it is typified by a growing apathy and indifference to the needs of government rather than by a desire to impose new forms. In this sense, the future of the liberal nation-state is maintained by an inertia in place of a positive attraction.

It is impossible to foresee what the consequences of further destabilization might be, or to judge the effectiveness of palliatives that could be applied. One wide remedy is to secure a substantial decentralization of state power, and this line has several recommendations. The territorial dispersion of state power counteracts the remoteness of central government and by enforcing a more local responsibility for decision-making it helps to overcome the alienative features of the modern state. Decentralization by itself is hardly a panacea for all the ills of the nation-state, but it is particularly relevant to one symptom: the rise of 'sub-national' movements that, in varying degrees, challenge the hegemony of the uni-national state. In conceding to demands for local autonomy, the threat of an ultimate fragmentation can be avoided, but the admission has to be made that the historical concept of the indivisible nation is no longer valid. That concession may be traumatic, yet the functional value of a unified nation-state has also declined: the passing of the hard-shell state implies that the binding force of strong national loyalties is no longer needed in the era of the inadequate state.

Such reflections apply to the old liberal-democratic states, but their problems and forms of resolution have no bearing on the situation of states that are not based on the principles of competitive political choice. In the absence of a system allowing for the free presentation of demands or the open expression of dissent, the 'symptoms' of weakness will also be absent, and in an efficient authoritarian regime the controls exercised over society will suppress social discontents for considerable periods. Does this mean that only the liberal democracies are affected by a crisis of the state?

The answer is almost certainly 'no'. The precise nature of a regime does not diminish the salience of the central problem of the contemporary state, and we have seen that the question of declining external adequacy is a general phenomenon. Nor does the absence of the liberal-democratic 'ungovernability' syndrome mean that other forms of state system escape the basic pressures. It is important also to take into account the extent to which the vast majority of the world's states now base the legitimacy of rule on the ethic of social welfare and rely on mass support: the demands may be throttled or closely controlled but they are still presumed to be there, and governments are bound by the imperative of their satisfaction. That imperative is strengthened by what we may call the 'competitive — emulative' link that exists between societies ruled by antagonistic ideologies: there is a continuous pressure to catch up or to out-perform the others, and the impossibility of securing a national isolation in the present structure of the world economy means that all states are made intimately aware of the progress and setbacks elsewhere.

Such similarities do not amount to an argument for a 'convergence' in the types of solution sought, least of all that there should be a convergence in political evolution. The communist states — those belonging to the authoritarian-ideological family of states — should not be expected to follow the path of political liberalization. Quite apart from the ideological constraints that stand in the way of accepting a pluralist view of society, the effect of introducing 'bourgeois freedoms' might well lead to the communist political systems being swamped by the force of demands unleashed. This difficulty is evident in the uneasy relationship that communism bears to nationalism. On the one hand, Marxism must in principle reject nationalism as a determining factor of the state or world order and must always seek to ensure that it is safely harnessed to the dictates of ideology. Yet, on the other hand, that subordination is never complete. Whatever the ideals of 'proletarian internationalism',[7] the power of communism is expressed through its organization on the basis of the nation-state, and the communist nation-state shows a remarkable persistence and an ability to represent its own national interests. Moreover, the national element supplies a principal source of latent opposition to communist rule, whether against the dominance of the Soviet Union or within the individual states. Thus nationalism that is a prop in helping to legitimize communist regimes may also act as the focus for an otherwise fragmented opposition.[8] Either way — whether the communist states encounter greater internal stresses or not — it is evident that nationalism continues to have a potency that has been lost in the capitalist systems based on liberal democracy.

In a world of nation-states, those that have newly achieved their independence or have rid themselves of their traditional rulers can scarcely avoid growing up in the same mould. A description of their forms of government as being in the 'authoritarian-pragmatic' style is certainly too sweeping, but it expresses their general rejection of the competitive model of democracy, and their authoritarianism is modified by the undeniably popular basis of government as well as in the presence of charismatic leaders who 'democratize' regimes by their hold over the masses. Their contribution is often of critical importance: the 'nation' may still be largely artificial, and for the nation-building process to be successful there must be a unifying force to overcome the resistance of traditional society and of ethnic minorities. The need to promote a national identity is not reduced by the availability of wider appeals — Pan-Africanism or the great galvanizing shock of the Islamic Revolution — for they do not provide the means of tight political organization, although they can usefully be employed to bolster up the national appeal.

The new nation-states have no real alternative to following the route already taken by others, but there is a substantial difference: they need not suffer any disability from their external inadequacy and may even be able to profit from apparent weakness by operating at the critical margins of superpower interests. Yet they do face the perils of internal over-extension. The pressures to raise standards of living are intense, and they are magnified by the competitive— emulative imperative. The spectre of 'ungovernability' — suppressed in communist systems, 'managed' by liberal democracy — lurks as a revolutionary force, waiting for the regime and its leaders to falter in their efforts.

Where do these comparisons lead us? One conclusion must be that there is no one model for the nation-state and another is that there are no overwhelming reasons for predicting its decline. In their different ways, all three types of regime we have considered show that they are vulnerable and none can produce a golden rule for survival in their present form. Yet blueprints for a possible alternative to the nation-state do not carry much conviction: neither the 'technical' superiority of supranational solutions, nor the idealism of utopian schemes to create a new political order. The rational-irrational admixture of the nation-state may accord better with man's social and political nature, and that quality could guarantee its survival. There is, however, a cautionary rider to be added against making predictions in the field of politics — and, after all, Mark Twain is no longer with us.

NOTES AND REFERENCES

1. The fate of the national idea in Germany is an exemplary case of malleability. See G. Schweigler *National Consciousness in Divided Germany* (Farnborough: Saxon House, 1975) and 'Whatever happened to Germany?' in E. Krippendorff and V. Rittberger (eds) *The Foreign Policy of West Germany* (London: Sage, 1980).
2. The expression used by J. Rothschild 'Political legitimacy in contemporary Europe' in B. Denitch (ed.) *Legitimation of Regimes: International Frameworks for Analysis* (London: Sage, 1979).
3. On the concept of the 'hard shell', see J. Herz 'Rise and demise of the territorial state' in H. Lubasz (ed.) *The Development of the Modern State* (London: Macmillan, 1964).
4. The title of an early and influential treatise: E. B. Haas *Beyond the Nation State* (Stanford, Calif.: Stanford University Press, 1964).
5. The economic tensions are probably the most fundamental, as is evident in the European Community. See M. Hodges (ed.) *Economic Divergence in the European Community* (London: Allen and Unwin, 1980).
6. For a fundamental treatment of legitimacy problems in capitalist society, see J. Habermas *Legitimation Crisis* (London: Heinemann, 1976).
7. 'Proletarian internationalism' is often used as a euphemism for the claim by the Communist Party of the Soviet Union to primacy over other communist parties.
8. A recent account of oppositional forces is R. Tökés (ed.) *Opposition in Eastern Europe* (London: Macmillan, 1979). See also, T. McNeill 'State and nationality under communism' in J. Hayward and R. Berki (eds) *State and Society in Contemporary Europe* (Oxford: Martin Robertson, 1979).

FURTHER READING

Many of the books already cited in earlier chapters are relevant. Basic on the formation of the nation-state are R. Bendix *Nation-Building and Citizenship* (New York: Wiley, 1969) and C. Tilly (ed.) *The Formation of National States in Western Europe* (Princeton, NJ: Princeton University Press, 1975). A good introductory account of state theory is G. Poggi *The Development of the Modern State: A Sociological Perspective* (London: Hutchinson, 1978), and see also, K. Dyson *The State Tradition in Western Europe* (Oxford: Martin Robertson, 1980).

On the question of legitimacy, an excellent, broadly based collection is provided in B. Denitch (ed.) *Legitimation of Regimes* (London: Sage, 1979). A general and historical perspective is given by N. Birnbaum *The Crisis of Industrial Society* (London: Oxford University Press, 1970).

The related theme of ungovernability is examined by Richard Rose, 'Ungovernability: is there fire behind the smoke?' *Political Studies* (September 1979) with a guide to recent literature.

Ernest Gellner's account of nationalism in *Thought and Change* (London: Weidenfeld, 1964) should certainly not be missed and it supplements A. D. Smith's *Nationalism in the Twentieth Century* (Oxford: Martin Robertson, 1979). See also: J. Krejci 'Ethnic problems in Europe' in S. Giner and M. S. Archer *Contemporary Europe: Social Structures and Cultural Patterns* (London: Routledge and Kegan Paul, 1978).

A recent contribution to the considerable literature on the dispersion of state power is L. J. Sharpe (ed.) *Decentralist Trends in Western Democracies* (London: Sage, 1979).

Index